TH
ELECTRON... BRAIN

"Shelli Joye's book raises one of the fundamental problems of philosophy— what is the display that appears to us when we look at ourselves and the world? Something does, and we call it mind or consciousness. This book claims that it is the electromagnetic field. Her book merits being read, pondered, and explored in reference to the ever-increasing storehouse of knowledge about the physical world in general and the electromagnetic field in particular."

ERVIN LASZLO, AUTHOR OF *THE IMMORTAL MIND*

"*The Electromagnetic Brain* is a bold, brave effort to pull together and present important alternative views to what has become the dominant paradigm in the fields of neuroscience and brain science—a paradigm that arbitrarily assumes that consciousness and the mind arise from physical, neuronal activity in the brain and that they are limited to these processes. The nature of consciousness or subjective awareness is a challenge to science and to much of what we take for granted in our ordinary lives. Joye's work is thorough, extensive, well written, and fascinating. It will ultimately challenge its readers to examine who we truly are, and this is why it is so important."

MENAS C. KAFATOS, PH.D., COAUTHOR OF
THE CONSCIOUS UNIVERSE AND *YOU ARE THE UNIVERSE*

"Joye dives into the epic, unsolved scientific question—not simply of the nature of the observed, but rather observation itself. The unfolding story of enfolded field theories of consciousness is delivered with Joye's unique genius and heart. These consciousness insights are presented with a minimum of specialist jargon; thus the book connects subtle concepts to a wide audience."

CHRISTOPHER PAPILE, PH.D., FOUNDER OF BRANECELL

"In clear, cogent prose Joye has written the first book to survey electromagnetic theories of consciousness. Long neglected by the academic establishment in favor of more material models, electromagnetic perspectives stand poised to make substantial contributions to our scientific understanding of consciousness. Joye's knowledge and writing style render complex topics readable and accessible for a general audience, thus facilitating the cross-disciplinary dialog necessary to approach the complex phenomena of consciousness."

KERRI WELCH, PH.D., AUTHOR OF *A FRACTAL TOPOLOGY OF TIME*

"Beautifully written and comprehensive in scope. Pribram and Bohm are the two major figures here, and you will not find a better description of their work anywhere. It is clear that current approaches to the brain and consciousness are several orders of magnitude too simple, and this book is perhaps the best way to begin to rectify that."

SEÁN Ó NUALLÁIN, M.SC., PH.D., AUTHOR OF *THE SEARCH FOR MIND*

". . . Shelli Joye's most complete and informative work to date. This is a fascinating book! Shelli has a way of making the technical and controversial easily digestible—and enjoyable. The material collected here will be a great aid for anyone interested in the nature of consciousness—scientist and layperson alike. Highly recommended!"

MICHAEL PRYZDIA, PH.D., SENIOR LECTURER
AT ARIZONA STATE UNIVERSITY

"*The Electromagnetic Brain* bridges the world of consciousness research with physics, electrical engineering, and stories about those exploring human consciousness. These approaches to an understanding of electromagnetic fields of consciousness are presented with fascinating biographies, references, and numerous diagrams to reveal new frontiers of research."

LAUREN PALMATEER, PH.D., ELECTRICAL ENGINEER

"In *The Electromagnetic Brain*, Joye takes the daring position that consciousness is not only generated in the brain but also partly received by the brain, being embedded in a physical information field as earlier proposed in the holographic approaches of David Bohm and Karl Pribram. These pioneering ideas are now reborn in the era of quantum biology, with its groundbreaking concepts in modern biophysics. An excellent presentation that mirrors the ongoing quest for understanding our participatory role in bringing the cosmos we live in to self-understanding, emphasizing our own responsibility for the survival of our precious planet."

DIRK K. F. MEIJER, M.D., M.SC., PH.D.,
PROFESSOR EMERITUS AT THE UNIVERSITY OF GRONINGEN

"At this time when the limitations of a purely materialist approach to comprehending consciousness are increasingly evident, *The Electromagnetic Brain* reads like a breath of fresh air. Joye describes top cutting-edge theories delving into how consciousness might best be viewed in terms of energetic fields. While many of these theories do not yet include complete physical mechanisms by which interaction between fields of consciousness and human brains occur, Joye's new book constructs a foundation upon which future consciousness research in this most promising direction can emerge."

CYNTHIA SUE LARSON, PH.D., AUTHOR OF
QUANTUM JUMPS AND *REALITY SHIFTS*

THE
ELECTROMAGNETIC
BRAIN

EM Field Theories on
the Nature of Consciousness

SHELLI RENÉE JOYE, PH.D.

Inner Traditions
Rochester, Vermont

Inner Traditions
One Park Street
Rochester, Vermont 05767
www.InnerTraditions.com

SUSTAINABLE FORESTRY INITIATIVE
Certified Sourcing
www.sfiprogram.org
SFI-00854

Text stock is SFI certified

Originally published in 2018 by the Viola Institute under the title *Ten Electromagnetic Field Theories of Consciousness*

Cataloging-in-Publication Data for this title is available from the Library of Congress

ISBN 978-1-64411-091-1 (print)
ISBN 978-1-64411-092-8 (ebook)

Printed and bound in the United States by Lake Book Manufacturing, Inc. The text stock is SFI certified. The Sustainable Forestry Initiative® program promotes sustainable forest management.

10 9 8 7 6 5 4 3 2 1

Text design and layout by Debbie Glogover
This book was typeset in Garamond Premier Pro with Columbia Serial and Gill Sans MT Pro used as display fonts

Material in Chapter 10 is based on the author's 2016 Ph.D. dissertation, "The Pribram-Bohm Holoflux Theory of Consciousness: An Integral Interpretation of the Theories of Karl Pribram, David Bohm, and Pierre Teilhard De Chardin," and also appeared in her books published by the Viola Institute in 2017: *Tuning the Mind: Geometries of Consciousness* and *The Little Book of Consciousness: Holonomic Brain Theory and the Implicate Order*.

To send correspondence to the author of this book, mail a first-class letter to the author c/o Inner Traditions • Bear & Company, One Park Street, Rochester, VT 05767, and we will forward the communication, or contact the author directly at **https://shellijoye.net/**.

Contents

Groundbreaking Theories of Consciousness

Dean Radin, Ph.D.

The Electromagnetic Brain: EM Field Theories on the Nature of Consciousness is an important book because it reminds us that when faced with a stubbornly persistent mystery, like the nature of consciousness—by which I mean subjective (personal) awareness—we are obligated to consider a very broad range of explanatory theories.

The prevailing theory of consciousness in the second decade of the twenty-first century is that consciousness is a side effect of neuronal activity in the brain. That is, essentially, an electrochemical theory of consciousness. An extreme interpretation of this theory is that consciousness is a meaningless epiphenomenon, or as philosopher Daniel Dennett puts it, we are zombies. That is, no one is conscious. There's just an appearance of something going on inside our skulls, but it's just an illusion. Based on this theory, we (and presumably, Dennett) are mindless machines made of meat.

Less extreme models suggest that consciousness is a real phenomenon, but it is thought to emerge somehow out of brain architecture. Other models suggest that the brain is a quantum computer, and that quantum concepts are somehow compatible with consciousness, or that it's all about the manipulation of information. In fact, there are no widely accepted models that persuasively explain how three pounds of warm, wet tissue gives rise to subjective awareness.

When it comes to cognitive activity—meaning brain-centric information processing—that is another matter. Our understanding of the neural correlates of cognition have matured to the point where the brain-computer interface is quickly evolving into the fledgling technology of "synthetic telepathy." Those successes have led some neuroscientists to expect that we are also on the cusp of figuring out how consciousness works.

I believe they are right about much of what we call mind or cognition, but they are wrong about consciousness. Neural correlates are not going to explain why we have intimate internal knowledge of the subjective *taste* of a lemon, or why a sunset can evoke such felt emotion that it brings tears to our eyes. When we attempt to trace how we know our own experiences, by following signals from our senses to brain, nowhere do we find the taste of a lemon, or an emotion sparked by beauty. The awareness of these experiences does not appear to be located anywhere spatially specific in the brain region. The locus of awareness has not been established anywhere within human physiology.

Consider a 2015 article in the *Philosophical Transactions of the Royal Society*. There we find Giulio Tononi and Christof Koch, both influential thought leaders in the neurosciences, musing as follows:

Is consciousness—subjective experience—not only in other people's heads, but also in the head of animals? And perhaps everywhere, pervading the cosmos, as in old panpsychist traditions and in the Beatles' song?[1]

Scientists are not supposed to suggest that consciousness might "pervade the cosmos," so Tononi and Koch felt obligated to apologize in that same article for daring to mention such radical ideas. Such obsequious behavior is understandable from a sociological perspective, but it's a pity. Science has made magnificent strides in understanding the physical world, but in the process it has developed blinders that make it difficult to think about what lies beyond the physical. Fortunately, that taboo is beginning to break, as seen in a less formal 2014 article in *Scientific American,* where Koch was more forthcoming. He wrote:

> The mental is too radically different for it to arise gradually from the physical. This emergence of subjective feelings from physical stuff appears inconceivable and is at odds with a basic precept of physical thinking, the Ur-conservation law—*ex nihilo nihil fit* [out of nothing comes nothing]. . . . The phenomenal hails from a kingdom other than the physical and is subject to different laws.[2]

Philosophers, like Jerry Fodor, have been worrying about this problem for far longer than scientists. For example, Fodor wrote:

> I think it's strictly true that we can't, as things stand now, so much as imagine the solution of the hard problem [of explaining subjective awareness]. . . .
> . . . I would prefer that the hard problem should turn out to be unsolvable if the alternative is that we're all too dumb to solve it. Nobody has the slightest idea how anything material could be conscious. Nobody even knows what it would be like to have the slightest idea about how anything could be conscious.[3]

Here's where Shelli Joye's book comes to the rescue. It provides a clearly articulated bridge between purely physical concepts based on electrochemical activity of neurons, and nonphysical concepts like panpsychism and idealism. The bridge involves *field models* of consciousness. Fields are an important concept in physics, but they are not quite as physical as the everyday notions of matter or energy.

Fields may be described as regions in space-time that mediate interactions between objects through forces, and forces are actions that tend to maintain or alter the motion of a body. These two concepts are so closely related that they give rise to the concept of a "force field," which refers to an object that exerts a force into the space around it, and then that force in turn influences the object.

From this perspective, field models of consciousness may be thought of as recursive processes whereby:

- the electrochemical brain creates an electromagnetic force,
- that in turn influences the electrochemical brain,
- which in turn modulates the electromagnetic force,
- which in turn . . .

The picture painted by this recursive force field is partially physical, but it is also not quite physical. It's more like reverberating, self-reflective energetic loops that form quasi-stable informational patterns in space-time.

How these loops might solve the "hard problem" of explaining subjective awareness is not entirely clear, but that's not the point. What *The Electromagnetic Brain* does is open doors into new ways of thinking about the problem. As those doors open, even a crack, we get glimpses of vistas that were previously unthinkable. And that's the first step toward solving seemingly intractable problems.

Now let's open those doors and see the world anew.

DEAN RADIN, PH.D., is Chief Scientist at the Institute of Noetic Sciences and Distinguished Professor at the California Institute of Integral Studies. He holds an M.S. in electrical engineering and a Ph.D. in psychology and has published numerous books and scientific papers on consciousness. He is the author of *The Conscious Universe: The Scientific Truth of Psychic Phenomena* (1997), *Entangled Minds: Extrasensory Experiences in a Quantum Reality* (2006), *Supernatural: Science, Yoga, and the Evidence for Extraordinary Psychic Abilities* (2013), and *Real Magic: Ancient Wisdom, Modern Science, and a Guide to the Secret Power of the Universe* (2018).

PREFACE

How Entheogens Made Me Conscious of Consciousness

As a young college student, the word *consciousness* had never registered in my vocabulary as something worthy of much consideration. I certainly have no recollection of any mention of consciousness in any of my engineering classes. In fact, "consciousness," being a word bandied about by hippies meant that it was seldom found in academic circles at the time. As a contemporary neurophysiologist mentions in her book on electromagnetic consciousness: "In 1972, use of the word 'consciousness' was regarded by neurophysiologists as unacceptably New-Age."[1] The nearest I had come to considering consciousness as a concept in its own right was during an elective course on Romantic poetry (Wordsworth, Byron, Keats) where I mused over various poetic metaphors and similes, each trying to capture various states of consciousness. Yet even in an English class, I seldom encountered the use of the specific word *consciousness* in lectures and discussion.

That all changed on a California beach just south of Big Sur, on a mild Pacific night in July 1967. Having completed my third year of electrical engineering, I had been offered a summer intern job to program in FORTRAN at a U.S. Navy base near Point Mugu, California, just north of Los Angeles. Catalyzed by an epiphany that night on the beach, the word *consciousness* became a real "thing" for me, an undeniable mystery calling out for further exploration.

Henceforth, "consciousness" was no longer some vague abstract term.

Having recently married, neither of us yet twenty-one, we had traveled from Texas to California for the summer to live three blocks from the pure white-sand beach where Ventura Boulevard ends. We found ourselves among a local artist-hippie beach crowd. Earlier that summer, the Beatles had come out with *Sgt. Pepper's Lonely Hearts Club Band,* and we soon found ourselves burning incense and listening to records of Ravi Shankar, the Grateful Dead, and Jefferson Airplane. A surging wave of peace and love was rising, a counterpoint to a country in the throes of assassinations, urban riots, and the Vietnam War. It felt as if we were in the throes of a major cultural shift where everything could be questioned; a transformation seemed to be occurring, and young people were rising up in demonstrations from coast to coast, working to stop the Vietnam war machine, drowning it with waves of peace, love, and music.

Early in July we took a three-day trip to San Francisco, driving up the Pacific Coast Highway with a friend with the goal of finding "Owsley acid" (little yellow pills of LSD-25 often distributed at Grateful Dead "love-ins" in Golden Gate Park). I had read articles in *Time* and *Life* magazines relating how people experimenting with the new drug LSD had "seen God." Though I was an engineering student, I had been raised in a Catholic family, and even though I had drifted away from Sunday church services, I was really intrigued by the idea of being able to "see God," if that were at all possible, or at least find out firsthand what others had seen as God.

Arriving in San Francisco, we went directly to the Haight-Ashbury neighborhood near Golden Gate Park, and found many of the streets blocked off by the shoulder-to-shoulder crowds of wandering young hippies, many newly arrived in San Francisco with beads, leather vests, and flowers behind their ears. The smell of incense and cannabis was everywhere, and the sounds of Jefferson Airplane's *White Rabbit* and sitar music could be heard issuing from innumerable apartment crash-pads. It felt good to be alive, and as we wandered in and out of Indian cotton-print tents set up in a warren that lined the streets, we heard rumors that George Harrison had been seen earlier that day.

Later that Saturday, the three of us left San Francisco having acquired ten small yellow tabs of LSD-25, and with rising expectations we wound our way back south along the coastal highway, enjoying the spectacular views of the Pacific Coast and the blue waters breaking on the beaches below. Excited, but somewhat apprehensive, I could not stop thinking of what I had read about people "seeing God" on LSD and could not imagine what I might experience that night.

Around twilight we found ourselves parked by the ocean side of a road high above the Pacific, with a view of the wide beach far below. We were soon scrambling down the rugged cliffs, carrying sleeping bags and backpacks down to the wide beach formed by the mouth of Little Sur Creek, feeding an enormous shallow pool of fresh water, forming a mirrorlike lake on the beach before flowing into the Pacific. Sheltered by the sand dunes and an enormous rocky cliff, which looked to me like a Buddha lying on his side, we built a small fire of driftwood and talked about what we might soon experience. At around 9:00 p.m., I swallowed three of our little yellow LSD pills with a sip of water. I remember becoming slightly apprehensive when our friend Roscoe mentioned that the Owsley acid would give us a spectacular trip, and I worried that perhaps I had taken too much. Yet I took the three doses to ensure that I would be able to experience the various things I had read about in *Life* and *Time*.

But I had no idea! Over the next thirty minutes or so, my teeth began to feel strange, and my gums felt as if they were bubbling or buzzing somehow. Next I noticed, or suspected, that time and space were beginning to wobble slightly. I could no longer focus my thoughts, and as each new thought arose, I realized that I had lost what I had previously been thinking. Soon I began to notice little sparks of light moving into and out of my awareness. The sparks began to form little geometric structures that moved and rotated like small glowing 3D wire-frame objects. When I tried to look at them, they quickly changed and moved away, and I had to then shift my focus on other such structures moving in strange configurations, like rotating pinwheels and spinning polygons. I began to hear high-pitched whistling and buzzing sounds floating in and out of my awareness, and the small colored patterns began to look like some kinds of checkerboard, floating and weaving spatially in different locations in my visual field. I concluded that the LSD was starting to work after all!

I soon lost touch with my body. I sensed that I was a disembodied center of awareness floating in a multidimensional ocean of energy, surrounded by swirling currents full of an amazing array of strange and compellingly energetic entities. As my vision continually shifted, the cartwheeling electric wire-frame shapes, which became ever more frequent and vivid, seemed to emerge out of nowhere and then vanish. They began to remind me of the lights of a carnival at night. I was also surprised by unexpected sounds, deep bass sounds that seemed to come from the distance or from far below my hearing.

Things grew stranger and stranger until suddenly I was gone, hurled into a vast ocean of roiling awareness, as if I were soaring through some torrential rapid, turbulent with energy. And this went on for what seemed like years, or an eternity. I had lost track of time and space. Occasionally I experienced fear verging upon panic, worrying that I might never return to my familiar regions and modes of consciousness, but the fear would vanish as ever more surprising phenomena emerged into my awareness, new feelings and sights and sounds. Perhaps the most amazing realization was that all of these energetic things I was seeing and sensing were alive and aware, beyond any doubt! This was not a dead universe that I was observing, but one filled everywhere with a *living awareness* presenting itself in innumerable emotional flavors and modes, as if I were cast into an ocean of sentient beings—angels everywhere. It was not unlike my recollection of dreamworld experiences during sleep, but much more vivid, like my dreamworlds on steroids, yet a thousand times more intensely perceived, and I could not help but be convinced that somehow it was "real," even more real than my normal waking state. At least that is my recollection of how it seemed to me at the time, and it is how I now recall that night of wandering through those many new domains of perception on the beach.

At some point I managed to reconnect with my physical body, and

I stood up and began slowly walking on the flat sand beach. Suddenly I found myself standing in the middle of a mirrorlike lake of shallow warm water, and immediately was transfixed by the crystalline image of an ocean of stars reflecting in the pool of water under the clear moonless night. It was like looking into a cosmic mirror; yet each point of light seemed to have a life of its own as a unique being.

This single night, far beyond the familiar everyday bounds of awareness, set my path firmly on a lifelong journey to explore these incredible regions and to try to interpret them in terms of what I had been studying: physics, electronics, mathematics, and cybernetics. Later I came to realize that to fully understand these experiences would require more than science, and I was eventually led to study the writings of saints, mystics, contemplatives, and philosophers. But that would be many years later.

Several months later, back in Austin, I found myself again in my familiar engineering department, enrolled in senior elective classes including laser communication theory, electromagnetic field properties, and so on. But most weekends I continued to explore firsthand these astonishing new regions of consciousness opened up to me after ingesting entheogens, and I continued to experiment not only with LSD, but with a wide range of consciousness-amplifying substances, including mescaline, peyote, and psilocybin *cubensis* mushrooms. At dusk I would drive out into the Texas Hill Country to find isolated forested areas where I could spend the rest of the night exploring these vast new worlds revealed during expanded states of consciousness.

My early love of science fiction and radio had previously influenced my hopes of earning a Ph.D. to qualify me to enter a career of research, hoping to discover new phenomena in the area of electronics and physics. Those initial sparks of interest for exploring the unknown through science, though slightly diverted, had fully ignited in a roaring flame of enthusiasm to explore firsthand the incredible world of consciousness.

Naturally, the hundreds of hours I had spent studying electromagnetic theory in physics and engineering classes influenced my initial attempts to understand consciousness. For example, just "how" was I seeing these glowing, jeweled objects, frequently referred to as "visuals" in the written accounts of other psychedelic voyagers? What part of my physical organism was involved in the display of these incredibly clear, colorful, and dynamic visual images emerging out of the darkness of "inner space" during the early parts of each psychedelic voyage? I did not think it was occurring within my eyes themselves, which were often closed, unless the rods and cones were processing things not normally sensed. An alternative would be that it was some interior activity that I was perceiving using an as yet unidentified organ or system of perception; could it be that my pineal gland (often referred to by anatomists as a vestigial eye) might be observing subtle low-level activity (what might be called machine-language activity in a computer system) operating within the clear, ionized, cerebrospinal fluid of the brain's cerebral cavity in the third ventricle, referred to in traditional yogic texts as Brahma's cave?

It seemed obvious to me that these clearly observable, sharply focused, visual presentations of colorful neon three-dimensional objects rotating and floating within some dark inner space must involve some photonic energy processes. However it might be accomplished, some process could be seen as organizing these glowing phenomena into a distinct visual field clearly perceivable by my own "center of consciousness," wherever that might be! In fact, I reasoned, it must be the same mechanism that filled my dreams with clear, colorful visual images. And what were these strange alien sounds I heard during psychedelic exploration? Where did the sounds come from, and why was I able to hear them only under the influence of the entheogenic substances in my bloodstream? The mysteries multiplied.

During weekdays, especially in class sessions and at the library, I found that I could not stop trying to relate what I was studying in electromagnetic physics to the phenomena of consciousness I was directly exploring on weekends. From an engineering standpoint, I wondered what might be the mysterious mechanisms of "internal perception," both visual and audible, experienced during psychedelic trips and every night while dreaming. My senior engineering advisor had been urging me to choose an area of specialization to guide my future career choices, and now it quickly dawned on me that here was a fascinating goal, here in this new and intense focus—one of trying to understand what consciousness might be and how it might "work" according to physics and engineering principles.

Here lay an area rich with potential new discoveries, real mysteries that had not yet been uncovered by modern science. As an engineer, I realized that even a partial solution to the phenomenon might lead to the construction of previously unimaginable electronic devices for amplifying consciousness that might radically enhance communication, provide new modes of entertainment, and perhaps even amplify and refine intelligence, perception, memory recall, and emotional sensation. Ultimately one might even be able to communicate with the strange and innumerable alien entities I had encountered during each of the many psychotropic explorations. Perhaps even more direct communication could be established with some of the conscious entities I had sensed during my psychonautic voyages of discovery.

Having established my goal to search for a link between electromagnetism and consciousness, I began to seek out graduate programs in the area of consciousness studies, but, to my surprise, I could find no consciousness study programs of any sort. When I searched the technical literature I was even more surprised that I could find no such research efforts being supported by any of the sciences.

At the time, it seems that psychology departments almost universally regarded the behavioral approach as the primary way to study consciousness. I found numerous studies of human behavior that focused upon classical Pavlovian stimulus-response observations, analyzing the data using statistical methods. From conversations with my friends studying in psychology departments, I knew that they were never required to enroll in calculus, physics, or electronics courses. From this I reasoned that research psychologists were not sufficiently familiar with the calculus, physics, or electromagnetic theory to be able to approach research from the hard-sciences point of view that I felt was vital for any serious research into the phenomenon of consciousness. Conversely, neither could I find any interest in consciousness research (or psychedelic drugs) among physicists, electrical engineers, or biologists. A friend in a philosophy program tried to convince me that philosophers were studying consciousness, and to some extent I had to agree, yet their methodologies depended primarily on verbal logic and involved none of the hard-science laboratory approaches that I felt would be vital in any serious effort to uncover, verify, and master the actual mechanisms of consciousness. Eventually I learned that a primary reason for the lack of interest in exploring any possible electromagnetic component of consciousness in the hard sciences stems from a misguided conclusion published in the 1950s.

In the early twentieth century there was a concerted effort to explore consciousness through a method championed by the great American psychologist William James, who published numerous books and essays on the value of "introspection" as an appropriate methodology for studying human consciousness. James himself even experimented with the ingestion of consciousness-altering substances such as nitrous oxide (laughing gas). However with the advent of successful stimulus-response experiments of the Russian Ivan Pavlov (1849–1936), behavioral studies and observation overtook introspective methods as the favored mode of research.

In the 1930s, with the rapid development of electromagnetic modulation of radio waves for communication, new interest arose in approaching consciousness as an electromagnetic phenomenon. This interest peaked in 1940, when William Köhler (known as the father of Gestalt psychology), theorized that there must be an electromagnetic basis to consciousness. However, changing priorities arising from World War II meant relevant research was put on hold as government funding for such projects vanished.

Shortly after the war, Karl Lashley (1890–1958), a psychologist of the behaviorist school at Harvard, seemingly discredited Köhler's idea through a series of experiments seeking to discover whether he could detect any evidence for Köhler's theorized electromagnetic flow of information in the brain. Though Lashley's experiments themselves have now been discredited for their exclusive focus on the detection of direct current flow, they were at the time widely accepted by the scientific community, and this acceptance effectively put an end to interest in research projects designed to explore the relationships between electromagnetism and consciousness.

Though somewhat surprised and slightly discouraged by this all-too-brief history of consciousness research, my own fascination with what I believed to be a likely connection between electromagnetic fields and consciousness was not dimmed, and I continued with my own "experiments" using the technique of direct introspection, the approach pioneered by James in *The Principles of Psychology,* published in 1890.

Primarily through the ingestion of psychotropic substances alone at night in my dark study or in the dark Hill Country forests many miles from Austin, I continued to explore these incredible dimensions firsthand while doing my best to recall the esoteric experiences in my journals the next day. The new worlds that opened up under the influence of entheogens were powerful, direct, and rich in both visual and emotional content. This gave me the impression that something vast and mysterious was trying to communicate with me, but I did not know the language or have the voice with which to reply.

Back at school I was puzzled by friends who would take the substances in the daytime at home or even at weekend beer parties. I was certainly not interested in using these amazing tools for amusement, but instead felt that I was on the cutting edge of an exploration of previously unknown worlds that exist all around us, ones that we are unable to see without the aid of various entheogens. More than ever, I was increasingly convinced that the various vividly glowing apparitions that moved in and out of my vision must be electromagnetic in nature, and that understanding their mechanism would be the key to understanding consciousness itself.

I began to read everything that I could find that might provide a key to relate electromagnetism with the phenomenon of consciousness, and I spent hours in the engineering library searching through material in various journals of physics, biology, and electronics. I not only wanted to know how consciousness worked in the most general sense, but hoped to gather enough specific evidence to discern a model that might act as a guide for psychonautic exploration and might provide clues that could explain variations in the multiple flavors of consciousness: thinking, dreaming, aesthetic experience, contemplative practices, pleasure/pain, and psychotropic perceptions. It was now clear to me that at the very top of my own "professional hierarchy of needs" was that of acquiring sufficient information to develop a feasible model, a framework for an even more detailed architecture of human consciousness—one that could not only be reconciled with all that we know through science, but also compatible with the many accounts of consciousness described in the words of mystics, saints, artists, shamans, and psychonauts.

But it was my second encounter with John Lilly (1915–2001) that clarified the general technique I would follow in my search to understand the physics of consciousness. After graduation I had moved to New York City, where a wide range of resources dealing with consciousness, meditation, and entheogenic exploration seemed to have converged. One day I noticed a small announcement in the *Village Voice* of an upcoming lecture on "Consciousness and the Human Biocomputer." Several days later, in a small hotel room on 53rd Street, I found myself listening to John Lilly's presentation of ideas from his new book, *Programming and Metaprogramming in the Human Biocomputer: Theory and Experiments*.[2] After the lecture I introduced myself and mentioned that we had met a few years earlier in California, where I had worked as a summer engineering student for the Naval Pacific Missile Range. During lunch breaks I often went to the beach area of the base to watch porpoises being trained for the Navy, and I soon met the original custodian of the porpoises, John Lilly. Somehow we discovered our mutual interest in electromagnetic communication theory and that we were both licensed amateur radio operators. Now in New York, his interests had evolved from studying interspecies communication (between humans and porpoises) to introspectively exploring consciousness through the use of what he called isolation chambers, meditation techniques, and entheogenic drugs, primarily ketamine and LSD. Following his guidance, I constructed an isolation chamber in my loft on Greene Street, and began practicing various techniques for exploring consciousness, my goal being to supplement my speculations on the physics of consciousness with firsthand experience.

In my search over the last thirty years or so, to my delight, I have been able to find published evidence that directly supports my early experience and speculation that an invisible electromagnetic field in the brain, perhaps throughout the body, is the primary substrate and basis for human consciousness. The search has been difficult owing to the tendency in the scientific community to ignore ideas falling outside of the currently accepted mainstream assumption that consciousness will soon be found to be some complex epiphenomenon of electrical impulses moving between individual neurons in the brain. This book strengthens an alternate approach by offering the theories of twelve scientists and two philosophers whose conclusions point unequivocally to the electromagnetic field as the basis for consciousness. Mention of their papers has been largely absent from mainstream scientific publications, and their ideas, accordingly, have been largely missing from notice in the larger scientific establishment.

The basic fundamental principle being proposed here is that consciousness is identical with certain spatiotemporal patterns in the electromagnetic field.

SUSAN POCKETT,
THE NATURE OF CONSCIOUSNESS

The field characteristic of a living system is a basic property of life. It can be argued that the Universe is an electrical field and that everything that exists in it is a subsidiary or component part of the total field.

HAROLD SAXTON BURR,
THE FIELDS OF OUR LIFE:
OUR LINKS WITH THE UNIVERSE

1

Twelve Electromagnetic Field Theories of Consciousness

The material in this book provides insight into the assertion that consciousness, in all of its modes (e.g., thinking, dreaming, remembering, and the more esoteric modes of self-awareness induced by contemplative techniques or the ingestion of entheogenic substances) operates primarily through the modulation of multidemensional electromagnetic energy fields in space-time.* To support this conjecture, we examine twelve field theories of consciousness, each of which points to the electromagnetic field as being the underlying physical substrate of consciousness in living organisms.

Because consciousness appears to be a property related to brain processing, the tacit assumption in Western research has been that consciousness depends solely upon the brain and its neurophysiological activities. This book embraces a somewhat different paradigm. It is the contention here that the underlying source of consciousness may be found beyond the observable activity of mind-brain processes, and is most likely to be found in areas where our modern scientific tools are not able to detect unsuspected phenomena, or in areas where few researchers have yet been

---

*Space-time, in physical science, is a single concept that recognizes the union of space and time, first proposed by the mathematician Hermann Minkowski in 1908 as a way to reformulate Albert Einstein's special theory of relativity (1905). Common intuition previously supposed no connection between space and time. (Britannica online s.v. space-time)

motivated to look. Might it be that we are looking for the source or sources of consciousness in all the wrong places?

Part of the problem is the entrenched belief that the source of consciousness lies within the activity of neurons in the brain, that consciousness itself is a rare epiphenomenon that emerges from physical activity. The British researcher Max Velmans here points out that other cultures have taken a different approach:

> While Eastern philosophical/psychological writings entirely accept the existence of phenomenal conscious experiences that have been shaped by the workings of the mind and sensory systems, they do not take the view that these exhaust or even reveal the true essence of consciousness. For example, in both Samkhya and Advaita Vedanta these mentally conditioned phenomenal contents are said to obscure the actual source from which they arise.[1]

In seeking to understand consciousness from a materialistic point of view, the scientific community has unnecessarily narrowed its own range of search by excluding an insight such as the one Velmans describes regarding what the essence of consciousness might be. Modern neurophysicists thus see consciousness as an epiphenomenal—and thus mechanical—result of neuronal activity, assuming that there is indeed no "ghost in the machine." Of course, mystics, saints, and psychonauts down through the ages would strongly disagree. Velmans describes the reasoning behind the scientific community's rejection of something beyond the currently measurable material domain of brain activity.

> Consciousness is commonly thought of as a state or property of the mind (which may or may not be manifest under given conditions)—while "soul" continues to have its more classical meaning, that is, some essence of human identity that survives bodily death. Teased apart in this way, mind and consciousness have become major topics of scientific research, while soul has been largely left to theologians.[2]

It is clear that few scientists are interested in researching "soul" or investigating possible domains of awareness beyond death. Instead, the focus is exclusively upon observable, measurable activities of neuronal tissue, particularly in the brain. But philosophers are also burdened with their own form of myopia, lacking access to the many powerful conceptual tools that result from deep familiarity with the hard sciences.

The contention of this book is that the current study of consciousness is constricted by these mutually exclusive approaches. What is needed is a wider, more cross-disciplinary effort, a more comprehensive approach built upon concepts from the hard sciences but focused with the ontological insights offered by philosophers. One of the common characteristics of the theories developed by the fourteen researchers in this book is that their ideas are all the products of unusually wide cross-disciplinary interests and training, opening doors to new maps and paradigms of consciousness.

In fact, several of the major ideas discussed in this book arose from researchers who were not working within the confines of the neurophysiology community. For example:

- Alfred North Whitehead: Known as the "process philosopher," Whitehead's early background was in pure mathematics, and it was not until he turned his interest to philosophy at the age of sixty that he began to articulate the possibility of "electromagnetic societies" and "absolute entities."
- Harold Saxton Burr: A professor of anatomy at Yale, whose interest extended so far into electrical phenomena that he eventually published over ninety-six papers on the bioelectric phenomena of embryos and plants.
- William Tiller: A Stanford professor emeritus of material science and engineering, a Physics Fellow of the American Association for the Advancement of Science, a world authority on the physics of crystallization, and the author of the widely used textbook, *The Science of Crystallization.*
- Ervin Laszlo: A philosopher of science, a systems theorist, a

concert pianist, and a two-time nominee for the Nobel Peace Prize.

- David Bohm: A theoretical physicist, a world-class expert in the dynamics of plasma (his work on plasma under Robert Oppenheimer led to the development of the first operational atomic bomb), and early in his career he became a close associate of another giant whose thinking was "out of the box," Albert Einstein. In 1953 Bohm authored the 646-page textbook *Quantum Theory,* still used in physics departments throughout the world.

Others discussed in this book include individuals specializing in such diverse fields as biochemistry, neurophysiology, anesthesiology, and genetics.

OBJECTIONS TO AN ELECTROMAGNETIC FIELD THEORY OF CONSCIOUSNESS

Before proceeding, it is important to address several erroneous ideas that for over a half century have been used to dismiss efforts to investigate the role of a purely electromagnetic field in the manifestation of consciousness, thus biasing research efforts and leading to an almost exclusive focus upon the role of neurons and neuronal wiring in the brain.

Köhler's Electric Field Theory of Consciousness

Until recently an electromagnetic field theory approach to consciousness was largely dismissed owing to a misreading of the work of one of the founders of Gestalt psychology, Wolfgang Köhler (1887–1967).[3] An "electric field theory of consciousness" was allegedly put forward by Köhler in 1940, but in actuality Köhler did not posit an electromagnetic field of consciousness, but only the observational discovery that sensory stimulations (both auditory and visual) initiated complex, widely distributed field changes in voltage patterns on the brain surface, as measured between different regions on the cerebral cortex.[4]

Lashley and Sperry Refute Köhler's Theory

Köhler's correlation of perception and voltage change was thought to have been refuted by Karl Lashely (1951), and later by Roger Sperry (1955), in laboratory experiments that have since been found to be questionable in light of contemporary developments in brain research.[5]

In the early 1950s, Lashley sought to discover whether he could detect any evidence for Köhler's theorized electromagnetic flow of current over the surface of the brain.[6] Operating on monkeys, Lashley drilled holes in their skulls and inserted interconnected gold pins into multiple areas of each monkey's cerebral cortex. His assumption was that the gold pins would short-circuit and disrupt any existing electric fields involved in monkey consciousness and result in observable behavioral changes in the monkeys. When no behavioral impairment or effect of any kind was noted, Lashley concluded (erroneously) that there was no electromagnetic field component of consciousness.

This conclusion is highly suspect for a number of reasons. Lashley assumed that electrical currents would flow along the surface of the cerebral hemispheres, but never considered the possibility of currents flowing at different physical levels internally, within the brain (or within electromagnetic fields external to the brain's neurons). Lashley's experiments did not account for the possibility that brain activity might consist of high-frequency, three-dimensional electromagnetic field activity that would be undetected by his equipment, which had been designed primarily to measure direct current (DC), or at most, very low frequency alternating current (AC) signals.

Though widely accepted even now, Lashely's conclusion that consciousness cannot be an electric field phenomenon is suspect for a number of reasons: (1) Lashley only considered voltage changes between macro areas of the cerebral hemispheres, that is, the thin, outermost region of the brain; and (2) he ignored the fact that complex three-dimensional electromagnetic fields of extremely short wavelengths fill the human neuronal tissue at wavelengths such as the "thermal" infrared found throughout the body, or the even higher-frequency ultraviolet wavelengths. Such high-frequency signals would not be affected by the presence of randomly positioned gold pins poking into the cerebral hemispheres. High-frequency waves in the ultraviolet range are produced by biophotons that have since been detected in numerous experiments.

Though none of Lashley's experiments were definitive, nevertheless the electric field approach to consciousness was widely perceived as having been discredited, and this misperception continues to this day.

Libet's "Preconscious" Action Timing

In a series of famous experiments at the University of California, San Francisco, Benjamin Libet (1916–2007) examined the timing relationship between neuronal activity in the brain and a spontaneous action. His results astonished neurophysiologists and psychologists by repeatedly proving in numerous experimental designs that the readiness potential of motor neurons fired an average of 300 milliseconds before the subject reported consciously willing it into action. These results were taken to mean that voluntary acts are always initiated "preconsciously," and, accordingly, that consciousness does not influence actions.[7]

However, there is a potential flaw in this reasoning that has to do with the distinction between the words *consciousness* and *awareness,* and the assumption that there is only one variety of consciousness operational within the human neuronal system. It is more likely that there are multiple systems of consciousness operational in the human mind-brain complex beyond what is termed "awareness." Certainly myriad biological systems within the body continue to operate while the individual sleeps or is in a state of coma. Consciousness is much vaster than its "awareness" component; it might be more accurately said that there are various states of "unconscious consciousness" in parallel operation.

A good analogy can be found in the operational levels of computer architecture, where innumerable "decisions" occur at relatively low levels of high-speed machine language, whereas the resulting "action" occurs after a significant time lapse: higher-level languages (such as FORTRAN or C) take more time to carry out higher-level operations than those implemented by their subroutines at the machine-language level, to say nothing of the additional time required for storage and retrieval of memory traces.

The Faraday Cage Fallacy

Another objection to any electromagnetic theory of consciousness is the widely accepted but somewhat erroneous belief, held by both the general public and many biologists and neurophysiologists, that a Faraday cage will block all electromagnetic fields, and thus will prevent any electromagnetic signals from either entering or leaving the enclosed space. The 1944 photograph in figure 1.1 shows a soldier being treated by a diathermy machine within a Faraday cage. A diathermy machine is used to warm and relax cramped muscle groups through the action of high-intensity radio waves in frequency ranges from 100 MHz to 2 GHz (shortwave to microwave, see fig. 1.2). The soldier was placed in the cage so that the machine would not interfere with other electronic equipment in the immediate area. But the assumption that such a cage blocks all electromagnetic signals at every wavelength is patently false.

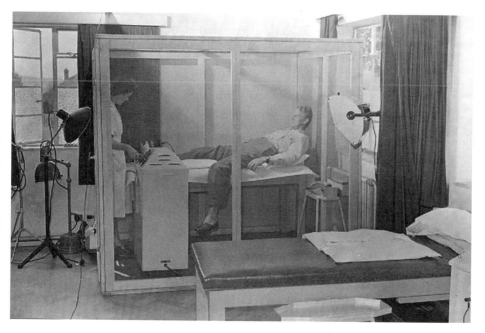

Fig. 1.1 A Faraday cage.

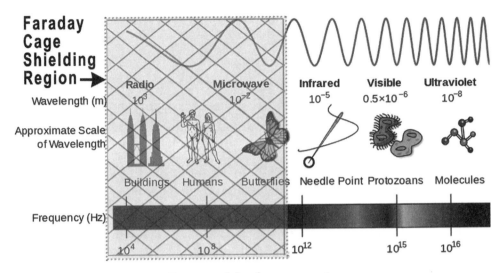

Fig. 1.2. Portions of the electromagnetic spectrum.

This erroneous belief was widely accepted among scientific researchers back in the 1960s, before radio frequencies in the gigahertz range became widespread.

While it is true that a Faraday cage will block external electromagnetic radiation if the metallic wire that makes up the cage is thick enough and if the gaps between the wires are significantly smaller than the wavelength of radiation, it cannot block electromagnetic fields of smaller, higher-frequency wavelengths.

A Faraday cage does indeed shield some electromagnetic radiation, in particular that of radio waves (AM and FM radio), but these are only a small subset of the vast electromagnetic wavelength spectrum, a portion of which can be seen in fig. 1.2.

The Faraday cage will not stop the higher-frequency electromagnetic waves that can be seen to the right in the spectrum (infrared, visible, ultraviolet, and cosmic rays). Even the closest woven strands of metallic wire are filled with enormous holes compared to the smaller wavelengths, for which a Faraday cage becomes totally transparent. Light waves, which are in the terahertz frequency range, are clearly visible as they pass through the cage to reveal the nurse and soldier within.

CONGRUENT FIELD THEORIES
OF CONSCIOUSNESS

While Lashley and his many followers rejected Köhler's suggestion that consciousness manifests as dynamic electromagnetic patterns flickering over the brain's surface, others agreed with Köhler. Each of field theories in table 1 adds support to Köhler's idea that consciousness is a phenomenon of the distributed electromagnetic field itself, *not* in the activity of individual electrical pulses passing from neuron to neuron.

TABLE I. CONGRUENT FIELD THEORIES
OF CONSCIOUSNESS

Year of Publication	Proponent(s) of Theory	Published Theory: congruent with an Electromagnetic Field Theory of Consciousness
1929	Alfred North Whitehead[8]	Electromagnetic Societies and Actual Occasions
1932	Harold Saxton Burr[9]	Electric Fields of Life
1995	Mari Jibu & Kunio Yasue[10]	Quantum Brain Dynamics
1997	William Tiller[11]	k*Space
2000	Susan Pockett[12]	Electromagnetic Field Theory of Consciousness
2002	Johnjoe McFadden[13]	CEMI Field Theory of Consciousness
2004	Stuart Hameroff & Roger Penrose[14]	Orchestrated Reduction (OrchOR) Model of Consciousness
2007	Ervin Laszlo[15]	Akashic Information Field or A-Field
2012	Rupert Sheldrake[16]	Morphic Fields / Morphic Resonance
2013	Karl Pribram[17]	Holonomic Brain Theory
2013	David Bohm[18]	Holomovement and the Implicate Order
2016	Shelli Joye[19]	Holoflux Field Theory of Consciousness

THE TWELVE THEORIES

The theories discussed in this book are all directly related to consciousness, and each makes an attempt to correlate the phenomenon of consciousness with an articulated hypothesis based upon principles of modern science. The proposed models are sufficiently different to provoke thought: at one extreme, two are the product of philosophers (Whitehead and Laszlo), while at the other, neurophysiologists (Pockett and McFadden) propose a patterned electromagnetic field that manifests human consciousness.

It is unfortunate that none of these twelve theories of consciousness have been investigated further or even generally acknowledged by current established communities of neurophysiologists, quantum theorists, and philosophers—but there are exceptions, and it is hoped that the collection of ideas in this book will be a springboard for the thought of others. The theories discussed in this book are listed in table 1 on the previous page, "Congruent Field Theories of Consciousness."

PRESENTATION OF THE THEORIES

In presenting the various theories explored in this book, care has been taken to develop each in terms that might be more readily understood by the general reader. Wherever possible, the subject matter has been supported with diagrams in a way that will render them more easily accessible to those who are unfamiliar with the arcana of modern physics, electromagnetism, advanced mathematics, or metaphysics. The chapters presenting the work of David Bohm and Karl Pribram are somewhat more extensive than other chapters owing to the fact that Pribram and Bohm published over one thousand technical papers and thirty-eight books. They also spent time together exploring concepts of mind and consciousness experientially with the philosopher and mystic Jiddu Krishnamurti at conferences and retreats both in England and in California.

Though these theories of consciousness have been developed by individuals with markedly different research interests, they are all (with the exception of Ervin Laszlo, a philosopher of science and systems theorist) credentialed science professionals holding university degrees in one or more of the hard sciences (i.e., electronics, mathematics, engineering, biology, or physics).

Each of the theories discussed in this book supports the conviction that consciousness has an electromagnetic basis or substrate, and that further research in this area will pave the way toward development of devices in the future that will interact with human electrophysiological systems to enhance, heal, project, expand, and empower human consciousness in ways currently unimaginable. Accordingly, the book also includes a chapter offering a glimpse into the range and history of hardware devices that have been developed in the effort to modify mind-brain activity through the application of electromagnetic fields.

The concluding chapter, "Optical Networks in the Brain and Future Research," is an effort to integrate and extend the material in earlier chapters, and points the way to new directions in consciousness research.

2

Pockett's
Electromagnetic Field Theory

In 2000, Susan Pockett, a neurophysiologist by training and a researcher in the field of psychophysics and consciousness at the University of Auckland, New Zealand, put forth the idea that consciousness manifests *not* in some collective configuration of neurons, but as a spatiotemporal electromagnetic field.[1] In her book *The Nature of Consciousness* Pockett stresses that consciousness is a *thing* and not a *process*. She believes that researchers have been looking for consciousness in all the wrong places, and they have been putting too much emphasis on the assumption that consciousness is merely an epiphenomenon, a by-product of neuronal processing that is a recently evolved phenomenon manifesting through the integrated activity of billions of neurons. In the opening of her book she states unequivocally that:

> The basic fundamental principle being proposed here is that consciousness is identical with certain spatiotemporal patterns in the electromagnetic field.[2]

This assertion runs counter to prevailing theories of consciousness as an epiphenomenal neuron-driven *process*. By contrast, Pockett says that consciousness is *not* some peripheral by-product of brain activity, rather:

The electromagnetic field theory of consciousness posits that conscious experiences are not abstract entities, but actual things: spatially patterned electromagnetic fields.[3]

One of the most intriguing assertions Pockett makes concerns the possibilities for implementation of hardware systems that would be able to "generate consciousness."

All neural processing is unconscious. . . . Conscious sensory experiences are not processes at all. They are things: specifically, spatial electromagnetic (EM) patterns, which are presently generated only by ongoing unconscious processing at certain times and places in the mammalian brain, but which in principle could be generated by hardware rather than wetware.[4]

CONSCIOUSNESS AND INFORMATION PROCESSING

Pockett argues that consciousness is separate from the actual information processing of the mind. The mind may be viewed as a local computer, but consciousness is that which operates the computer-mind. Not only does consciousness exist at a level or domain that lies *beyond* the data manipulations and display mechanisms created by the mind, this consciousness also continually absorbs information displayed by the mind. For Pockett, the mind exists as an interface allowing an observing consciousness to view the universe of space and time.

The brain researcher Karl Pribram and the physicist David Bohm, discussed at length in later chapters, would have agreed with Pockett's observations. Bohm pioneered the concept of the implicate order, a transcendental region outside of space and time but one containing additional dimensions as predicted by string theory (a mathematical theory in modern physics). In a 1978 interview, Bohm states, "Let me propose that consciousness is basically *in* the implicate order."[5]

To Pockett, Pribram, and Bohm, consciousness might be understood

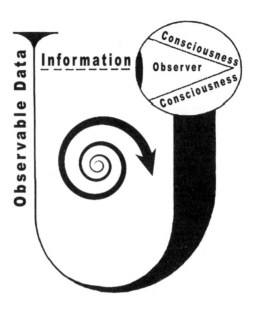

Fig. 2.1. The self-observing U:
Observable data → Information → Observer → Consciousness.

as an observer peering out at observable data while absorbing this information to expand its being. A simple diagram of such a process is given
in figure 2.1. The image is a visual metaphor used by the father of black-
hole physics, John Wheeler, in many of his lectures.[6] The diagram presents a feedback loop emphasizing the distinction between the *observing
consciousness* absorbing *information* from the *observable data* in the universe. This modified version of Wheeler's famous "U diagram" of the
universe depicts the universe growing in a process of self-observation
through which the universe co-creates itself in a continuous feedback
loop. Starting small (the thin portion of the U) the observable universe
grows in time giving rise to ever more complex tangible realities (the
thick portion of the U).

Pockett insists that consciousness *is* this third entity, beyond mere
data and information, one that transforms "raw data" into "understood
data." We call "understood data" by another name, "knowledge," when
inert information suddenly triggers that certain feeling of "Aha!" that is
sensed during moments of comprehension.

Conventional wisdom holds that information is *content* that can be encoded and transmitted. This information is contained in what is called a *signal,* which is independent of the coding scheme or transmission details. Contemporary theories of consciousness tend to identify consciousness in an imprecise way, equating it to some undefined macro-property that is thought to emerge during the processing of information. Such an approach seeks to equate consciousness with information processing, and this unsupported assumption results in efforts to generate consciousness through use of advanced computing hardware and software. For example, Max Velmans, a professor exploring the psychology of mind at the University of London, states:

> All talk of mind (including consciousness) can be translated, without scientific loss, into talk about information processing.[7]

CONSCIOUSNESS AS SPATIAL ELECTROMAGNETIC PATTERNS

Pockett disagrees with this information-processing paradigm, and instead proposes that conscious experiences are spatial electromagnetic patterns. Her reasoning is as follows:

> In general terms, the parallels between consciousness and electromagnetism are striking. First, consciousness appears to be produced by the brain—and it is well accepted that patterns of electromagnetism are produced by the brain. Secondly, consciousness appears on the face of it to share the same area of space-time as the brain—and it is well accepted that electromagnetic fields share the same area of space-time as matter.[8]

Pockett takes exception to the widespread assumption held by her peers that sensory consciousness is a completely neural process. She points to recent laboratory experiments in which various areas of the brain have been temporarily inactivated by transcranial magnetic stimulation (TMS) applied at approximately 100 milliseconds after the initiation of the sensory stimulus in question. This stimulation by a strong magnetic field works to block the normal activity of the sensory-associated neurons and prevents the stimulus from reaching what she refers to as the "global workspace," an electromagnetic field that has been posited to operate beyond the neuronal system and is thought to be the actual locus of conscious awareness. The global workspace theory was originated by the neurobiologist Bernard J. Baars in 1997 at the Neurosciences Institute in San Diego.[9] Pockett states, "If activity in the relevant primary sensory area is blocked at this time, conscious perception of the stimulus does not occur."[10] Her reasoning here is that there has been an interruption in the normal offloading sequence of neuronal information into the global workspace EM field.

CONSCIOUSNESS AND THE NEOCORTEX

The neocortex (commonly called "gray matter") is the newest evolutionary addition to the central nervous system. It is located at the outermost surface of the brain, just below the bone of the skull, and consists of a thin sheet, the *meninges* (fig. 2.2), which is approximately 2.5 millimeters in thickness (about the thickness of four sheets of copier paper), and contains 80 percent of the neurons of the entire central nervous system. Strong local connections between neurons are formed within this sheet, exhibiting local field potentials.

Neurophysiologists have identified six layers of the neocortex, labeled in the figure from 1 to 6, with 1 being the outermost. These layers can be seen in figure 2.3 in relation to a single pyramidal neuron that spans the inner and outer layers of the cerebral cortex. The locus of the complex electromagnetic field generation of interest to Pockett has been identified as the outer layer, layer 1, at the surface of the brain, just below the bone of the skull. It is here that complex, dynamic, three-dimensional electromagnetic fields have been observed, where they are generated and sustained by the synchronous firing of pyramidal neuron axons in synapses at the brain's surface.

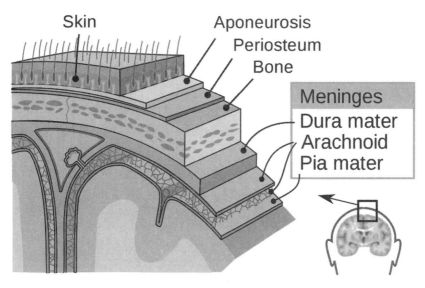

Fig. 2.2. Neocortex showing the meninges just below bone.
Graphic by Mysid.

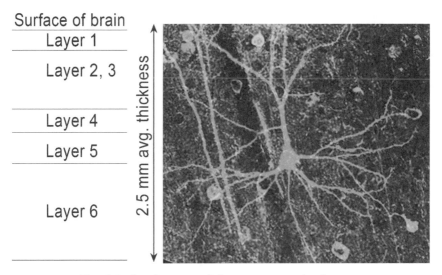

Fig. 2.3. Single pyramidal neuron in cerebral cortex.
Graphic adapted by author from an image by Nrtes (2006).

Pockett also points out that it is here, at the surface of the brain within layer 1, that electromagnetic correlates of consciousness exist as *dynamic local field potentials* (three-dimensional electromagnetic field configurations), generated when large populations of neurons fire synchronously in a feedback response to external sensory or internal stimuli. From such evidence, Pockett claims the following:

> It is thus a reasonable hypothesis that conscious experiences may actually *be* transient spatial patterns of LFPs [large field potentials]: in other words, transient spatial patterns of electromagnetism.[11]

THE CONSTRUCTION OF ARTIFICIAL CONSCIOUSNESS AND ITS IMPLICATIONS

Pockett's hypothesis, that human conscious experience should be identified with detectable, transient, three-dimensional patterns of local electromagnetic field potentials, leads to striking implications for future technologies intent upon generating "artificial consciousness." She believes that it is not too far-fetched to anticipate that concerted exploration of this electromagnetic approach to consciousness research will likely result in the production of systems of "artificial consciousness" through skillful implementation of new modes of hardware-generated electromagnetic (EM) fields.

> With regard to the possibility of producing artificial consciousness, it is relatively easy to produce EM fields artificially. The EM field theory of consciousness predicts that correctly configured EM fields that are produced by hardware will be just as conscious as similarly configured fields that are produced by wetware. So according to this theory, artificial consciousness is definitely in the cards.[12]

There are various other practical implications if the EM field theory of consciousness is correct, such as the possibility of pain-cancelling devices. Pockett explains:

If the EM field theory of consciousness is right, unwanted sensory experiences like chronic pain could be treated by measuring the associated brain EM field and then intervening to cancel it out, by imposition of an inversely patterned field (on the same principle as that used by noise-cancellation headphones on sound waves).[13]

3

McFadden's Conscious Electromagnetic Information Field

The British scientist Johnjoe McFadden agrees with Susan Pockett that consciousness is a three-dimensional electromagnetic field phenomenon associated with activity in the brain. McFadden, a genetics researcher at the University of Surrey, proposed his observation in 2000 when he published *Quantum Evolution,* in which he first referred to the "conscious electromagnetic field (CEM) theory."[1]

McFadden proposes a theory similar to Pockett's, but one that integrates the current fascination with information while clearly supporting Pockett's theory of the electromagnetic (EM) field as the seat of consciousness. McFadden proposes:

> that the brain's electromagnetic information field is the physical substrate of conscious awareness.[2]

Like Pockett in *The Nature of Consciousness,* McFadden reasons that a three-dimensional electromagnetic field, encoded with dynamic information, must coexist with human brain tissue. Powered by the activity of 100 billion electrically active neurons, this plasma-like dynamic processes, McFadden tells us, is consciousness as electromagnetic information.

THE CONSCIOUS ELECTROMAGNETIC INFORMATION FIELD

McFadden calls his theory CEMI (conscious electromagnetic information). Based on experimental evidence, McFadden hypothesizes that the brain generates an electromagnetic field that influences neuronal brain function through electromagnetic field-sensitive voltage-gated ion channels in neuronal membranes. By this mechanism, information in neurons might be pooled, integrated, and reflected back into neurons through the brain's electromagnetic field and its influence on neuron firing patterns.

In a 2011 article in the *Journal of Consciousness Studies,* McFadden writes:

> The electrical mechanism of neural firing ensures that all the information encoded in the neurons of the brain is reflected into the brain's EM field where it will be unified: that is what we mean by a field.[3]

One of the arguments critical of Susan Pockett's electromagnetic field theory of consciousness had been the lack of evidence that nerve cells could be causally influenced by electromagnetic fields within the brain. McFadden reasoned that if an electromagnetic field consciousness "entity" could not influence the physical neurons of the brain, then this field entity would be a "ghost in the machine," and that this does not correspond to our experience of consciousness.

McFadden points out that increasing evidence of the synchronous firing of neurons has been seen as a strong correlate of conscious perception.[4] In fact studies have provided hard evidence for assemblies of synchronously firing neuron areas in widely distributed regions of the brain to be strongly correlated with attention and awareness.[5] McFadden takes these findings a bit further by positing that there are two mechanisms at work and notes that they reflect the distinction between *unconscious processes* and *conscious processes.*

A *conscious process* creates a *percept,* an experienced conscious mental impression. *Unconscious processes,* however, such as those that regulate the digestive system, do not usually result in percepts (you are normally unaware of activity in your digestive tract). McFadden discovered that these unconscious—often called subconscious—processes are not associated with an observable, coordinated, synchronous firing of neurons. When recorded, subconscious processes exhibit seemingly random firing of neurons, or *asynchronous firing.*

However, when neurons fire *synchronously,* the information in distant neurons is bound through resonance into a single field, raising the information into cognitive awareness as a *conscious percept.* When neurons fire synchronously, the peaks and troughs of their oscillations reinforce one another to generate a strong net EM field oscillation. McFadden tells us that subconscious or preconscious information, of which one is *not* aware, is encoded within the mechanism of asynchronously firing neurons and that identification of consciousness with the brain's EM field "naturally and elegantly" accounts for why synchronous firing can be correlated with conscious percepts.[6]

New facts emerging in 2007 strengthened McFadden's hypothesis. Clinical experiments by a team of Japanese neurophysiologists demonstrated that neurons themselves are definitely influenced by the activity of electromagnetic fields through resonance at various frequencies, and McFadden was able to bolster his CEMI theory and extend it. Here, he alludes to the plasma-like nature of an electromagnetic field, which exhibits the Fourier transform properties of having a dual nature: one manifesting in the space-time (three-dimensional) field, and the other exhibiting a complementary existence in the nonspatial, nontemporal region called the frequency domain.

> From the frame of reference of an electromagnetic field there is neither time nor space between any part of an EM field. So the vast quantity of information in the EM field of the human brain (surely the most complex object in the known universe) has the same level of unity as a single electron or photon. It is in this information-rich dimensionless point that, I claim, the seat of our experience is located.[7]

McFadden's CEMI field theory emphasizes the existence of a feedback loop whereby neurons both generate and are affected by the EM field itself.[8] He describes a series of experiments conducted at the California Institute of Technology wherein the researchers were able to simultaneously monitor both extracellular and intracellular electric fields using small electrodes, one set *within* neurons and the other set *between* (outside of) neurons. The experiment called for inducing a constant low current into the cell bodies of the neurons sufficient to stimulate them to spike at a rate of 4 Hz. The researchers then moved on to phase two of the experiment, which examined the effect of applying an additional extracellular field to fill the volume outside of the neuronal tissue. Application of the external oscillating electromagnetic field yielded totally unanticipated results! The researchers had expected to observe, if anything at all, an increase in the frequency of neuronal firing due to the exogenous field; however, what their recordings revealed was not an increase in the frequency of firing but an observable change in the timing patterns of firing through a distinct phase shift in which the neurons almost immediately fired in phase, directly modulated by the changing external-field signal. In short, the external field drove the neurons to fire *synchronously,* in resonance with the electromagnetic pulses coming from the external field. McFadden points out that these results are sufficient to conclude that endogenous EM fields *can and do recruit neurons* to act in unison as networks capable of receiving signals from external EM fields.

According to McFadden, findings of the 2011 experiment at Stanford provide the key to understanding the mechanism of a direct cybernetic feedback loop between neurons and external EM fields. Within the wiring system of the brain, external electromagnetic field changes (the 4 Hz pulses in the experiment) are "seen" by the neurons as a detectable time-varying signal, driving the neurons' own signals into resonance with the external signal. Conversely, the three-dimensional external, plasma-like EM field, which encases the physical brain, receives these electromagnetic signals that radiate outward from within the neurons when they fire. When numerous neurons fire as a synchronous collective, their signals modulate the external EM field throughout the volume of the cranium.

In summary, results of the Stanford experiment support the phenomenon of two-way resonance (feedback looping) between the external EM field activity and internal neuronal EM field activity, and these resonating pulse trains may contain information encoded at the much higher frequency harmonics contained in the pulse. These findings are key to McFadden's CEMI theory in that:

> They clearly indicate that endogenous EM fields play an important role in recruiting neurons into networks of synchronous firing which are the strongest known correlate of attention and consciousness.[9]

AWARENESS AND INFORMATION

When it comes to the actual phenomenal *experience* of consciousness, McFadden is on less sure ground when he tries to conflate or superimpose awareness upon information.

> What I propose is that information/awareness may be experienced as information from the reference frame of an observer external to that information but is experienced as awareness from the reference frame of the particles/fields that encode the information. In this view, all information possesses an awareness aspect.[10]

In explaining the ground of consciousness, the sense of awareness itself, McFadden argues that this awareness is "what complex information encoded in electromagnetic fields feels like from the inside."[11] Unfortunately, his phrase "feels like from the inside" adds nothing that might provide a mechanism or an operational hypothesis clarifying the link between electromagnetic information and the awareness or the immediate experience of the content conveyed by the information.

SEVEN CLUES TO
THE NATURE OF CONSCIOUSNESS

In 2006, McFadden published an essay examining what he describes as the "Seven Clues to the Nature of Consciousness."[12] He articulates the following seven propositions in an approach to understanding consciousness:

1. Consciousness impacts upon the world.
2. It is a property of living brains but no other structure.
3. Brain activity may be conscious or unconscious.
4. The conscious mind appears to operate serially.
5. Learning requires consciousness, but recall does not.
6. Conscious information is bound.
7. It correlates with neurons firing synchronously.

Let us now take up these seven propositions in more detail, examining them each in turn.

1. Consciousness Impacts upon the World

McFadden's first proposition, that consciousness "impacts upon the world," seems self-evident and needs little discussion. Consciousness *does* seem to impact the world we live in, at least consciousness of the human cognitive and ego-based flavor. Human consciousness certainly reveals impacts upon the world in the manifestations of tools, art, and books, to mention only a few.

2. Consciousness Is a Property of Living Brains

McFadden's second clue, that "it is a property of living brains but no other structure," is more troublesome and certainly would find objection among the many panpsychists, both in philosophy as well as quantum physics. Here he seems to contradict himself by first declaring that "it is supposed that the consciousness is merely an epiphenomenon. I don't for one moment believe that this is the case." Yet he subsequently states that the brain "generates" the phenomenon of consciousness. He writes:

> Not all living flesh is conscious. Our livers aren't conscious. Neither is our colon nor our kidneys. Only brains are conscious. So it must be something about the structure of brains *that generates* the phenomenon of consciousness.[13]

3. Brain Activity May Be Conscious or Unconscious

To elaborate his third proposition, that "brain activity may be conscious or unconscious," McFadden goes on to distinguish three modes of human brain activity (see fig. 3.1):

- Obligate unconscious
- Facultative conscious
- Obligate conscious

In McFadden's scheme, *obligate unconscious* processes are *not* accompanied by awareness. These processes include such important biological system activities as temperature regulation, digestion, endocrine control, and memory storage and retrieval.

His second category of brain activity consists of what he terms *facultative conscious* processing, which may or may not include a sense of awareness. This mode he identifies with such activities as breathing, eating, and various learned activities, such as riding a bicycle. In many instances, facultative conscious processing (such as driving a car) eventually transitions into obligate unconscious processing, whereas other instances of facultative conscious processing (for example, playing a game of chess) never pass into the obligate unconscious mode.

The *obligate conscious* mode of brain activity is associated with such learned pursuits as reading, writing, speaking, performing arithmetical operations, and so on. Obligate conscious activities *always* proceed with the inclusion of some sense of awareness.

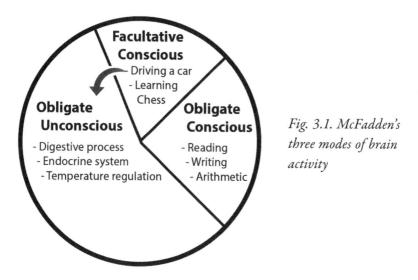

Fig. 3.1. McFadden's three modes of brain activity

There is clearly a tendency for the more primitive activities—those we share with lower animals and even plants—to be performed unconsciously and the more specialist activity—the strictly human actions, like use of language—to be accompanied by awareness.[14]

4. *The Conscious Mind Appears to Operate Serially*

McFadden's fourth proposition points out that processes that do not require cognitive awareness *operate in parallel,* while those processes that require concentration, or at least some degree of awareness, *operate sequentially.* As McFadden puts it, "Any theory of consciousness must explain why our unconscious mind appears to be massively parallel but our conscious mind is infuriatingly serial."[15]

Bernard J. Baars, a neurobiologist conducting research at the Stanford Neurosciences Institute, mirrors McFadden's interest in the sequential nature of awareness-consciousness versus the parallel nature of unconscious processes. Baars asks how it is that "a serial, integrated and very limited stream of consciousness emerges from a nervous system that is mostly unconscious, distributed, parallel and of enormous capacity."[16] Clearly both Baars and McFadden view awareness itself as an epiphenomenon of brain activity.

5. Learning Requires Consciousness

Many processes requiring sequential, focused learning (such as memorizing the multiplication tables or individual Morse code letters) eventually operate unconsciously in parallel with all the other sub-awareness activities of the body and mind. McFadden notes that "learning a skill seems largely to be about driving its accomplishment into our unconscious mind."[17]

McFadden points out that the relationship of *awareness* to *memory* is also a sequential process. It appears that a focused, sustained awareness on a particular perception is required for the generation of a long-term memory.

> Our visual system is constantly analyzing the changing scenery as we go through our day, but we only recall those items that we thought about. The memory of everything else is lost. Any theory should explain why our conscious mind appears to be the conduit for delivering information to our memory, but is not required for its retrieval.[18]

Here McFadden disregards the fact that a certain level of consciousness is required to provide the impetus for a specific memory retrieval, and it is only the subsequent search/retrieval mechanism process that is unconscious. The memory storage/retrieval mechanism falls under McFadden's category of *obligate unconscious*. This memory storage/retrieval system is not something that is learned, though some claim that there are techniques that can be learned to improve certain memory operations. However, the basic memory storage and retrieval process is operational at birth, possibly via DNA-inherited mechanisms.

6. Conscious Information Is Bound

McFadden's sixth clue is that somehow myriad separate neuronal input systems are bound together into single perceptual units. The example he gives is that of seeing a "tree" as a single percept out of the myriad individual leaves, colors, textures, and so on. The conscious mind thus binds together these innumerable details into a single familiar concept. The big question he suggests here is: Where in the brain does this binding occur?

7. Consciousness Correlates with Synchronously Firing Neurons

In his final proposition, McFadden's focus is again upon perceptual binding, and here he tells us that consciousness and awareness are associated not with the firing of individual neurons but with vast collections of neurons firing in synchrony.

THE BRAIN'S ELECTROMAGNETIC FIELD

Having stated his seven propositions—or "clues," as he sometimes refers to them—McFadden dives into proposing that the brain's electromagnetic field (as described in his CEMI field theory) addresses these seven issues.[19]

> The electrical field at any point in the brain will be a superposition of the induced fields from all of the neurons in the vicinity and will depend on the geometry and the dielectric properties of neurons and tissue. The combined activity of all the neurons in the brain generates a complex electromagnetic field.[20]

He explains that any such electromagnetic solution definitely runs contrary to the near-exclusive approach found in contemporary brain research, in which "neurobiology has focused on the chemical signal that is transmitted from one neuron to another." This is not to say that the chemical-signal transfer approach is not valid, but that it is may not be the only valid approach. It is quite possible, and even probable, that there are multiple modes of communication operating simultaneously within human bio-systems.

While the "chemical signal modes" of information processing may be quite adequate to meet the requirements for processing at the speed needed for operation of physiological systems (measurable in seconds or millisecond ranges), it is likely that substantially higher processing ranges may be required for consciousness and its varied cognitive processes (thinking, remembering, comparing, speculating, and so on).

Since the 1948 publication of a paper by Claude Shannon (1916–2001, also known as the "father of the digital revolution"), it has been mathematically understood that information-handling capacity—the frequency bandwidth of an information signal—depends directly upon the frequency rate of the specific data transmission mode.[21] Accordingly, frequencies required for processing complex real-time operations of human consciousness (cognitive vision or audition, thinking, making decisions among multiple alternatives, specific memory retrieval operations, etc.) necessitates significantly higher signal frequency rates than those available in chemical signaling. McFadden suggests, in full agreement with Pribram and Bohm (discussed in later chapters), that human consciousness must emerge from some holonomic process, that it appears to operate as superpositioned three-dimensional holographic-field modulations operating in the extremely high frequency ranges provided by light, infrared, or ultraviolet signals.

> Optical holograms can perform convolution, deconvolution, and Fourier transforms at the speed of light, acting on massively parallel data sets. Conversely, I suggest that it is their inability to process gestalt information holistically that accounts for the failure of digital computers to handle meaning, understanding, or common-sense knowledge.[22]

At this point, however, McFadden makes a questionable leap to the assumption that such information is "digital" when he categorically states:

> Digital information within neurons is pooled and integrated to form an electromagnetic information field. Consciousness is that

component of the brain's electromagnetic information field that is downloaded to motor neurons and is thereby capable of communicating its state to the outside world.[23]

While he does not elaborate on the source of his digital information assumption, it is likely that he views neurons as providing digital information by either firing or not firing their electrical spikes, though this is a tenuous assumption. Information encapsulated in a hologram is not digital; it is analog information.

In another of his "clues," McFadden says that brain activity may be conscious or unconscious, which he accounts for by saying that there are two systems operational in the human brain, both involving electromagnetic fields.

> The theory of natural selection predicts that over millions of years a complex brain will evolve into an electromagnetic field-sensitive system and a parallel electromagnetic field-insensitive system. These systems correspond to our conscious and unconscious minds, respectively.[24]

McFadden describes what he calls the "electromagnetic field-insensitive system" as one that could only be operational in the neuronal wiring system of the brain; it would only require relatively slow operational speeds (long time periods) such as the familiar beta-wave range (12.5 Hz to 30 Hz) measurable with EEG recordings. Distinct-frequency EM bands might eventually be found to control and monitor the various physiological subsystems, such as breathing, heartbeat, and so forth.

In contrast to the slower, field-insensitive EM ranges, awareness and cognitive processing are identified with the "electromagnetic field-sensitive system" operating at the much higher frequency ranges of infrared and light, in the ranges of 10^{14} Hz.

Of course any given frequency has the mathematical and electromagnetic potential to contain numerous harmonic frequencies of energy. These increasing frequencies correspond to wavelengths that would be smaller and smaller, down to the limit of the Planck length (10^{-35} m).* Thus, a beta wave EM signal has an almost infinite range of potential higher superimposed harmonic frequencies that can increase up to the Planck-length wavelength limit. Within this enormous frequency range may lie many bands of frequencies within which modulated signals are exchanged between the endogenous field and the neuronal system, each separate band communicating with and controlling various subsystems of human physiological processes.

In summing up his arguments for the CEMI field theory, McFadden states:

> Equating consciousness with a real physical field may initially seem an outlandish suggestion, but it is in fact no more extraordinary a proposal than claiming the commonplace materialist position that consciousness is identical with certain configurations of the matter of the brain: its neurons.[25]

McFadden surmises how the forces of evolution might, through natural selection acting over millions of years, take advantage of the mechanism of signal transfer between neurons and EM fields to evolve a process of information interchange. He concludes his 2011 essay, "The CEMI Field Theory: Closing the Loop," with the following:

> I suggest that advantage was captured at some crucial stage of human evolution and provided our ancestors with conscious minds.[26]

---

*The *Planck length,* determined in 1899 by the father of quantum mechanics, Max Planck, is recognized by physicists as the absolute smallest length possible in space, below which space has no meaning. The Planck length is generally expressed either in meters (10^{-35} m) or centimeters (10^{-33} cm).

4

Sheldrake's Morphic Resonance and the Morphogenetic Field

If a truly unified theory is ever to emerge, living organisms and conscious minds must be included within it along with the particles and fields of physics. There is a need for a new natural philosophy that goes further than physics alone can go but remains in harmony with it.

RUPERT SHELDRAKE,
THE PRESENCE OF THE PAST

The plant physiologist Rupert Sheldrake (b. 1942), educated both in biochemistry and cell biology, developed the radical new theory of morphic resonance at the end of fifteen years of laboratory research at Cambridge University and several years of subsequent field study in India. Sheldrake had been intrigued with the way plants and animals develop form and structure, and was puzzled as to what might be the mechanism by which simpler configurations, such as those found in the fetus, egg, or seed, were able to change over time into radically new forms, thereby producing extremely complex organisms at maturation. For example, how is it that an acorn receives the sequence of instructions that eventually transform the acorn into an oak tree? Genetic research in DNA points to the possibility of some sort of blueprint encoded in the DNA, but the intermediate mechanisms of growth and transformation remain completely unknown. He was particularly interested in the phenomenon that has often been noted when one individual in a species transforms into new and unexpected configurations, a phenomenon known as mutation; it has frequently been observed that other organisms of the same species, even those separated by vast distances, synchronously exhibit the same changes. Sheldrake wondered where the pattern or template for the form and structure might be located, and what mechanism might be involved in order for these characteristics to be transmitted to the growing organism, not only from its direct parents and ancestors, but from geographically remote members of the same type of organism. His focus upon this mystery led to the hypothesis of "formative causation" and "morphic resonance," both ideas an outgrowth of the concept of morphogenetic fields, which were first hypothesized in 1910 by Alexander Gurwitsch. Morphogenetic fields were thought to exist as a middle ground between genes and their expression. According to this theory, genes were thought to act upon these morphogenetic fields, and the fields themselves subsequently provided the sequenced patterns to guide the developing organism.

MORPHIC RESONANCE

Sheldrake's theory of morphic resonance declares that memory is somehow inherent in nature; all animals and plants inherit their structure and functional programming through resonant links with the collective memory of the species' ancestral experience. Sheldrake holds that DNA and genetic material are not enough to account for the complex structural and behavioral features of plants and animals, and that there must exist some additional field mechanism whereby these features are transmitted directly to the developing organism, a field mechanism that has not yet been detected in the laboratory.

Sheldrake's theory drew immediate criticism from the scientific community. In particular, his use of such descriptive phrases as "telepathy-type interconnections between organisms" drew outright condemnation from more conservative scientists. His overt criticism of the scientific community's highly mechanistic approaches in exploring the phenomenon of life only exacerbated the rift. As an example, he wrote:

> At present, the orthodox approach to biology is given by the mechanistic theory of life: living organisms are regarded as physicochemical machines, and all phenomena of life are considered to be explicable in principle in terms of physics and chemistry.[1]

The persistent denigration of Sheldrake's published work highlights the extent of the scientific community's power to censure new hypotheses whenever a theoretical approach is judged to fall too far outside the bounds of what is currently considered "proper" scientific speculation. Such condemnation effectively banishes the individual from subsequent professional publications, and it has the effect of discouraging further inquiry by others in what otherwise might be new avenues of research.

In a 2005 issue of the *Journal of Consciousness Studies,* one devoted exclusively to Sheldrake's ideas, the editor expressed this phenomenon as it has affected Sheldrake's career:

> In September 1981 the prestigious scientific journal *Nature* carried an unsigned editorial (subsequently acknowledged to be by the journal's senior editor, John Maddox) titled "A book for burning?". . . It reviewed and damned Rupert Sheldrake's then recently published book *A New Science of Life: The Hypothesis of Causative Formation* . . . and raised a storm of controversy whose fall-out is still very much with us. Up to this time Sheldrake was a well-respected up-and-coming plant physiologist and the recipient of academic honors including a fellowship at his Cambridge college. The furor that grew out of the assault in *Nature* put an end to his academic career and made him *persona non grata* in the scientific community. Over

twenty years later this journal still runs the risk of ostracism by publishing his work.[2]

Yet it is not only Sheldrake, but a growing number of research scientists, independently trying to put forth a coherent science of consciousness, who have also encountered major difficulties in disseminating nonmainstream ideas. Nevertheless, Sheldrake stands out for having retained the courage to pursue his ideas without the support of the scientific establishment, and he has continued conducting new experiments designed to collect data related to morphic resonance. He has also been able to publish popular books outside of normal scientific channels, and continues to give public lectures at colleges and universities.

ANIMAL TELEPATHY

In a 2010 summer lecture at Schumacher College, Sheldrake stated quite clearly, "what I'm arguing is that telepathy is a normal part of animal communication, it's the way animals communicate with one another at a distance." He went on to reference a 2010 research paper published in the Proceedings of the National Academy of Sciences, "Scale–Free Correlations in Starling Flocks."[3] After analyzing ultrahigh-speed digital photographic recordings of the three-dimensional movement of flocks of starlings through a wide range of flock size and spatial dimensions (from ten-bird to two-thousand-bird flocks), the authors arrived at the startling conclusion that flock motion response speeds were *completely independent* of the space-time separating the birds. The results proved unequivocally that reception and response occurs simultaneously in every member of a flock, as described below:

By reconstructing the 3D position and velocity of individual birds in large flocks of starlings, we measured to what extent the velocity fluctuations of different birds are correlated to each other. We found that the range of such spatial correlation does not have a constant value, but it scales with the linear size of the flock. This result indicates that behavioral correlations are scale free: The change in the behavioral state of one animal affects and is affected by that of all other animals in the group, no matter how large the group is. Scale-free correlations provide each animal with an effective perception range much larger than the direct inter-individual interaction range, thus enhancing global response to perturbations.[4]

Such action-at-a-distance behavior among birds can be explained if they are communicating via an electromagnetic field, or, even more esoterically, if we view a component of their communication as occurring within another domain related to electromagnetism outside of space and time. Such dimensions are known to quantum physicists from the results of high-energy particle physics experiments.

According to M-theory, the most recent version of string theory, there are an additional seven dimensions that exist beyond space-time. In other words, the data might be explained by the existence of actual dimensions beyond those of the time dimension (t) and the three spatial dimensions (the x, y, and z axes of a point's location) in space-time. One of the M-theory dimensions is the frequency domain (f_d), an important part of an electromagnetic field in space-time. The frequency dimension is used by electrical engineers to encode information onto radio waves by modulating the waves with unique combinations of frequency. In fact frequencies can be used to modulate and transfer information through various mediums (e.g., water, rock, air, space, etc.). One example is sound, a combination of frequencies that modulate air.

The frequency domain is completely outside of space-time, and yet embedded within space and time at every point in the universe. This is a difficult concept to grasp when first encountered and is discussed at greater length in the next chapter (on Laszlo's A-dimension). It is enough here to know that any frequency encoded as an information signal in space-time (such as a radio-station program, a song, or the call of a humpback whale) resonates identically as the same frequency within the spaceless, timeless frequency domain. A key concept is that there is neither space nor time in the frequency domain, every frequency within

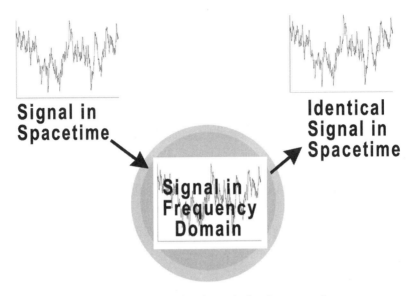

Fig. 4.1. Signal transfer through the frequency domain

that domain is simultaneously "superimposed"* upon every other frequency in the universe; there is neither space nor time separating the frequencies, they all become one frequency vibration. The implications are mind-boggling: if every frequency vibration in our space and time universe is superimposed within the transcendent frequency domain, where there is no spatial separation, then there is no reason that information cannot travel faster than the speed of light by ducking out of space-time and into the frequency domain where it then has the possibility of popping out into space-time again *anywhere* in space-time (fig. 4.1). This would be, in effect, instantaneous communication, information traveling faster than the speed of light.

Sheldrake said that the birds in the flock move "as if they have one mind," and went on to state, "I think that the field through which these effects takes place, the field of the social group, is an actual field, is a means through which communication can pass, just

---

*To *superimpose* means to lay one thing on top of another such as in music notation where multiple notes are layered at the same moment of time to create a chord, or in photography where several photographic images are superimposed through multiple exposures.

as iron filings line up, so the field can affect the way the birds line up."[5] These fields he calls *morphic fields,* and he describes how they have a kind of memory.

Though Sheldrake and his followers have not yet postulated an observable mechanism for the morphogenetic field, it is possible that the mechanism for morphic resonance lies in the operation of the frequency domain. Electromagnetic fields, though commonly detected and measured within space and time (t_d), can also be measured and mapped in terms of pure frequency in the frequency domain (f_d), a fact that can be seen in the widespread application of Fourier transform mathematics (see fig. 4.2).

It is thought that the elegant beauty and applicability of the Fourier transform supports the existence of the frequency domain as an onto-logical reality in its own right. The Fourier transform equation is shown in the center of the figure to indicate the central role that it plays in bridg-ing the two separate and quite distinct dimensions: frequency and time. Communication engineers design information signal processing systems within the frequency domain where the mathematics is greatly simplified. They then use the Fourier Transform to move their design solutions into the time domain where the actual electromagnetic field signals can be dynamically generated in space-time by electrical circuitry hardware. This approach has been used ubiquitously in the design and implementation of our various electronic communication devices over the past century.

Assuming that this frequency domain is a fundamental part of the

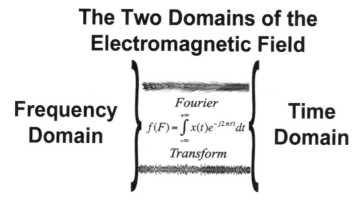

The Two Domains of the Electromagnetic Field

Frequency Domain

Fourier

$$f(F) = \int_{-\infty}^{+\infty} x(t)e^{-j2\pi ft}dt$$

Transform

Time Domain

Fig. 4.2. The two electromagnetic domains

cosmos, it would be safe to assume that living organisms have evolved in parallel with frequency information residing in this nonspatial, nontemporal dimension. Thus the frequency domain might not only be seen as providing a field that resonates with and coordinates flocks of birds and schools of fish, but also that it might offer an invisible template, a pilot mechanism that steers the growth, development, and evolution of individual organisms through resonance with electromagnetic fields in space-time.

Sheldrake's hypothesis of morphic resonance might then be explained as the direct ubiquitous influence of information from the frequency domain affecting and guiding all changes in the space-time domain. Since the Fourier transform is a two-way transformation (resonance causing both sides of the equation to remain synchronized), we can imagine that *all* information generated within the space-time universe is being simultaneously stored within the frequency domain *ākāśa* (see Laszlo's theory of the akasha or "A-dimension" in chapter 5), which then becomes an enormous memory depository for events occurring in our "outside" space-time universe

Through morphic resonance, individuals of each species contribute *all* of their unique experiences to the frequency domain as pure frequency information. The life of each "being" is fully recorded. The entirety of all information is immediately available for processing, in parallel (through superposition), to compute the next iteration of the universe and each individual living species currently within it. The resulting iteration would then collapse *out of* the frequency domain *into* the next immediate configuration of the observable space-time universe via the operation of the Fourier transform.

Thus we see how morphic resonance between space-time and the frequency domain may be guiding the evolution of organic matter and our own individual lives. According to this hypothesis, a feedback loop exists between the experience of organisms in the time domain and information from previously existing organisms now stored in the timeless absolute of the frequency domain. This information, preserved outside of time and space, can be seen as a vast repository of cosmic memory available for guiding organisms as they evolve in space-time.

5

Laszlo's Theory of the Akasha and the A-Dimension

A graduate of the Sorbonne and a professor of philosophy, systems sciences, and future studies, Ervin Laszlo (b. 1932) has been twice nominated for the Nobel Peace Prize. Laszlo, a prolific writer, supports the hypothesis that the universe is *nonlocally coherent,* that it is part of a unified field of consciousness.[1] The primary operating paradigm in modern science is that the universe is believed to be locally coherent, but not necessarily coherent at vast distances of separation in time and space. Science has been able to describe in great detail how material forces and objects interact locally, within measurable distances in space and time. However, Laszlo's claim that everything is nonlocally coherent implies that *everything is interconnected,* an idea that material science has not been able to prove, but one often found in metaphysics and mysticism.

THE "A-DIMENSION" AND THE "M-DIMENSION"

In explaining how the universe is nonlocally coherent, Laszlo proposes that reality consists of two domains or dimensions: an "A-dimension" and an "M-dimension" ("A" for *akasha* and "M" for "material").[2] Laszlo has described his "A-field" as an "information field," and he tells us, paradoxically, that this information field exists outside of space-time, yet is somehow omnipresent. He goes further to say that this information field (the dynamic field within the A-dimension) has been continuously interacting, dynamically, with all material that has manifested (and is manifesting) in our enormous (expanding) galactic region of space-time since the very beginning of the cosmos.[3]

In Laszlo's cosmology, the universe is the interaction of these two dimensions, the A-dimension and the M-dimension. The M-dimension contains that which manifests in space-time, that is, our familiar universe of the stars in the cosmos, the billions of galaxies in space-time, and so on. And it is here, in the M-dimension, that material science has been primarily focused since the time of Newton.

It is clear that Laszlo's use of "A" in naming his A-dimension stems from his use of the term *akasha,* an ancient Sanskrit term (*ākāśa*). Widely discussed in Vedic texts in India as early as 5000 BCE, the *akasha* denotes a vast region of vibrational information that is said to be perceivable by contemplative mystics and that is believed to underly the manifest universe.[4] It is likely that the same region has been referred to by early Christian mystics as "the Word," and by Buddhist contemplatives as "the Void." In the ancient Vedas its function is identified with *shabda,* the very first vibration, the first ripple that began our universe. *Shabda* is described by the contemporary authority on yogic philosophical terms, Ian Whicher, as "vibration/movement of consciousness."[5] The *akasha* has been described by I. K. Taimni as a sort of space out of which integrated energy vibrations emanate.

There is a mysterious integrated state of vibration from which all possible kinds of vibrations can be derived by a process of differentiation. That is called *Nāda* in Sanskrit. It is a vibration in a medium called *Ākāśa* which may be translated as "space" in English. But the conception of *Ākāśa* is quite different from that of Science. It is not mere empty space but space which, though apparently empty, contains within itself an infinite amount of potential energy. . . . This infinite potentiality for producing vibrations of different kinds in any intensity or amount is due to the fact that at the back of *Ākāśa* or hidden within it, is consciousness.[6]

Laszlo tells us that not only is all information stored in the Akashic or A-field, but that this field is a property of the quantum vacuum itself; within this domain of reality exists the fundamental information-carrying capability that he sees as interconnecting all things in and between all dimensions, nonlocally, in a fractal series of multiverses. Laszlo further identifies the A-field, which he says is currently unknown to physics, as being a "vacuum-based holofield."[7] But Laszlo again declares that any such posited field must be firmly rooted in what science already knows about the nature of physical reality.

> The concept of such a field cannot be an ad hoc postulate, nor can it
> be an extra–scientific hypothesis. It must be rooted in what science
> already knows about the nature of physical reality.[8]

THE CONTINUAL TWO-WAY FLOW

According to Laszlo, there is continual two-way interaction between the A-dimension and the M-dimension, between the Akasha and the material world. In a cybernetic feedback loop, the Akasha provides the information blueprint for outgoing changes in the material dimension that we also call space-time, while *information* recording these changes in space-time flows back into the transcendental center, where they add to all other information previously stored in the A-dimension.[9]

MORPHIC RESONANCE IN THE AKASHA

This model fits well with the theories of morphic resonance put forth by Rupert Sheldrake. Here, Sheldrake describes his conception of the mechanism of the morphic field's memory, relating it to the quantum vacuum field:

> All morphic fields have an inherent memory given by morphic reso-
> nance. Morphogenetic fields, the organizing fields of morphogenesis,
> are one kind of the larger category of morphic fields, rather like a

species within a genus. . . . Morphic fields must in some way interact directly or indirectly with electromagnetic and quantum fields. . . . Another possible point of connection between morphic fields and modern physics is through the quantum vacuum field. According to standard quantum theory, all electrical and magnetic forces are mediated by virtual photons that appear from the quantum vacuum field and then disappear into it again.[10]

While Sheldrake tells us that information stored in the morphic field *outside* of space-time is interacting with electromagnetic fields *within* space-time, Laszlo supports and extends Sheldrake's biological model to include an actual mechanism that clearly parallels Sheldrake's morphic resonance model. Laszlo describes the effect of a long-term interaction of a living, evolving species with the A-dimension.[11] In the following passage, he describes how this species-specific pattern may act as a natural attractor for morphic resonance within the A-dimension.

The information generated in this interaction is conserved in the A-dimension. The A-dimension is the memory of the M-dimension; it is the manifest world's Akashic record. The sea of Akashic information includes the species-specific pattern that is the natural "attractor" of healthy functioning in an organism. This pattern results from the long-term interaction of a species with the A-dimension; it is the enduring memory of those interactions; and it codes the generic norms of viable species.[12]

Laszlo describes a two-way information transfer between the Akasha and a living species in space-time. The Akasha thus provides a blueprint for the living organism, while simultaneously providing an information-recording mechanism and nonlocal storage facility for species-specific evolutionary changes as they occur in space-time. Laszlo states:

According to the Akasha paradigm the information that coordinates the functions of a living organism is a specific pattern in the sea of A-dimensional information. This corpus of information governs action, interaction, and reaction throughout the manifest world. It also governs the functions of the living organism. It is a blueprint of normal organic functioning.[13]

Sheldrake's morphogenetic field thus mirrors Laszlo's A-dimensional field, but while Sheldrake makes explicit a possible relationship or inter-action of morphic fields with electromagnetic fields, Laszlo has not attempted to identify the A-field with any of the current fields known to physicists. Here he states that the "Akashic Field" is, as yet, unknown to the physical sciences:

> The evidence for a field that would conserve and convey informa-tion is not direct; it must be reconstructed in reference to more immediately available evidence. Like other fields known to modern physics, such as the gravitational field, the electromagnetic field, the quantum fields, and the Higgs field, the in-formation field can-not be seen, heard, touched, tasted, or smelled. . . . In his previous books this writer named the in-formation field the *Akashic Field,* or *A-field* for short.[14]

Unfortunately, although Laszlo states clearly that his concept must be rooted in science, he provides no clear connection between the A-field and the tenets of modern science, neither through mathematics nor physics, and this leaves his theory incomplete.

Nevertheless, the brilliantly intuited metaphor of the A-field being some sort of "blueprint" can be used to explain why evolu-tion is not a random process. If we assume that there is a mechanism whereby the arc of the creating cosmos is guided by information stored in the A-field, then all of the "fine-tuned constants" discov-ered in our universe, and marveled at by cosmologists, might be more readily explained. If we assume that the A-field contains (and shares) information from billions upon billions of experimental attempts in previously evolving space-time universes to create new forms (new forms of particles, new forms of galaxies, new forms of matter, life, and consciousness), then it is the influx of this information collapsing from the A-field into the M-field that produces the exquisitely tuned constants that provide the underlying structure for our particular universe, observable in zebras, blossoming flowers, and iridescent nebulae. Such a viewpoint accords well with the recent ideas of the theoretical physicist Lee Smolin that "for cosmology to progress, physics must abandon the idea that laws are timeless and eternal and embrace instead the idea that even they may evolve in real time."[15]

LASZLO'S AKASHA AND BOHM'S IMPLICATE ORDER

Where might we look in physics to find some support for Laszlo's hypothesis of the two domains? While Laszlo does not mention the electromagnetic field, his two domains can be seen as possible descriptions of the two domains associated with what physics knows as the electromagnetic field and frequency domain, or as mapped by Fourier mathematics: the time domain (t_d) and the frequency domain (f_d). Laszlo's M-dimension can also be seen to be congruent with David Bohm's *explicate order,* which is projected out of what Bohm has called the *implicate order* (see chapter 11), a domain associated with the quantum vacuum. Laszlo's other dimension is the A-dimension, the Akashic dimension, which, we have seen, lies outside of space-time, but which we can identify with Bohm's implicate, enfolded order.[16]

In addition to supporting the theories of the biologist Sheldrake and the quantum physicist Bohm, Laszlo's theory brilliantly points the way toward a truly new paradigm for material science and future research directions. Unfortunately, his use of the Vedic term *akasha* and the Theosophical term "Akashic record" serves only to undermine his theory among the scientific community. Laszlo's occasional use of "spiritual" and "yoga" in his essays would seem also to limit the dissemination of his work within a broader scientific community, as seen here:

Our bodily senses do not register Akasha, but we can reach it through spiritual practice. The ancient Rishis reached it through a disciplined, spiritual way of life, and through yoga.[17]

Laszlo's frequent use of the phrase "Akashic record" gives ammunition to his critics, as it is found to be a phrase used by the famous Theosophist Alice Bailey in the mid-nineteenth century in her discussion of Patañjali's *Yoga Sutras*: "The ākāshic record is like an immense photographic film, registering all the desires and earth experiences of our planet."[18]

ADDITIONAL SUPPORT FOR LASZLO'S THEORIES

Yet another support for the concept and term "Akashic record" (again influenced by the Theosophists) can be found in the extensive writings of the Austrian philosopher Rudolf Steiner (1861–1925), who identifies the Akashic records to be the source of information obtained through his own supersensory perception, by means of which he was able to delve into the history of the planet.[19] Steiner taught a theory, which he claimed to practice himself, whereby through conscious development of latent organs of perception we can go beyond the ordinary space-time sensory systems into various modes by which we can directly access cosmic memory.

Everything which comes into being in time has its origin in the eternal. But the eternal is not accessible to sensory perception. Nevertheless, the ways to the perception of the eternal are open. . . . We can develop forces dormant in us so that we can recognize the eternal. . . . In gnosis and in theosophy it is called the "Akasha Chronicle." Only a faint conception of this chronicle can be given in our language. For our language corresponds to the world of the senses. . . . The one who has acquired the ability to perceive in the spiritual world comes to know past events in their eternal character.[20]

More recently, the American clairvoyant Edgar Cayce (1877–1945), known as "the sleeping prophet," writing in the mid-twentieth century, also used "akashic records" to describe the source of ideas with which he claimed to have connected during his deep trance and sleep states.[21]

Thus Laszlo's theories find a great deal of support in writings and traditions outside of the scientific field of inquiry, based as they are upon participatory, experiential data, which is not normally of interest in the material sciences. However, Laszlo is not averse to discussing such participatory experiences of his own, and uses his direct observations to extend his theory.

> When we enter an altered state of consciousness images, ideas, and intuitions flow into our consciousness that transcend the range of our sensory perceptions. These elements are part of the totality of the information in the cosmic matrix: the Akasha. This information is in a distributed form, as in a hologram.[22]

Here the idea of information distributed as a hologram is directly supported by years of brain research conducted by Karl Pribram (1919–2015), which provided a great deal of evidence that memory is a holographic processes, a holonomic flux of information stored in the frequency domain, a nontemporal domain equivalent to Bohm's implicate order. Pribram and Bohm, working together for almost two decades, eventually came up with the holoflux theory, which posits that the "whole" of reality is made up of two domains, an explicate space-time domain explored by the material sciences, and an implicate, transcendental, nonspatial, nontemporal frequency domain explored by mystics and psychonauts. According to this theory, the explicate domain, located in space-time, is populated by "material" consisting of vibration-frequency configurations of the electromagnetic field, whereas the implicate domain (equivalent to Laszlo's Akasha) is replete with information consisting of holonomic flux, or what Pribram and Bohm referred to as "holoflux." In this theory, holoflux in the implicate domain is the correlate of electromagnetic energy in the space-time domain, and the two are mapped mathematically by the Fourier transform relationship.[23]

Bohm insisted on considering the "whole" as an unending movement of information within the implicate order "unfolding" out into the explicate order of space-time. Conversely, the information mapping the changes in space-time are "folded" back from space-time *into* the implicate order. This cybernetic loop or flow is called *holomovement* by Bohm, and an image which captures this movement quite well is the wu-wei symbol from Taoism (also known as the yin-yang symbol). The process can also be viewed mathematically as a continual Fourier transformation of energy resonating between the two orders, manifesting in space-time (the explicate order) as electromagnetic field "objects," while in the transcendental implicate order the energy manifests as superpositioned holoflux information.

Like Bohm, Laszlo also insists on the importance of the need for understanding the whole, rather than exclusively focusing upon its separate parts, and he agrees with Bohm that information is never lost, but that it is conserved (within the Akasha, the Bohmian implicate order). In *Science and the Reenchantment of the Cosmos,* Laszlo basically sums up Bohm's view when he states:

Information is conserved and conveyed in nature at all scales of magnitude and in all domains.[24]

Laszlo argues that a shift in the materialist science approach is required for any real progress to be made in understanding consciousness, and that the new paradigm he offers would release modern science from its self-imposed restrictions to matter, space, and time.

It is a paradigm where information rather than matter is seen as the basic reality, and where space and time, and the entities that emerge and evolve in space and time, are manifestations of a deeper reality beyond space and time.[25]

6

Tiller's k*Space

William A. Tiller, a professor emeritus of materials science and engineering at Stanford University, is another rare example of a brilliant and well-respected mainstream physicist moving beyond the normal constraints of the physical sciences to a serious investigation of the physics of consciousness.[1]

Tiller received his doctorate in physical metallurgy in 1955. At Stanford, Tiller, department chair from 1966 to 1971, published over 250 papers on the physics of materials, and in particular on the process of crystallization in material substances.

Prior to his thirty-four-year career at Stanford, Tiller had spent nine years as a research physicist at the Westinghouse Research Laboratories in Pittsburgh, during which he began to explore the practice of meditation with his wife, Jean. By the end of his tenure at Stanford, he had become a daily meditator, and a growing set of nonordinary experiences led him to read *Psychic Discoveries behind the Iron Curtain.*[2] Tiller describes this turning point in his scientific interest.

> I was asked to be Department Chairman in 1965–66 while Jean and I continued our private inner explorations of the seemingly non-orthodox realms of nature in parallel with my very orthodox science research and teaching at Stanford. We took a sabbatical leave from Stanford in 1970 with a Guggenheim Fellowship to Oxford University in order to write one or two books in my orthodox science area, *The Science of Crystallization.*[3]

In the summer of 1970, Tiller was offered an invitation to speak on his more esoteric ideas at a conference in Oxford, and subsequently he and his wife traveled from California to London. Here, in his own words, we see Tiller moving from a previously orthodox scientific career in material science to a serious, enthusiastic focus upon the science behind metaphysical phenomena.

> On the flight to England, I read the book *Psychic Discoveries behind the Iron Curtain* by Ostrander and Schroeder and, although I knew a great deal about this subject by that time, I was impressed with what the Soviets had accomplished. . . . A key thought kept returning to my mind during this time period: "How might the universe actually be constructed to allow this seemingly crazy kind of stuff to naturally coexist with the orthodox science research that I was doing every day at Stanford with my Ph.D. students?" I reflected on this question a great deal via my daily meditative process while in England and eventually came to the conclusion that . . . competent, serious scientists needed to carefully study this area of research.[4]

Tiller reached the conclusion that there were phenomena being ignored by conventional scientific avenues of research, and decided to devote serious work to the field.

> I thus embarked upon a dual path in my search for knowledge and understanding of nature that I conducted in both orthodox and nonorthodox science in parallel with each other for 30 years (until my last Ph.D. student completed her thesis and passed her oral defense in 2000).[5]

In 1991, during his final year as a physics professor at Stanford, Tiller published a well-received textbook on crystallography, *The Science of Crystallization: Macroscopic Phenomena and Defect Generation.*[6] Unfortunately, this was to be his last manuscript accepted for publication by the mainstream scientific press.

FORTY YEARS OF DAILY MEDITATION
AND INTROSPECTION

Tiller's personal experiences, acquired over forty years in practicing daily meditation, led, after his retirement, to a full-time focus on research into the physics of consciousness. Subsequently, he published four significant books in the decade following (1997 through 2007), though none of them were reviewed in scientific journals as all of his previously published scientific work had been. His new books described, in detail, his experimental strategies, results, and theoretical conclusions in his research into the physics and architecture of consciousness.

Unfortunately, Tiller's books, replete with equations from integral calculus, technical diagrams and charts, and concepts from chemistry and crystallography, are difficult to follow for readers without a substantial background in mathematics and physics. Conversely, his work makes use of terms from popular esoteric terminology, such as "subtle," "spirit," "ether," and "magic," which make his work easy to dismiss among more technically trained readers. While such terms lack any consensual meaning in the wider scientific community, his choice of words stems directly from traditional nonscientific sources. In one of his glossary entries, for example, he defines his use of "subtle domains" as follows:

> Subtle Domains: Potential cognitive domains of the universe beyond the domain of physical cognition by humans or present physical instruments. Some humans presently sense these domains, most do not. Here, they have been labelled etheric, astral, mind, spirit, divine.[7]

Unfortunately the contemporary split between science and mysticism (physics and metaphysics) leaves the research of open-minded explorers such as Tiller in the unenviable position of being largely unexamined and undeservedly underappreciated by members of both communities.

THE TWO LEVELS OF PHYSICAL SUBSTANCE

In Tiller's words, "there are at least two unique levels of physical substance, not just one, occupying the same general space in our physical bodies but, normally, they are minimally interactive with each other." Tiller uses the following two terms for these two levels:

"k-Space" and "k*Space."[8]

The term "k-Space" is widely used in magnetic resonance imaging (MRI) technology to describe a three-dimensional array of numbers representing the distribution and relative intensities of electromagnetic field frequencies in space that are displayed during the generation of a magnetic resonance image.[9] Thus Tiller's k-Space designates information within our familiar space-time dimensions where electromagnetic fields propagate throughout space and time. However his k*Space designation (with an asterisk) indicates a domain of information that exists outside of (beyond) space and time, within the frequency domain.

The Akashic cosmology discussed in the previous chapter is fully aligned with Tiller's own conclusions. In 2014 Laszlo describes his A-dimension much as Tiller describes k*Space, though Laszlo goes further by suggesting that consciousness originates in the A-dimension and is then transformed into space-time as it flows into the brain hemispheres. Laszlo states:

Consciousness originates in the A-dimension, and it infuses the manifest world by interaction with that dimension. The neural networks of the human brain resonate with the information present in the A-dimension. In a more technical vein we can say that the brain performs the equivalent of a Gabor transform in regard to signals from the A-dimension: it translates the information carried in that dimension in a holographically distributed form into linear signals that affect the functioning of the brain's neural networks. This—nonlocal—information first reaches the subneural networks of the right hemisphere, and then, if it penetrates to the level of consciousness, also reaches the neuroaxonal networks of the left hemisphere. Given that this information is a translation of holographically distributed information in the A-dimension, it conveys the totality of the information in that dimension. Thus our brain is imbued with the totality of the information that pervades the cosmos.[10]

THE "THREE SELVES" OF HUMAN CONSCIOUSNESS

Tiller believes that consciousness acts as an interactive triad of quasi-independent "selves":

- the source self
- the soul self
- the personality self

In diagramming these "three selves" of human consciousness, Tiller theorizes, in a process of centration moving from an outer layer to an inner, several distinct domains. The first, the outer layer, consists of an electric domain, followed by a magnetic domain, and finally, the inner domain, k*Space or the "source self" or "fully spiritual" domain, equivalent to the frequency domain in electromagnetic-holoflux field theory. Tiller's model can be seen in figure 6.1.

Tiller here gives his answer to the question of what is the meaning of life's conscious experience in this universe:

My working hypothesis is that consciousness is a byproduct of spirit entering dense matter and that spirit can only attach or bond to information that has been built into the various layers of the whole person. I see this as one of the major reasons for our life experience in this particular classroom. One of the goals of our whole person appears to be to develop a state of coherence at the two interfaces between the three selves.[11]

Tiller's Diagram of the Three Domains

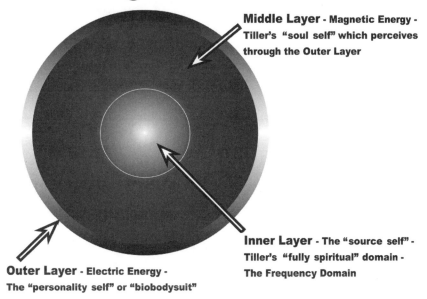

Middle Layer - Magnetic Energy - Tiller's "soul self" which perceives through the Outer Layer

Inner Layer - The "source self" - Tiller's "fully spiritual" domain - The Frequency Domain

Outer Layer - Electric Energy - The "personality self" or "biobodysuit"

Fig. 6.1. Tiller's three domains of the human being

Tiller makes an interesting dichotomy between "absolute reality" found in the innermost zone, what he terms the "source self," as contrasted with "relative reality," identified as functioning in the outermost zone of the "personality self," which primarily inhabits and controls the "biobodysuit." It is this outer layer, the avatar-like personality self with its physical senses and neural circuitry, that communicates the outer space-time phenomena of the universe to the inner, nontemporal dimensions of reality, which Tiller calls "a frequency domain."[12]

TILLER'S FREQUENCY DOMAIN

Tiller's frequency domain and space-time domain are dimensional reciprocals of one another, and it is the Fourier transform that maps the relationship between the two. He explains:

Mathematics requires a unique and quantitative connection between the different materials in the two layers of the personality self. One is automatically led to simultaneous particle-type behavior in one subspace connected to wave-type behavior in the other. This type of wave/particle behavior is a cornerstone of present quantum mechanics. In addition, this reference frame shows that a unique connectivity exists between any two points in one subspace via the totality of the other subspace and vice versa.[13]

In other words, all of these domains intersect at every "point" in existing reality. The unique connectivity Tiller describes, which can also be seen to explain Bell's theorem, can be seen as a function of the frequency domain, which is "outside of" or perhaps "not in the same dimensional ranges as" the time-space domains, because in the pure frequency domain there is neither time nor spatial dimensions.*

TILLER'S WRITING STYLE

But again, in describing his model, Tiller's choice of words is clearly influenced by his years of studying contemplative philosophy written by nonscientists, all of whom tend to fall into clearly nonscientific, "New Age" terminology, no matter how adept the writers might be. Tiller writes, for example, "The third, and inner zone, I call the high spirit self or the 'God Self,' whichever label one wishes to use." Such terms are not well defined, discussed, or tolerated in publications within the scientific community, and can only distance Tiller's research from mainstream science. On a less dogmatic level, however, and in comparison to the tone of the typical scientific publication, Tiller's work is often refreshing, as shown in the following quote:

---

*Bell's theorem: In a 1964 paper, "On the Einstein Podolsky Rosen Paradox," the physicist John Bell provided evidence which seemingly proves David Bohm's interpretation of quantum mechanics, which requires that all particles in the universe be able to instantaneously exchange information with all others.

Thus, the whole person is made up of three very different selves! The soul self, consisting of the still higher dimensional domains of emotion, mind and an aspect of spirit, is the entity that is importantly evolving in this overall process. It is much more durable than the personality self and is the repository of all the key experiences from a long succession of personality selves. When the various world classrooms have little more to teach the soul self, it graduates and transfers all of its essential information to the God Self. In this way the God Self is thought to keep expanding. . . . As to the God Self, when I was considerably younger I had many wonderful theories about God. *Now that I am older, and perhaps more awake, I realize that my personality self is not sufficiently conscious to even begin to seriously understand what that concept means!*[14] (Emphasis in original.)

7

Harold Saxton Burr's
Electric Fields of Life

Nature keeps an infinite variety of electro-dynamic "jelly-moulds" on her shelves with which she shapes the countless different forms of life that exist on this planet.

HAROLD SAXTON BURR,
BLUEPRINT FOR IMMORTALITY

Harold Saxton Burr (1889–1973) was a highly respected Yale neuro-physiologist who accumulated strong evidence that electric fields unify and direct the development of biological organisms at every stage of growth, from pre-ovulation to adult. With over forty years of precise laboratory measurements, Burr proved that patterned electromagnetic fields do exist, that they can be measured and mapped, and that these patterns can be used to predict future outcomes such as the time of ovulation and the onset of tissue malignancy.

It should be noted that Burr's findings, like those of so many in this book, have remained largely invisible to mainstream scientific research, as Burr himself commented near the end of his life. He wrote:

Surprisingly enough, these findings were never picked up in the literature and have not been extended further or repeated under other conditions.[1]

In many ways, Burr's research supports Rupert Sheldrake's hypothesis of morphic resonance; however, whereas Sheldrake assumes that the cause of morphic resonance is some as yet unknown esoteric mechanism beyond the boundaries of contemporary science, Burr views the electromagnetic field as the fundamental mechanism guiding morphic development and tissue regeneration. Burr's hypothesis is found to be supported by decades of hard evidence obtained from a number of different research programs conducted both by himself and by colleagues at various medical centers in New England.[2]

Burr was born in Massachusetts and was awarded his Ph.D. in neuroanatomy from Yale at the age of twenty-two, and he spent the next forty-three years as a faculty member of the Yale University School of Medicine. As an adolescent he was interested in electrical theory and amateur radio, and this early enthusiasm for electronics led to his lifelong passion for exploring the intersection of electricity and neurophysics in living organisms. During his years at Yale, Burr initiated a completely new field of research that he at first referred to as bioelectricity, and that eventually became the field of bio-electrodynamics. During his lifetime, Burr published over ninety-three major technical papers exploring and mapping the interaction of electromagnetic fields and living organisms.[3]

When Burr was appointed full professor at Yale in 1929, he set up his own laboratory and began his own research program. His initial goal was to explore the electromagnetic properties associated with the development of the central nervous system in animals and humans, but in order to do this he required electronic instrumentation not available in conventional laboratories at the time. It was virtually impossible to measure the minute voltages thought to be associated with a cell without affecting the cell itself, particularly those changes that he suspected would be found in neurons within a growing embryo. Up until the mid-1920s, the filaments in vacuum tubes that controlled the flow of electric current in an electronic device could become quite hot, with tungsten filaments in such tubes reaching temperatures as high as 2,200°C. Even by the early 1930s filament temperatures had only been reduced to about 700°C,[4] which was still much too hot, adversely affecting the living embryos being measured. In the early 1930s, Burr collaborated with the head of the Physics Department at Yale to design and construct a new and highly unique type of voltmeter with extremely high sensitivity. More importantly, the new instrument used special vacuum tubes that emitted very little heat. With this new device Burr could now measure extremely small voltages associated with living cells without having to worry about excessive heat damaging the living cells and delicate tissues being examined. With this new vacuum-tube voltmeter he was able to develop a new technique to detect complex electrical field changes at the cellular level.

> With our "navigational instruments"—a high impedance amplifier and silver-chloride electrodes working through a salt bridge in contact with living systems—we have been able to develop a technique which gives reliable results. With this it soon became clear that every living system possesses an electrical field of great complexity. This can be measured with considerable certainty and accuracy and shown to have correlations with growth and development, degeneration and regeneration, and the orientation of component parts in the whole system.[5]

With this new instrument, Burr was able begin collecting electromagnetic data during each stage of the growth and development of living cells. His research objective sought to understand two phenomena that had long puzzled physiologists: (1) the problem of how cells acquire the guiding information necessary to develop into specific physiological patterns, and (2) how cells are guided to replace damaged tissues. At the time it was understood that the information itself lies within some type of coding of genetic material carried by the chromosomes of each cell. What was not known, however, was the mechanism by which the stored, encoded information was subsequently used to guide the overall pattern of new cell formation during initial growth and subsequent regeneration of living systems. The most common assumption was that some type of unknown chemical-messenger molecules must be used to transfer specific information from the genes to guide cell construction at every stage of growth and transformation. Indeed, it was obvious that whatever the mechanism, it must be pervasive throughout the body as growth, repair, and regrowth is continual throughout living organisms. Commenting on this mystery, Burr wrote:

> Materials of our bodies and brains are renewed much more often than was previously realized. All the protein in the body, for example, is "turned over" every six months and, in some organs such as the liver, the protein is renewed more frequently. When we meet a friend we have not seen for six months there is not one molecule in his face which was there when we last saw him.[6]

Burr began his early experiments by determining the range of voltage differentials that might be discovered in human subjects by attaching silver-silver chloride electrodes to the tips of their index fingers. Each finger was immersed in a separate small cup filled with a saltwater solution.

After several hundred candidates had been measured repeatedly over a period of four months, Burr determined that the range of measured voltage gradients fell into four distinct groups: 0–1 millivolts, 2–4 millivolts, 5–6 millivolts, and 9–10 millivolts. The output voltage for each individual remained stable within their particular range over weeks of repeated testing. While Burr's chosen initial research subjects all happened to be men, shortly after a female associate pointed this out, he turned his focus to female subjects and measurements were consistently made on female members of the laboratory group.[7]

To his surprise the data revealed a difference in voltage-measurement sequences recorded from men and women: one day each month, "the female voltage gradients showed remarkable increases, a sharp rise for a period of twenty-four hours."[8] This indicated to Burr the possibility that he might be able to prove that a change of magnitude in voltage gradient might be associated with a fundamental biological activity.

To determine if the change in voltage actually occurred during the same time period as ovulation, Burr began working with rabbits. It was known that stimulation of the cervix in female rabbits results in the appearance of ovulation approximately nine hours after the stimulus. Eight hours after stimulating a rabbit's cervix, Burr surgically opened the rabbit's abdomen and introduced a salt solution around the ovary and an electrode close to the ovary itself. Using a microscope, the surface of the ovary was continuously viewed while the changes in voltage between the electrodes were recorded. The results were spectacular.

> To our delight the moment of rupture of the follicle and the release of the egg was accompanied by a sharp change in the voltage gradient on the electrical recorder.[9]

After numerous successful repetitions of the experiment on rabbits, Burr was able to convince a colleague running a research laboratory at Bellevue Hospital in New York to devise a similar experiment with a human subject. A young woman who was scheduled for a laparotomy was willing to be the subject, and in the middle of her menstrual cycle her voltage was monitored by Burr's instrument. After fifty-six hours, a marked change in voltage gradient was noted (which researchers suspected indicated a ruptured follicle in the ovary), and she was immediately moved to the operating room.

> Under the skillful hands of Dr. Luther Musselman, a laparotomy was performed, an ovary uncovered, and a recently ruptured follicle noted. This obviously confirmed the findings in the rabbit [that a spike in electrical activity indicates a ruptured follicle].[10]

Another physician in the same hospital, Dr. Louis Langman, noted the results of the experiment and with Burr's permission began to use one of Burr's devices with great success to determine the best time for artificial insemination. However, Langman's primary research interest lay in "the possibilities for detecting the problem of malignancy in the generative tract of women."[11] Langman had his research staff spend over a year to examine the voltage gradients of over one thousand female patients throughout all the wards of the hospital. The results were startling.

> There were a hundred and two cases where there was a significant shift in the voltage gradient, suggesting malignancy. *Surgical confirmation was found in ninety-five of the hundred and two cases.*[12] (Emphasis in original.)

Further experiments conducted by Burr in his own laboratory on hundreds of mice confirmed that voltage anomalies were to be found associated with the onset of tumors in the mice, whether implanted directly into the tissues or implanted as fetal material, or in those mice that developed tumors through other laboratory means of inducement.[13]

ELECTRODYNAMICS OF EMBRYOS

After years of experimenting with ovulation and malignancy detection, Burr began to focus upon mapping direct voltage patterns on growing embryos in living animals, beginning with frog eggs and salamander embryos. In examining voltage changes on the surface of frog eggs as they developed into more complex embryos, Burr discovered that the eventual development of nerve pathways occurred precisely where he had previously detected the largest voltage gradients.

> We explored the field of frog's eggs. . . . We marked the axis of the largest voltage gradient with spots of Nile blue sulphate and later found, as the eggs developed, that the frog's nervous system always grew along the axis with the highest observed voltage gradient. This was an indication that the field is primary—the matrix that shapes the living form.[14]

In his mapping of the voltage gradients in the developing salamander eggs by meticulously mapping electric-voltage potential along many points over the surface of spherical eggs, Burr, to his surprise, found the following:

> Using a moving electrode around the equator of the egg in the four quadrants of the development . . . there was one point on the equator of the egg which showed a marked increase in the voltage drop between the reference electrode and the point. . . . It was eventually found that this marked the head end of the developing salamander.[15]

FROG'S EGGS IN BIOMORPHIC FIELDS

In his laboratory, Burr and his colleagues made careful measurements of the voltage gradient at different parts of an egg, calling the results "electro-metrification."

> We explored the fields of a frog's eggs . . . not only to satisfy ourselves that something so small and relatively simple possessed a field but also to find support for our theory that the field controls the growth and development of the form.
>
> Using micropipettes filled with salt solution and connected to the voltmeter we found different voltage gradients across different axes of the eggs.[16]

After examining frog eggs, Burr and his team moved on to studying the gradients on salamander eggs, using silver-silver chloride electrodes "immersed in micropipettes and connected to the high input impedance of a suitable amplifier with a . . . recording galvanometer in the output."[17]

Again, measurements revealed voltage gradients on the surface of the salamander eggs, clearly revealing a main axis and subsidiary branches of electromagnetic patterns on the egg surface. Over the next two years the team proceeded to measure not only fields on the surface of the salamander eggs, but took measurements at each stage of the eggs' development into a salamander embryo and fetus. In a paper titled "An

ElectroDynamic Theory of Development," Burr described how he was able to detect the direction of regrowth in missing salamander limbs purely through mapping pregrowth voltage gradients.

During the later stages of his studies on salamanders, one of Burr's colleagues, Leslie F. Nimms of the Brookhaven Laboratories, made a fascinating discovery:

> as the micropipette electrodes were pulled away from the surface of the [salamander] embryo, a voltage gradient could still be recorded. In fact, drop-off of voltage gradient carried on as far as one or one and a half millimetres from the embryo.[18]

To determine if these fields changed in magnitude over the life of an organism, Burr persuaded a marine biologist at the Marine Experimental Station at Cape Cod, F. S. Hammett, to conduct a study of electro-metric fields over the life of a marine polyp, the Obelia, due to its extreme short-cycle life span. The results were astounding.

> During the early growth and differentiation of the animal, increasing voltage gradients were recorded until a peak was reached at the time when the animal was fully developed and feeding.
> . . . During the first third of the animal's life, voltage gradients increase fairly steadily. During the middle third, voltage gradients tend to level off and form a plateau. The last third of an animal's life shows evidence of regression with a consequent falling off of voltage gradients until death itself ensues.[19]

Burr reached the conclusion that electromagnetic fields emerged to radiate even *beyond* the boundaries of the embryo: "The *field properties of the embryo radiate through the medium of the liquid environment in which the embryo lives*" (emphasis in original).[20]

Eventually, to his surprise, he discovered that voltage gradients representing bioelectric fields of all organs could be measured "*at a distance from the affected organs.*"

It is sometimes possible to measure field-voltages with the electrodes a short distance from the surface of the skin—not in contact with it. *This shows that it is a true field that is measured and not some surface potential.*[21] (Emphasis in original.)

PANPSYCHIST INTERBIOLOGICAL INTERACTION

All of these results convinced Burr that the omnipresent electromagnetic fields must be acting in some way to control the pattern of organization and provide the design framework for biological systems, and thus they were acting with some degree of consciousness. But what might be the nature of this field of consciousness? Burr began to take a panpsychistic approach, hypothesizing that the electromagnetic field at its widest reaches might be the substrate of consciousness guiding the evolution, growth, and maintenance of biological organisms, that life in this universe might be based upon the intentional drift of electromagnetic fields.[22]

In the later part of his research career, to determine the extent to which electromagnetic fields might influence biological organisms, Burr switched from examining electromagnetic interactions within individual biological organisms to an exploration of mega-interactions of biological systems with external geomagnetic phenomena. In planning this next phase of his research, he realized that he needed to find some living subject that could be measured every day over a time period of at least a single diurnal cycle (one year) and preferably several years in duration.

In an intriguing chapter written in 1972, "Antennae to the Universe," he explains why he ultimately chose trees as the object of his long-term experimental monitoring.

We chose a tree as the most suitable subject for this investigation, because, in many ways, a tree has enormous advantages. It always stays put in a particular place; it requires no special feeding; it does not have to be anaesthetized when making the measurements; and there is no problem of cleaning up after the experiments, as there is with animals in the laboratory.

We hoped, then, that trees would not only offer a steady and reliable baseline from which to measure ordinary environmental influences but would also serve as antennae—so to speak—to pick up any extraterrestrial or Universal forces that might influence the living forms of this planet.[23]

TREES AS ANTENNAE TO THE UNIVERSE

Through long-term recording of the electric potential in trees (frequent measurements of the voltage gradient between electrodes bridging the deep central tree core and the outer rings), Burr collected over twenty years of data that support his theory that all living organisms are influenced through the activity of wider electrodynamic geomagnetic fields. His data revealed that bioelectric voltages measured in trees clearly synchronize with geophysical phenomena, such as solar flares, phases of the moon, and to some extent, earthquakes.[24] In the 1970s he switched from referring to the field phenomena he was measuring as "an electromagnetic field" to what he believed to be a more suitable term: the "field of life," or the "L-field."[25] At that time he was in his eighties and somewhat discouraged that he had not seen any signs of continuing interest in his research.

In the concluding chapter of his 1972 book, Burr summarized his hypothesis that these fields are *intentional,* that behind them is some form of consciousness.

> They are not just haphazard interactions between the component entities but forces which apparently are involved in a directional control of growth and development. In other words, the forces have directive properties.[26]

My own belief is that Burr's renaming of the electromagnetic fields he had measured so carefully was not in the best interest of his legacy. A careful literature search does not find reference to any "L-field" in the biological sciences. Nevertheless, the extensive data that Burr collected supports his theory that it is the electromagnetic field that guides the direction of growth and regeneration of living tissue in a way that implies conscious intention and awareness at every stage. In fact his recasting of the "EM-field" as the "L-field" indicates only that electromagnetic fields and living fields may be one and the same.

From 1916 to 1956, Burr published, either alone or with others, ninety-three scientific papers, yet his work is not well known either among modern biological sciences or in the recent field of consciousness studies. Burr's legacy, however, is a courageous one and should not be neglected by modern researchers. His work suggests the efficacy of a strongly multidisciplined approach to exploring the dynamics of life, consciousness, and the electromagnetic field, and it was Burr's conclusion that it is the ubiquitous electromagnetic field that most directly displays the power to control and direct the complex inception, structural growth, and healing processes found in biological life itself.

8

Penrose, Hameroff, and the Brain as Billions of Computers

One of the few proposed theories of consciousness that have not found outright rejection within the wider scientific community is "orchestrated objective reduction (Orch OR)," a model of consciousness that has been jointly developed by Sir Roger Penrose (b. 1931) and Stuart Hameroff (b. 1947). Orch OR is a biological theory of human consciousness that postulates that awareness originates at the quantum level, within microtubules. This goes against the conventional view that consciousness is a product of the firing of electrical impulses within networks of neurons in the brain. Yet they have been able to publish in scientific journals where their theory of consciousness has gained significant traction.

HAMEROFF AND PENROSE: THE ANESTHESIOLOGIST AND THE QUANTUM THEORIST

Brain as Billions of Computers
Hameroff is a medical anesthesiologist by training. Early in his career, while conducting cancer-related research, he became fascinated by the active and complex role that microtubules played during cell division. This led him to suggest that microtubules must be controlled and guided by some form of computational mechanism, and that perhaps

the problem of consciousness could be approached by understanding how microtubules might process information within the structure of neurons in the brain. In his 1987 book *Ultimate Computing,* Hameroff puts forth the hypothesis that the brain is not necessarily a single organ that produces consciousness, but perhaps should be understood to perform as a complex system of separate bio-computational devices acting in coherent unison. In his book he states:

> Thus *each of the billions of neurons in the brain is a computer.* Similarly, single cell organisms which have no synapses and are independent agents perform complex tasks involving rudimentary decision making, behavior, and organization. Thus, the basic irreducible substrate of information should reside *within* biological cells, and the brain may then be viewed as an organized assembly of *billions of computers* in which collective emergent properties may be specifically related to consciousness. The hierarchy of brain organization may thus have a secret basement—a new "dimension."[1] (Emphasis in original.)

Microtubules and Consciousness

In 1988, shortly after the publication of Hameroff's book, the distinguished mathematical physicist Sir Roger Penrose was awarded the prestigious Wolf Prize for physics along with his colleague Stephen Hawking for the development of the Penrose-Hawking singularity theorems, which, among other things, prove that the collapse of a star will always result in the formation of a black hole.[2] Penrose had earned his Ph.D. in mathematics at Cambridge, and in his twenties gained popular notoriety through presenting an unusual drawing that he himself called "impossibility in its purest form" (fig. 8.1), which was subsequently called both the "Penrose triangle" and the "impossible tribar."

As a student in 1954, Penrose was attending a conference in Amsterdam when by chance he came across an exhibition of Escher's work. Soon he was trying to conjure up such figures of his own and discovered the triangle that at first glance looks like a real, solid

Fig. 8.1. Penrose triangle

three-dimensional object, but upon closer inspection, becomes ever more impossible to resolve.[3]

In viewing the Penrose triangle we see an example of bistable perception caused by the unresolved superposition of two different perspectives that are unable to collapse into a single percept. In many ways this parallels the operation of quantum events, where the superposition of numerous possibilities "collapses" into one resolution in space-time.

In 1989 (only two years after Hameroff had published *Ultimate Computing*), Penrose published *The Emperor's New Mind*, in which he argued, supported by the mathematics known as Gödel's incompleteness theorems, that laws of physics are simply inadequate to explain the phenomenon of consciousness. Gödel had proven that an algorithmically based system of logic could *not* reproduce such traits as human intelligence or mathematical insight. Instead, Penrose claimed, non-algorithmic processes must come into play in domains where quantum mechanical effects predominate, at extremely small dimensions and far below the regions where classical physics predominates. A major problem in quantum mechanics since its inception almost a century earlier was that of how quantum-state changes intersect the classical world of space-time.

By definition, the quantum state is discontinuous; it only supports operations in discrete units or *quanta* of both time and space. The smallest discrete unit of length (below which space has no meaning) is the Planck length at 1.616229×10^{-35} meter. It is a quantum of length, defined as the distance light travels in one unit of Planck time.

Conversely, the smallest unit of time, called Planck time, is granular at approximately 5.39×10^{-44} seconds, the time that it would take for one photon, traveling at the speed of light, to cross the distance of one Planck length in space.

Fundamentals of Objective Reduction (OR)

Penrose knew that a quantum particle can exist in two or more states or locations simultaneously, and that physicists had to resort to probability calculations to predict the observable space-time behavior of quantum objects. A mathematical description called the wave function, $\psi(x,t)$,[*] had been developed by quantum physicists to deal with the multiple coexisting superpositions of alternative probabilities for a quantum event. A peculiar quantum property came to be known as "nonlocal entanglement," in which separate components of a system appear to act as a single unified system, the entire collection of components being governed by one common wave function. The physicist David Bohm had noted this unusual behavior of plasma early in his career, and it became the subject of his dissertation.

The dual nature of quantum particles suggests that they exist simultaneously in two parallel worlds, that of space-time and that of a purely coherent frequency domain (Bohm's implicate order, a nonspatial, nontemporal frequency domain). The mathematics of the Fourier transform emphasizes this bimodal peculiarity, providing the mathematics to prove the equivalency of a wave function as it exists in space-time (one side of the equation as a particle) or the way it can be expressed in the frequency domain (the other side of the equation, as frequency holoflux). This dual relationship is of such importance to quantum mechanics that David Bohm's textbook, *Quantum Mechanics,* contains this caveat on page 1: "It seems impossible to develop quantum concepts extensively without Fourier analysis."

Prior to the collapse of a quantum wave function into our space-

---

[*]The wave function, depicted as $\psi(x,t)$ where x is position and t is time, is thought to completely describe a particle in space-time.

time reality, it is understood that the wave function occupies a vast number of possible solutions to the next emergent transformation of the wave function into space-time. The following question has been a major issue: Just what is the mechanism by which the myriad possibilities "collapse" into the subsequent manifestation that emerges into space-time? This has been called "the problem of indeterminacy." What is it that determines the outcome of a probability wave function's manifest collapse into space-time? How is the waveform "reduced" into one of the many possibilities? Currently there are four possible scenarios that have been proposed to solve the problem of objective reduction (Penrose offered the fourth proposal, quantum gravity):

1. The first attempt to handle the indeterminacy problem was in 1925 by Heisenberg, but it relied heavily on the mathematics of probability and stochastic processes to predict "the most likely outcome" of a range of probable outcomes. This eventually became the predominant approach used by quantum physicists to predict the outcomes of high-energy particle experiments, and it has become known as the "Copenhagen interpretation" of objective reduction.[4]

2. Another proposed solution to the indeterminacy problem that has found a significant amount of support among quantum physicists is known as the "many-worlds" interpretation or "multiple worlds hypothesis," and at first glance it sounds like science fiction. This solution holds that each possibility in the wide-ranging superposition of possibilities evolves to form its own universe, resulting in an infinite multitude of coexisting "parallel" worlds. As Penrose puts it in his 1989 book, "Each instance of the observer's consciousness experiences a separate independent world, and is not directly aware of any of the other worlds."[5]

3. A third solution to OR has been that of "environmental decoherence," in which interaction of a superposition with its environment supposedly "erodes" the quantum states, causing them to collapse fully into space-time.[6]

4. Penrose proposed a fourth possible approach to indeterminacy, which he termed "objective reduction" (OR), an approach that finds the bridge between quantum and classical physics in what is termed "quantum gravity." According to Penrose, OR is a "real physical phenomenon, occurring when a waveform of quantum-superpositioned alternatives is reduced to a single actual occurrence due to the gravitational self-energy of the difference between the two mass distributions of the superposition."[7] One way to imagine this might be to visualize a sphere with a surface made up of myriad "probability points," each of them equally likely to occur. Somewhere on the sphere appears a slight dip, a crevice, allowing the most adjacent probability to fall into the crevice and collapse into space-time.

As Penrose points out, one of the difficulties of formulating a theory of quantum gravity is that quantum gravitational effects only appear at length scales that are close to the Planck length at the bottom (or center) of space, around 10^{-35} meter, a scale far smaller and equivalently far larger in energy than those currently accessible by high-energy particle accelerators.

We recognize that the elements of proto-consciousness would be intimately tied in with the most primitive Planck-level ingredients of space-time geometry, these presumed "ingredients" being taken to be at the absurdly tiny level of 10^{-35} m and 10^{-43} s, a distance and a time some 20 orders of magnitude smaller than those of normal particle-physics scales and their most rapid processes.[8]

Now, incredibly, Penrose goes on to state that an individual occurrence of such an OR might be "an element of proto-consciousness."[9]

THE ORIGIN OF ORCH OR

Having reading *The Emperor's New Mind,* Hameroff contacted Penrose in 1990 to discuss his own hypothesis regarding the mechanism by

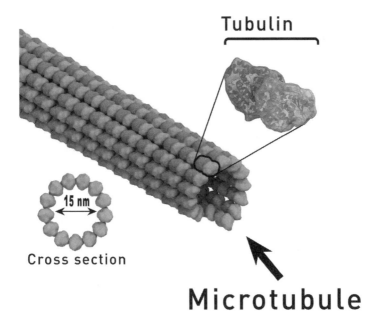

Fig. 8.2. Each microtubule is composed of tubulin protein.
Graphic by Thomas Splettstoesser.

which anesthesia blocked the operation of consciousness. Hameroff suggested to Penrose that microtubules (fig. 8.2) might provide the missing quantum environment in the brain in support of the sort of quantum operations sought by Penrose.

During the next several years, Hameroff and Penrose together developed a formulation for what is termed the orchestrated objective reduction (Orch OR) model of consciousness. According to their hypothesis, consciousness is associated with the quantum gravitational OR process, but human consciousness only occurs when many elements of proto-consciousness contribute in a coherently resonant process.

> The idea is that consciousness is associated with this (gravitational)
> OR process, but occurs significantly only when the alternatives are
> part of some highly organized structure, so that such occurrences
> of OR occur in an extremely orchestrated form. Only then does a
> recognizably conscious event take place.[10]

While Penrose had earlier been at a loss as to which structures of the physical brain might be possible candidates for Orch OR, it was Hameroff who recognized the potential of microtubules for the manifestation of consciousness.

Microtubules

Microtubules are the structural building material for all human cells and many bacteria. They are highly polarized, electrically, with one end having a plus charge and the opposite end having a negative charge. The length of a microtubule is about 1,600 times the width, which is approximately 25 nanometers. The inner diameter of a microtubule (fig. 8.2) is 15 nanometers, which as a wavelength is in the center of the wavelength range of ultraviolet light, and there are approximately 10^8 microtubules in each neuron. It is feasible that some or all of these microtubules could act as waveguides, shielding and channeling ultraviolet frequency signals in the range of 2.5 petahertz (1,000 times greater than microwaves).

Fröhlich Coherent Frequencies

The physicist Herbert Fröhlich (1905–1991), twice nominated for the Nobel Prize in Physics, proposed a theory of coherent excitation in biological systems known as the Fröhlich coherence. Fröhlich is famous for providing the first successful explanation of the microscopic theory of superconductivity, but perhaps of even greater importance for the understanding of conscious communication within the brain is his theory of the superconductor-like informational properties of coupled dipole excitation within small spatial regions of the brain. Hameroff describes these here:

> Collective nanosecond conformational states have been elegantly woven in a theory of *coherent* protein excitations by Professor Herbert Fröhlich. . . . Recognized as a major contributor to the modern theory of superconductivity, Fröhlich turned to the study of biology in the late 1960s and came to several profound conclusions. One is that changes in protein conformation in the nanosecond time

scale are triggered by a charge redistribution such as a dipole oscillation within hydrophobic regions of proteins. . . . Fröhlich's model of coherency can explain long range cooperative effects by which proteins and nucleic acids in biological systems can communicate. . . . Far reaching biological consequences may be expected from such coherent excitations and long range cooperativity.[11]

Bacteria, plants, animals, and humans are all known to emit radiation both in the infrared range (below the wavelength of visible light) and also in ultraviolet wavelengths (above the visible light range). While the primary frequency of human electromagnetic energy radiates in the far infrared band, peaking at a wavelength of 10 micrometers, the photons emitted by human cells in the ultraviolet have wavelengths in the range of 10 nanometers, slightly shorter than the inner diameter of a microtubule strand. It is not unreasonable to assume that the synaptic cleft between neurons, which ranges between 20 nanometers to 40 nanometers, would be resonant for EMF wavelengths that lie within the high ultraviolet range (the ultraviolet wavelength band of frequencies lie in a range from 380 nanometers to 10 nanometers). As the average inner diameter of a microtubule is 15 nanometers, were it to act as a waveguide it would resonate maximally at a wavelength of 15 nanometers, or equivalently, at a frequency of 2.5 PHz, definitely in the high ultraviolet range. In 2011 experimental evidence was published revealing strong Fröhlich coherence in microtubules at multiple resonant frequencies.[12]

While the Penrose-Hameroff orchestrated objective reduction model definitely offers a reasonable mechanism for the generation and sustaining of coherent, resonating electromagnetic frequencies of a very high order within the brain, it says nothing about *how such information might be modulated.* How is information *encoded* within these energy oscillations, and even more importantly, how is such encoded information actually "experienced?" Hameroff, like other contemporary brain researchers, has tended to assume that consciousness, at least mental cognitive processes, must function like modern computers—that consciousness must operate through some version of *digital information processing*. To this end, the word *qubit* has been created to capture the idea of the "quantum bit" of encoded information. In the universe of nature, however, nothing has yet been found that operates digitally. In the observable universe all processes in nature seem to operate in parallel as *analog* processes, not digital, and accordingly many brain researchers have instead explored holonomic models, focusing on analog patterns such as those found in holograms and fractal patterns, rather than trying to elicit some pattern of digital operations occurring within the brain.

At the conclusion of his book *Ultimate Computing: Biomolecular Consciousness and NanoTechnology*, Hameroff speculates on possible future developments:

> What technological device would be capable of receiving and housing the information emanating from some 10^{15} tubulin subunits changing state some 10^9 times per second? . . . Perhaps future consciousness vaults will be constructed in orbiting space stations or satellites. People with terminal illnesses may choose to deposit their mind in such a place, where their consciousness can exist indefinitely, and (because of enhanced cooperative resonance) in a far greater magnitude. Perhaps many minds can comingle in a single large array, obviating loneliness, but raising new sociopolitical issues. . . . Will it become reality like so much previous science fiction has? Probably not precisely as suggested; but if past events are valid indicators, the future of consciousness may be even more outrageous.[13]

9

Whitehead's "Electromagnetic Occasions"

In early life a mathematician and later in life a philosopher of metaphysics, Alfred North Whitehead (1861–1947) is known primarily as a philosopher, the father of a school known as "process philosophy." Early in his career he exhibited a distinct attraction to electromagnetic phenomena and theory, and much later in life this attraction spilled over into his philosophy of process, a flavor of which can be found in his own words, as shown here:

> There is urgency in coming to see the world as a web of interrelated *processes* of which we are integral parts, so that all of our choices and actions have consequences for the world around us.[1]

In his early years, Whitehead was clearly fascinated with the subject of electromagnetism. Whitehead's doctoral dissertation at Trinity College, Cambridge, was a treatise on what is now the cornerstone of electromagnetic theory and electrical engineering: Maxwell's equations.[2] To understand Whitehead's later philosophical fascination with "electromagnetic occasions," it is important to realize the significance of Maxwell's equations.

JAMES CLERK MAXWELL'S EQUATIONS

The first truly comprehensive solution to an understanding of the invisible phenomena of electricity and magnetism, and in particular the first set of equations that accurately map their dynamics, was discovered by the Scottish scientist James Clerk Maxwell (1831–1879). These equations opened the way to the development of electrical and electronic devices that are foundational to the functioning of our modern global society. To say that there are many uses for these mysterious invisible electromagnetic fields would be an understatement.

In 1862, the year after Whitehead's birth, Maxwell published his first paper revealing the mathematics presenting the long-sought-for relationship between these two mysterious and invisible phenomena: electricity and magnetism. The paper astounded the Victorian world of Maxwell, and yet only three years later his ideas leaped ahead even further, when he published a proof that electromagnetic fields traveling as waves through space and time move at the speed of light, 3×10^8 meters per second (671 million miles per hour). Our sun broadcasts an enormously wide range of electromagnetic energy waves from its surface, waves that require a full eight minutes in order to travel the 98 million miles before reaching planet Earth. Figure 9.1 shows the two sub-segments of the electromagnetic spectrum that are most familiar, the radio range and the visible light range.

It should be noted that the figure presents only a relatively small segment of the entire electromagnetic spectrum. The largest wavelength possible has a length that is the width of the entire universe itself, currently estimated to be approximately 10^{27} meters wide, though this value continues to expand at the speed of light. The smallest possible wavelength is that of the Planck length limit of 10^{-35} meter.

In 1872 (Whitehead was eleven years old at the time), Maxwell published his famous two-volume book, *A Treatise on Electricity and Magnetism*. In his new and more comprehensive treatment of electricity and magnetism, Maxwell revealed, in a brilliant set of interrelated mathematical equations, how all invisible electromagnetic phenomena

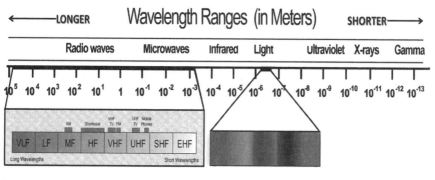

*Fig. 9.1. Radio and light segments of the
electromagnetic spectrum*

as well as visible light are all *one primary energy* radiating at vastly different wavelengths and frequencies.

In the history of physics, Maxwell's equations were as groundbreaking as Newton's laws had been two centuries earlier. However, whereas Newton's equations had accurately predicted the dynamics in the motion of solid visible objects in space and time, Maxwell's equations mapped the complex motion and dynamics of an absolutely invisible energy, one that fills the entire universe. Writing in 1931, Albert Einstein was especially impressed by the genius of Maxwell and his impact upon physics.

> Before Maxwell people conceived of physical reality—in so far as it is supposed to represent events in nature—as material points, whose changes consist exclusively of motions, which are subject to total differential equations. After Maxwell they conceived physical reality as represented by continuous fields, not mechanically explicable, which are subject to partial differential equations. This change in the conception of reality is the most profound and fruitful one that has come to physics since Newton.[3]

WHITEHEAD AND MAXWELL'S EQUATIONS

Whitehead entered Cambridge on a scholarship in 1880, only eight years after Maxwell had published his mathematical treatise proving the connection between electricity and magnetism. Initially attracted to pure mathematics, Whitehead was deeply intrigued by the precision with which Maxwell's set of mathematical equations so perfectly mapped the interrelated motion of electromagnetic energy as it moves through space-time. Accordingly, Whitehead chose to focus upon the published work of Maxwell for his dissertation research, and in 1884 Whitehead had completed, defended, and published his doctoral dissertation on the mathematics of Maxwell's equations. He immediately accepted an offer to become a fellow at his school, Trinity College, Cambridge, where he taught mathematics and physics and where he remained as a professor for the next twenty-four years.

In the early 1890s, the Serbian inventor Nicola Tesla visited London, offering visible public demonstrations of the incredible power of electromagnetic fields. Whitehead is said to have been particularly fascinated by the demonstrations of enormous electrical discharges that Tesla's apparatus was able to produce (fig. 9.2).

Whitehead spent much of the 1890s working to complete his first book, *A Treatise on Universal Algebra,* not publishing his book until 1898. However in 1900, he began collaborating with a former pupil, Bertrand Russell, working intensely to develop a three-volume tome eventually published as *Principia Mathematica*. Their mammoth project made a thorough attempt to present a set of axioms from which all mathematical truths could in principle be proven. This ambitious project established the reputation of both Whitehead and Bertrand Russell in the field of pure mathematics.

Near the end of Whitehead's participation in the *Principia Mathematica* project, his interest had begun turning from mathematics to metaphysics, and though he had not formally studied philosophy during his earlier formal education, he gave his first series of public lectures in philosophy in 1919 at the Tarner Lectures at Trinity College, subse-

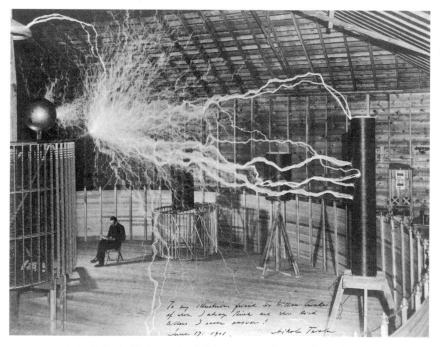

Fig. 9.2. Nikola Tesla in his laboratory with a Tesla coil producing 22-foot bolts of electricity. Graphic courtesy of Wellcome Images.

quently published as his first book on philosophy, *The Concept of Nature*.

In 1924, at the age of sixty-three, Whitehead was invited to teach philosophy at Harvard University, and he left England with his wife to live in Boston, where he spent the last twenty-four years of his life lecturing as a philosopher of metaphysics. In what is often thought to be his most important philosophical work, *Process and Reality* (first delivered as the Gifford Lectures at the University of Edinburgh during 1927–28), he declares, "Our cosmic epoch is to be conceived primarily as a society of electromagnetic occasions."[4] Just what, then, are "electromagnetic occasions"?

"ACTUAL ENTITIES" AS DROPS OF EXPERIENCE

In his Gifford lectures, Whitehead develops a speculative cosmology of consciousness based upon his own experience as a mathematician seeking to understand the integrated structure of cosmic reality. It is clear that he is fascinated by "process" (as seen in the very title of his book *Process and Reality*). However he goes beyond the simple view of process as a sequence of changing conditions within the space-time continuum by digging even beyond the concept of process in order to understand the relationship of change, existence, and consciousness through examining a similar term, *concrescence.*

The word *concrescence* comes from the Latin *concrescere,* which means "a growing together," "a formation," or "a coming into existence."[5] *Concrescence* is a term Whitehead uses in describing how a moment of experience comes into being. Each moment of experience Whitehead calls an "actual entity." His entire book, *Process and Reality,* as he tells us in the preface, "is concerned with the becoming, the being, and the relatedness of 'actual entities.'"[6] Whitehead describes actual entities as follows:

> "Actual entities"—also termed "actual occasions"—are the final real things of which the world is made up. There is no going behind actual entities to find anything more real. . . . The final facts are, all alike, actual entities: and these actual entities are drops of experience, complex and interdependent.[7]

Here, Whitehead considers actual entities as "drops of experience" or "moments of experience," with human life consisting of a series of these moments of experience stretching from conception through death. Actual entities are extremely "thin," temporally, and Whitehead regards them elsewhere as "quanta" of experience, undivided individual realities that occur as single undivided "now" entities. They are slices in time, and the passage of time measures the transition from actual entity to the next actual entity.[8] These actual entities are not to be confused with material objects; material things are actually "societies" of actual occasions. Actual occasions are the most basic units of actuality, Whitehead tells us:

> They are the final real things of which the world is made up. There is no going behind actual entities to find anything more real.[9]

On the other hand, these actual entities are not a static collection of "things"; they are dynamic and creatively alive, constantly developing in reaction to what has been and to what might be. And yet these actual entities are not separate from the rest of the universe—they are interdependent, related to all other actual entities in what he calls the "principle of relativity." It is this understanding, that the world is composed of an enormous set of interrelated living actualities of experience, that led Whitehead to call his philosophy "the philosophy of organism."[10]

Whitehead spends a great deal of time describing actual entities and how they concresce (come together or emerge) in space-time. He spends less time discussing nontemporal domains of reality, those outside of space and time; still, he proposes the existence of what he calls "Eternal Objects" as the source of creativity, the ultimate source of actual objects and the material world's "societies of actual occasions." An immediate problem is how to understand the word *existence* outside of or beyond our familiar dimensions of time and space. How can we understand Whitehead's "Eternal Objects" as existing outside of space and time?

ETERNAL OBJECTS AND
ELEVEN-DIMENSIONAL M-THEORY

Although modern science now accepts that there are additional domains beyond our familiar time and space dimensions, only four of these have been measured (or are measurable); physicists did not even suspect that another seven dimensions existed until quite recently. In scientific discussion, time (t), is represented as one single dimension, while space (with its three distinct x, y, and z axes) presents an additional three dimensions. Prior to the 1905 publication of Albert Einstein's theory of special relativity, scientists assumed that the time dimension was totally independent of the three space dimensions.[11]

However, Einstein's theory holds that time *cannot* be separated from the three dimensions of space. In addition, according to Einstein's paper, the speed of light itself is a constant (one that is often rounded up in scientific discussion to 3×10^8 meters per second).[12] Measuring these four dimensions has been so fundamental to the growth of scientific knowledge that the term "space-time" is now the accepted shorthand for referring collectively to these four dimensions. With the advent of particle physics experiments in the 1930s, however, new data revealed interactions of fundamental particles that were not predicted and could not be explained by space-time theory alone.

Over the next sixty years almost a dozen new theories were advanced in attempts to account for the new findings. These all converged in the early 1990s in a publication the American physicist by Edward Witten (b. 1951) that demonstrated that each of these earlier theories were different cases of an *eleven-dimensional theory,* which Witten called "M-theory." According to Witten, M should stand for "magic, mystery, or membrane," according to taste! Witten's theory resolved the mystery of the unexplained data by showing mathematically how there must be an additional *seven dimensions* beyond the four dimensions of space-time. The new field of M-theory has led to a groundbreaking understanding of quantum physics that implies that the cosmos is a projection from seven "internal" dimensions into our four "external" dimensions of space-time.[13]

Whitehead's "Eternal Objects," to exist outside of space-time, must accordingly exist in one or more (or all) of these additional dimensions predicted by M-theory. Yet they are not completely separate from space-time dimensions, as all things are interconnected according to both Witten and Whitehead, and everything in the universe is "concrescing process."

The process philosophy of Alfred North Whitehead can be seen to be congruent with electromagnetic field theories of consciousness. Other sections of this book illustrate how mathematics, physiology, and electromagnetic field theory can provide a mechanism by which the absolute entity concresces through creative resonance with eternal objects. Whitehead's work analyzes consciousness with almost mathematical precision in the universe, and yet there are two realms or domains for consideration in Whitehead's cosmology: a space-time domain and an eternal domain.

STRINGS AS ELECTRONIC ACTUAL ENTITIES

Whitehead's ideas provide a strong hint at an electromagnetic field theory of consciousness, as can be seen here in his observation that our age is characterized by "electronic actual entities":

> This epoch is characterized by electronic and protonic actual entities, and by yet more ultimate actual entities that can be dimly discerned in the quanta of energy. Maxwell's equations of the electromagnetic field hold sway by reason of the throngs of electrons and of protons.[14]

It should be noted that the theorized "strings" of vibrating energy, the fundamental entities of which the cosmos is composed (according to modern string theory), can be seen to be clearly compatible with Alfred North Whitehead's concept of "actual occasions" or "actual entities."*

Whitehead defines "societies" as collections of these concrescing actual occasions, and describes such collections of concrescence in time as emerging into "society in some portion of the universe."

> The term "order" evidently applies to the relations among themselves enjoyed by many actual entities which thereby form a society. The term "society" will always be restricted to mean a nexus of actual entities which are "ordered" among themselves. . . . The point of a "society," as the term is here used, is that it is self-sustaining; in other words, that it is its own reason.[15]

He talks about the endurance of a society—how it arises from disorder, grows, transforms, and changes in time—but concludes that "finally, after a stage of decay, passes out of existence."[16] Yet along with this image of the evolutionary arc of a society in space-time, Whitehead

---

*During his Gifford Lectures in 1928, Whitehead developed a speculative cosmology derived from his meditation upon direct experience, discussing at length his conception of the process of "concrescence" into "actual occasions" within the temporal domain.

strikes a subliminal note of pessimism and seems to voice regret in the image of "a system of 'laws' determining reproduction in some portion of the universe that gradually rises into dominance . . . has its stage of endurance" but gradually "passes out of existence with the decay of the society from which it emanates."[17]

But on what seems to be a new note of optimism, he goes on to say that now "we are in a *special* cosmic epoch" (emphasis added), one "characterized by *electronic . . . actual entities* (emphasis added).[18]

Unfortunately, Whitehead passes through this topic without significant development and begins discussion of the *Timaeus* of Plato and the *Scholium* of Newton.[19]

ELECTROMAGNETIC SOCIETY: A "MORE SPECIAL SOCIETY"

As if he were analyzing a mathematical proof, Whitehead spends significant effort to describe and contrast various configurations of societies. He proceeds with a discussion "largely conjectural, of the hierarchy of societies composing our present epoch."[20]

After developing a number of descriptions of various societies based on geometrical abstractions, he states rather surprisingly, but with great emphasis, that electromagnetic occasions presently dominate the cosmos in which we exist.

> Our present cosmic epoch is formed by an "electromagnetic" society . . . naming the members of the society "electromagnetic occasions." Thus our present epoch is dominated by a society of electromagnetic occasions. . . . The electromagnetic society exhibits the physical electromagnetic field which is the topic of physical science.[21]

Here it can be seen that Whitehead's electromagnetic occasions assume significant importance in his hierarchy of societies. It would be useful to explore the intersection of his concept of electromagnetic occasions with what is known of physics and physiology. Could the vast field dynamics of the electromagnetic spectrum in our space-time universe be the locus of electromagnetic occasions in an electromagnetic society?

Cosmologists do believe that long before there was matter in our space-time universe there were electromagnetic fields in the form of dynamic plasma. Eventually, as the universe cooled and the fields of electromagnetic plasma began to coalesce, elementary particles began to precipitate out of the void as quarks, eventually creating electrons, neutrons, and protons. Billions of years of evolution of electromagnetic field interaction with projected matter have culminated in the current configuration of the universe and what each of us experiences directly as "human consciousness."

Is it too much then to imagine that our consciousness is composed of electromagnetic occasions? Knowing that most of the cells in the human body die and are completely replaced multiple times within one lifetime makes it feasible to imagine that the primary feature of human physiology that survives throughout a lifetime is the electromagnetic flux (seen in the heat signature of the human body) that is unique in each one of us and that occupies a relatively wide bandwidth of frequencies centered in the infrared band of electromagnetic radiation. In the following three chapters the feasibility of consciousness manifesting as "electromagnetic occasions" will be explored in greater detail through a discussion of Pribram's holonomic brain theory, Bohm's theory of the implicate order, and the author's own sub-quantum holoflux theory.

ETERNAL OBJECTS AND
THE FOURIER TRANSFORM

So how and where do the eternal objects connect to concrescing electromagnetic occasions in space-time? Since the eternal objects are not ontologically within space-time, but are by definition eternal and thus in timeless eternity, they cannot be the issue, creation, or product of a society of occasions in space-time. Whitehead makes clear that a society of actual occasions in space-time "does not in any sense create the complex of eternal objects."[22] Thus, one can only infer that the complex of eternal objects itself is involved in the creation of societies.

But then by what vehicle or function do the eternal objects "reach out" from their domain of eternity to affect space and time? How do these eternal objects communicate with or project changes in the concrescing actual occasions that populate space-time? Unfortunately, Whitehead does not clearly answer this question in any of his lectures and essays, perhaps due to the limited conceptual tools available in his "pre-digital" age. The closest Whitehead seems to have come in his attempt to articulate a solution is when he states, "It seems as if the careers of *waves of light* illustrate the transition *from the more restricted type to the wider type*." (Emphasis added.)[23]

However, in subsequent chapters (exploring the ideas of the neuroscientist Karl Pribram and the quantum theorist David Bohm) this book offers a plausible answer to Whitehead's missing connection between the eternal objects and actual entities. The solution arrives via an identity equation discovered by the mathematician/scientist Jean-Baptiste Joseph Fourier in 1807 as a result of his research on the flow of heat energy during a project to help Napoleon cast cannon barrels more effectively. This remarkable equation has come to be known as the Fourier Transform, discussed at length later in the book, and it offers the plausible relationship between the eternal objects and actual societies sought for by Whitehead. In terms of the sub-quantum holoflux theory of consciousness discussed in chapter 12, the Fourier Transform describes the link of resonance that unifies electromagnetic fields in space-time with the holoflux fields that fill the implicate order.

10

Pribram's
Holonomic Brain Theory

My views stem from those proposed by Dirac, who noted that the Fourier transform describes a reciprocal relationship between formulations describing space-time and those describing a spectral domain. The spectral, holographic-like domain has enfolded space and time—and thus causality. A new vocabulary (such as talking in terms of spectral density) needs to be applied to fully understand the coherence/correlational basis of phenomena observed in this domain.

KARL H. PRIBRAM,
ORIGINS: BRAIN AND SELF ORGANIZATION

After decades of laboratory experiments seeking the location within the human brain of electromagnetic traces of memory, the elusive "engram," a holoflux brain theory based upon the mathematics of the hologram was published by Stanford professor emeritus Karl Pribram (1919–2015), who stated, "Holograms are examples of spectra, that is, of a *holoflux*."[1] Pribram's neurosurgical and mathematical search for a reasonable solution into the mnemonic aspect of the so-called hard problem advanced steadily during his seventy-year career of experimental research. His breakthrough metaphor, reinforced through subsequent experiment-driven research, came in the form of a hologram.

> Using the mathematical holographic process as a metaphor . . . my (1991) book *Brain and Perception* provides detailed review of experimental results that support the conjecture that holography is a useful metaphor in coming to understand the brain/mind relation.[2]

Pribram, who has been called "the Magellan of the brain," published in his lifetime over seven hundred papers and twenty books on pattern perception, cognition, and the brain. In 1972 he put forth a "holonomic brain theory," a mathematical model of brain function in which neurodynamics aligns with quantum theory.[3] Pribram here explains the use of the term "holonomic" in his theory:

> The term for the theory, *holonomic,* was first used by Hertz to describe linear transformations when they are extended into a more encompassing domain. I have here extended its meaning to cover the spectral domain.[4]

The Spectral or Frequency Domain

The spectral domain to which Pribram here refers is also known as the frequency domain in quantum physics and electrical engineering. The spectral domain is a concept that has been developed in the mathematics of the Fourier transform whereby information signals in a space-time domain are transformed into a complex of frequencies in a spectral domain.[5]

Early in his career, Pribram had become fascinated by the search for the engram, the suspected location of memory recordings in the brain.[6] In the 1920s the Canadian neurosurgeon Roger Penfield, while operating on the exposed cerebral cortex of patients with severe epilepsy, discovered that electrical stimulation of small areas of the parietal lobe would cause the patients, who were always awake during such operations, to recall specific memories, often in vivid detail.[7] According to Penfield:

> It was evident at once that these were not dreams. They were electrical activations of the sequential record of consciousness, a record that had been laid down during the patient's earlier experience. The patient "re-lived" all that he had been aware of in the earlier period of time as in a moving-picture "flashback."[8]

This discovery provided evidence to support the existence of the engram, a hypothesized physical storage location of memory traces whose mechanism and location has never been determined, in spite of decades of persistent research.[9]

Memory: The Search for the Engram

After graduating with an M.D. in neurosurgery from the University of Chicago at the age of twenty-one, Pribram began work with the renowned zoologist Karl Spencer Lashley, head of the Yerkes Laboratory of Primate Biology (a joint effort of Harvard and Yale), where the newly graduated neurosurgeon became Lashley's assistant, conducting research on memory in the brains of primates.[10]

Lashley had been searching for the elusive engram for over thirty years, but during his work with Pribram he reached the surprising conclusion that the engram did *not* exist in the cortex at all; he based his conclusion on the fact that no matter how much of a rat's cerebral cortex was removed, the rat would continue to remember its route through a maze that had been learned over a period of several weeks prior to the removal of massive sections of its cortex.[11] Lashley stated his conundrum as follows:

> Here is the dilemma. Nerve impulses are transmitted over definite, restricted paths in the sensory and motor nerves and in the central nervous system from cell to cell, through definite intercellular connections. Yet all behavior seems to be determined by masses of excitation, by the form or relations or proportions of excitation

within general fields of activity, without regard to particular nerve cells. It is the pattern and not the element that counts. What sort of nervous organization might be capable of responding to a pattern of excitation without limited, specialized paths of conduction? The problem is almost universal in the activities of the nervous system and some hypothesis is needed to direct further research.[12]

The search for such a hypothesis fired Pribram's research interest and, working with Lashley, Pribram discovered areas of the brain surface that when stimulated or removed significantly affected the processing of sensory information, even though no direct sensory links existed between neurons in the sensory organs and the areas in question. Pribram called these areas of the cerebral cortex "intrinsic," having no direct connection to the sensory organs, and contrasted these with "extrinsic" areas of the cerebral cortex in which could be traced identifiable, direct neuronal connections to sensory organs.[13]

Köhler's Theory of Geometric Isomorphism

In 1948, Pribram left Florida for New England to accept an offer to join the faculty at Yale, where he hoped to do research on the perception of sound by working with the Gestalt theorist Wolfgang Köhler.[14] Pribram was attracted to Köhler's approach to research, which had been formed by the Gestalt paradigm "that the whole is *different* from the sum of the parts."[15]

Pribram soon began working on an auditory cognition project at the laboratory run by Köhler, whose ideas reinforced Pribram's own; if the whole is discovered to be something much more than simply the sum of the parts of which it is comprised, then perception and cognition—in this case the psychoacoustic perception that interested Köhler—might indeed be something categorically different from the functioning of sensory neurons capturing light and sound.[16]

Pribram did not share Köhler's view of perception, a view commonly held among brain researchers at the time, that somewhere on the cerebral cortex would be found direct current electrical analogues, two-dimensional voltage images perhaps, having the same physical shape as the objects perceived; such a view, held in common by the Gestalt psychologists, is often termed "geometric isomorphism" (*iso* means "same," *morph* means "shape").[17] Pribram doubted Köhler's supposition that direct current fields would eventually be found to support the theory of geometric isomorphism but agreed that electromagnetic fields were somehow involved in visual, auditory, and cognitive perception, and in particular, in something Pribram termed "minding." As Pribram understood the term, "Minding is attending, looking out and ahead, grounded on looking back and within."[18]

For over two years Köhler and Pribram made extensive measurements, both of ape and human subject brains, trying to detect voltage changes between locations on the cerebral cortex surface that would correspond to changes in sensory stimulation.[19] Pribram's procedure was fairly simple, though it required access to the surface of the cerebral cortex, accessible immediately beneath the cranial bones.[20]

During the eight years Pribram worked with Köhler, a typical series of experimental procedures might involve holding up alternately white and then black cards while measuring any detectable and repeatable voltage changes between two adjacent surface areas of the cerebrum; to support his theory, Köhler sought to locate patterns of voltage gradient on the cerebral cortex itself that would be a mirror of the optical visual pattern falling upon the optic-field receptor neurons of the eye.[21]

After several years of research in Köhler's laboratory, Pribram (himself never having believed in geometric isomorphism) designed a successful experiment that provided a refutation of the assumption. In an amusing exchange afterward, Köhler asked Pribram, "Now that you have disproved not only my theory of cortical function in perception, but everyone else's as well, what are you going to do?" to which Pribram replied, "I'll keep my mouth shut."[22]

Brain Activity in Fine-Fibered Dendritic Networks

In the mid-1950s, Pribram's research led him to focus upon the neuroelectric activity associated with the fine-fibered webs formed by dendrites, rather than the more obvious electrical impulses that are seen to run along the much thicker axon trunks.

> At about the same time, in the 1950s, that Hodgkin had begun his work on the retina, I shared a panel at a conference held in 1954 at MIT with Stephen Kuffler of the Johns Hopkins University. . . .
>
> . . . Kuffler focused my thinking on the type of processing going on in the fine-fibered webs of the nervous system, a type of processing that has been largely ignored by neuro-scientists, psychologists and philosophers.[23]

Based upon his half century of research as a neurosurgeon, Pribram described how, it seemed to him, the thick, richly intertwining fine-fibered dendrite branch regions are where focused islands of complex frequency activity are to be found. He states:

> The fine fibers composing the web—the branches or dendrites of nerve cells—cannot sustain nerve impulse conduction the way axons can. The electrical activity of dendrites rarely "sparks" but oscillates between excitation and inhibition; thus, dendritic activity occurs locally, forming patches or nodes of synchronized oscillating activity. . . .
>
> When the formative processing web provided by the dendrites has to be accessed by the rest of the brain, axons relay the results of these interactions to other parts of the brain or to receptors and effectors in the body.[24]

The "form of the fine-fibered distributed web of the brain" became Pribram's passion and eventually led to his conclusion that the form of the ultra-deep structure of thinking is a holographic-like distributed process.

> According to the reasoning proposed . . . the potential of the ultra-deep structure of thinking is realized when the holographic distributed process becomes transformed by way of the memory-motive

and memory-emotive processes into cortically engendered complex verbal and nonverbal language and language-like cultural forms.[25]

In 1958, after ten years at Yale, Pribram accepted an offer from Stanford to continue his research in California as director of the Center for Advanced Studies. Over the next thirty years, Pribram published over two hundred papers mapping innumerable features of neuroanatomy and brain function.[26] The general consensus among neurophysiologists assumes that perception is a one-way street and that neuronal receptors in the external sense organs transmit information to the brain via neuronal impulses; however, during his years at Stanford, Pribram began to find evidence that the process is more of a "two-way" cybernetic transform, with information flowing both ways simultaneously, as described here:

> Critical to understanding is the acceptance of evidence that brain perceptual systems operate as top-down as well as bottom-up processors. It is this evidence that my colleagues and I have spent almost a half-century in amassing. Some 1,500 nonhuman primates, 50 graduate students, and an equal number of postdoctoral fellows have participated. The results of these researches have cast doubt on viewing brain perceptual processing as elementaristic, bottom-up, reflex-arc, stimulus-response—views that still characterize many texts in neurophysiology, psychology, and perception.[27]

Pribram would later put forth the critique that it is this very "neglect of a science based on pattern that has resulted in a science based on matter, an overarching materialism."[28]

During the course of his research, Pribram gathered sufficient evidence to convince him that not only visual reception of neurons seemed to exhibit top-down patterns of activity; auditory and motor systems in the brain showed similar distributed-field patterns of activity and response as well. As early as 1962, in a paper published on the work of Sigmund Freud, Pribram began to express his interest in focusing on the *pattern* of brain activity rather than tracing specific neuroanatomical circuit connections. He said:

> For Freud, a neuron may "fill"—i.e., become *cathected*—with excitation even though no transmitted activity results. . . .
>
> This emphasis on *cathexis** is one of those strokes of luck or genius which in retrospect appears uncanny, for only in the past decade have neurophysiologists recognized the importance of the graded nonimpulsive activities of neural tissue-graded mechanisms such as those of dendritic networks whose functions are considerably different from those of the transmitted impulsive activity of axons.[29]

The Holographic Paradigm

In 1965 Pribram was introduced to the holographic use of the Fourier transform through the widely reported implementation of three-dimensional holographic imagery, both in the United States and in the Soviet Union.[30] In the early 1960s engineers in both countries (working independently) created the first three-dimensional holographic images, feats that required the use of split beams of coherent laser radiation, a capability that itself had only just been discovered.

The mathematics of the hologram had been pioneered almost twenty years earlier by Dennis Gabor (1900–1979), a physicist and electrical engineer who used the mathematics of the Fourier transform to develop a novel optical approach for improving the resolution of the electron microscope. Gabor had earned his Ph.D. in Berlin by analyzing the properties of high-voltage transmission lines through the use of cathode-ray oscillographs, leading to his interest in electron optics. In 1933 he left Nazi Germany for London, recruited by the Thomson-Houston Electric Company (the British subsidiary of General Electric). There, in 1947, Gabor developed the mathematical basis of his holographic method, for which he was awarded the Nobel Prize in 1971.

Cathexis is a term used by psychoanalysts in describing an observed fixation in which a patient can be seen to be exhibiting an unusually strong degree of emotional attraction or charge to a particular person, object, or idea.

In referring to his predicted phenomenon, Gabor invented the name *holography* (from Greek *holos,* meaning "entire" or "whole," and *grafe,* "writing").[31]

However, Gabor did not produce an actual hologram. This had to await the invention of a perfectly coherent light source, the laser; instead, using a highly filtered mercury-arc light, Gabor was able to apply his holographic method to marginally improve the resolution power of electron micrographs. Unfortunately, Gabor's actual implementation of his holographic idea was not widely embraced; his technique was considered to be a somewhat awkward if theoretically intriguing variant of microscopy, which did not achieve financial success due to the time-consuming method required to produce an image.[32]

> Instead of the immediacy of seeing an image on a fluorescent screen (as some electron microscopes then produced), the reconstructed image was to be obtained more painstakingly via a half-hour exposure, followed by conventional photographic processing, unintuitive optical transformation, and observation through a conventional microscope eyepiece. . . . Gabor blamed lack of enthusiasm from his industrial collaborators and microscope manufacturers; . . . and microscopists dismissed [what they saw as] a hybrid and unfamiliar technique.[33]

In 1958, Yuri Denisyuk, a Russian engineer working at the Vavilov State Optical Institute in Leningrad, developed a holographic imaging system similar to Gabor's, also using filtered mercury-arc lighting. However, as Gabor had experienced in Britain, Denisyuk found little subsequent support in the Soviet Union for his holographic process.[34] In 1962, however, Emmett Leith and Juris Upatnieks, working in a highly classified laboratory near the University of Michigan campus where they were trying to develop a new form of side-looking optical radar, were able to run an experiment using the coherent source of light from a laser—a technology itself developed only in 1960.[35] Through use of laser light they were able to create a three-dimensional holographic image that could be viewed directly, without peering through a microscope. Their significant discovery, as well as the almost identical, simultaneous discovery of the holographic method in the Soviet Union, remained classified for almost two years before being revealed to the public.[36]

The creation of a hologram requires two fixed sources of radiation of the same frequency, often created in practice by splitting one original beam of electromagnetic radiation into two separate paths. The two resulting beams of energy (often infrared) are then aimed, from different angles of incidence, to fall upon a three-dimensional object, resulting in complex phase-interference fringe shadows upon a two-dimensional film plane where the patterns are recorded. These shadows form what are termed "holographic interference patterns." The information, captured in the recorded holographic image, can be subsequently reproduced by reversing the process.[37]

The full sequence of transformation is as follows: the three-dimensional information is first transformed into two-dimensional interference patterns of waves in space-time. The three-dimensional information has been transformed *out of* the space domain *into* a frequency-phase data, which can be stored on a flat two-dimensional film. From film, it can be transformed back again into the space domain through the focus of light energy of a single frequency through the complex fringe patterns imprinted on the film. This results in the formation of interference of light waves in space on the other side of the film from the source, and phase interferences in the light create a virtual three-dimensional image, identical to the one existing during the original recording. It is this resulting transmitted image that is termed a *hologram*.[38]

A major breakthrough in his search for a nonlinear frequency-based model occurred in 1965, when Pribram learned of the holographic method of memory storage in a *Scientific American* article written by the researchers Leith and Upatnieks.[39] What most impressed Pribram was that the article "described how the recording of interference patterns on photographic film had tremendously enhanced the storage capacity and retrieval of images."[40] The potential for rich data storage in holographic image technology intrigued Pribram, as it seemed to hold up new possibilities for visual processing and a new mechanism for memory storage.*

When Gabor was awarded the Nobel Prize in 1971 for his invention of the hologram, in his Nobel Lecture acceptance speech, he described the possible relationship of the hologram to human memory—likely much to Pribram's delight. Gabor noted that, in a hologram,

> the information is spread over the entire hologram area. . . . The appearance of such a "diffused" hologram is extraordinary; it looks like noise. . . .
>
> A diffuse hologram is therefore a *distributed memory,* and this has evoked much speculation whether human memory is not perhaps, as it were, holographic, because it is well known that a good part of the brain can be destroyed without wiping out every trace of a memory.[41]

That same year, 1971, Pribram published *Languages of the Brain,* summarizing the results of six years of experimental work at Stanford and supporting a new theory proposing cognitive holographic patterns in the brain. He proposed that while memories might not be localized in any specific brain cell, laboratory data indicates that memories are found to be spread, holographically, throughout wide regions of the fine-fibered web of the brain's dendritic synapses, like complex nets or networks.[42] Pribram's new hypothesis integrates the mathematical paradigm of optical holography with his observations that the processing of parallel information intercepted by sensory receptors is transformed

---

*A hologram is not necessarily limited to visual information. Each holographic imprinting can contain a complete snapshot of all current physiological, sensory, and cognitive activity at a particular moment of perception. These "snapshot holograms" of multidimensional information might be stored and chained sequentially, perhaps in layers, or filaments, or as overlapping shells as in the rings of a tree. Such holographic memory engrams would then be available for future retrieval and playback, triggered perhaps by selective neuronal activity retrieving strings of specific memory sequences.

orthogonally into horizontally interacting cortical fiber-mesh areas. He said:

> I propose that interactions among the patterns of excitation which fall on receptor surfaces become, after transmission over pathways organized in a parallel fashion, encoded by virtue of horizontally interacting processes. . . . The hypothesis is based on the premise that neural representations of input are not photographic but are composed not only by an initial set of feature filters but by a special class of transformations which have considerable formal resemblance to an optical image reconstruction process devised by mathematicians and engineers. This optical process, called holography, uses interference patterns. It has many fascinating properties, among which the facility for distributing and storing large amounts of information is paramount.[43]

In contrast to the prevalent neurosurgical research paradigm that focused upon tracing the activity and wiring diagrams of single neurons to tease out the answer to the memory problem within the brain, Pribram had chosen instead to search for evidence of some field or wavelike propagation in the junction of multiple neurons in the fine-fibered synaptic junction regions, where complex dynamic electromagnetic fields could provide the vehicle for information patterning, processing, and storage.[44]

> The arrival of impulses at synaptic junctions is never a solitary event. Axonal terminations are usually multiple—i.e., axons branch at their ends. As many as 1,000 synapses may characterize the junctional possibilities between a pair of neurons. Dendrites are tree-like almost by definition, displaying many fine fibered branches which crisscross, making multiple contacts among neurons to form a pattern. . . . Inferences about the nature of such a pattern can be made from the known fine structure of the brain and the electrical activity recorded from it. Several such inferences suggest that these patterns make up wave fronts . . . an advancing wave may sweep over 100,000 neurons in a single second. Such a wave has rich potentiality, and the

hypothesis that the mechanism of the junctional microstructure of slow potentials provides this organization.[45]

Pribram was also encouraged in 1964 when results of several independent research projects proved the general consensus—that there must be a single location for a memory engram—was false.[46] Computer systems had detected three-dimensional patterns over clusters of cerebral neurons, revealing the possibility of distributed, parallel processing, rather than simply (previously assumed) linear neuron-to-neuron processing. Pribram immediately related these patterns to the distributed geometric patterns he had observed in holograms, and he began referring to them as "holoscape contours."[47]

Pribram devised an experiment in which, through use of small spinning, notched gears, he measured the electrical response of a rat's buccal (lip) neuron to mechanical frequency stimulation of the rat's whiskers. The outcome revealed specific yet distinct complex three-dimensional contour patterns in response to different frequencies of whisker vibration.[48]

Such results strengthened Pribram's suspicion that perceptual processing would be found in patterns described by groups of neurons processing information in a spectral frequency domain, rather than by neuron-to-neuron impulse transmission.

> In my experience, each cortical neuron encodes several features of our visual environment, each neuron is like a person with many attributes, and thus our ability to recognize features had to depend on patterns displayed by groups of neurons for further processing.[49]

Pribram believed that he had found evidence that vision was undergoing two-way mathematical Fourier transforms in the processing of sight signals from photons striking eye cells to images perceived inside the brain. He relates a conversation he had just prior to attending a neuroscience conference in Boulder while climbing with colleagues on a hike in Colorado.

We had climbed high into the Rocky Mountains. Coming to rest on a desolate crag, a long meditative silence was suddenly broken by a query from Campbell: "Karl, do you really believe it's a Fourier?" I hesitated, and then replied, "No, Fergus, that would be too easy, don't you agree?" Campbell sat silently awhile, then said, "You are right, it's probably not that easy. So, what are you going to say tomorrow down there?" I replied, this time without hesitation, "That the transform is a Fourier, of course." Campbell smiled and chortled, "Good for you! So am I."[50]

Yet even in light of published, repeatable evidence, this Fourier transform–based theory met with substantial resistance within the mainstream research community. Neurophysiologists were reluctant to consider this mathematical frequency-field approach to perception and cognition when they were already invested deeply in biochemical and physiological approaches. This led to what Pribram here describes, rather amusingly, as the formation of two camps among researchers, those captivated by "feature creatures" versus the "frequency freaks":

Within the research community the contrast between these two views of perception was wittily joked about as pitting "feature creatures" against "frequency freaks." Feature creatures were those who focused on "detectors" within our sensory systems, of features in our external environment—a purely "bottom-up" procedure that processes particulars into wholes. Frequency freaks, by contrast, focused on similarities between processes in the visual mode and those in the auditory (and incidentally the somatosensory) mode. For the frequency freaks, the central idea was that our visual system responds to the spectral, frequency dimensions of stimulation very much as the auditory system responds to the oscillations that determine the pitch and duration of sound. The approach of the frequency freaks, therefore, is "top-down"—wholes to particulars. Within the neuroscience community, the feature creatures still hold the fortress of established opinion, but frequency freaks are gaining ascendance with every passing year.[51]

In the 1970s his theories continued to mature with the discovery of the Gabor function, in Paris, over a dinner with Dennis Gabor. What intrigued Pribram was not simply that Gabor found the Fourier transform important in the mathematics of communication, but that Gabor had pioneered an entirely new way of encoding and transmitting information using what came to be known widely as the "Gabor elementary function."[52]

When he discovered the Fourier holographic procedure, Gabor had been working on the problem of maximizing telecommunication across the newly laid trans-Atlantic cable.[53] He wanted to establish the *maximum* amount a message could be compressed without losing its intelligibility. To do this, Gabor developed the mathematics to model the two-way translations (movements) of Fourier flux (packets of information) through both space and time (in Gabor's application, a proposed undersea cable).[54]

This may be understood as the movement of the results of a Fourier transform, the transportation of a "packet" of frequency information that normally has no time component through time and space. Gabor designed a procedure to maximize information flow across the trans-Atlantic cable by first performing a Fourier transform on incoming frequency spectrum packets (typically milliseconds of audio conversation or music), and then transmitting the Fourier transformed information as electronic snapshot packets across the trans-Atlantic cable, where they could be received and de-encoded through application of a reverse Fourier transform.

A true mathematical Fourier transform requires an infinite range of frequencies, and in 1946 it was Gabor's challenge to determine the minimum number of frequencies that could be included in the transform to maintain intelligibility, while maximizing the amount of data being sent simultaneously across the cable.[55]

Over dinner, Gabor explained to Pribram how he solved the problem, using music as an example. While the pitch of a tone is dependent on the frequency of vibration and there may be many harmonics accompanying that tone in the frequency spectrum, the duration of the tone complex is not measured in any of those frequencies; instead, it is measured on a completely different time axis. Accordingly, the function Gabor sought must include coordinates describing a "windowed-packet" of tone information and *also* a set of space-time coordinates to map the packet flow.[56]

Gabor solved his problem through application of a "Hilbert space," a vector mathematical method capable of mapping an arbitrary number of dimensions beyond the usual four dimensions of space (x_d, y_d, z_d) and time (t). The Hilbert space is named after the German mathematician David Hilbert (1862–1943), who in 1926 described a way to extend the methods of algebra and calculus to any number of dimensions. Since 1926, quantum theorists had been able to use Hilbert's approach to represent classical concepts within the new quantum framework, and use of the Hilbert space also offered a computable framework for the Fourier expansions required by quantum mechanics.[57] Hilbert, a close friend and associate of Albert Einstein, was reputed to have an acerbic sense of humor; once, upon hearing that one of his students had dropped out of mathematics to study poetry, Hilbert was heard to reply, "Good, he did not have enough imagination to become a mathematician."[58]

The concept of a Hilbert space is essentially the consideration of a "space" having more than three dimensions, allowing the exploration of mathematical relationships involving an infinite number of dimensions (the topic is sometimes referred to as "infinite dimensional function spaces").[59] A simplified example of a Hilbert space is shown in figure 10.1, where the superposition of the two orthogonal dimensions found in the top half of the figure results in a Hilbert space of six dimensions shown at the bottom center. In physics and mathematics, each unique dimension is considered to exist at right angles (90 degrees geometrically, or "orthogonal") to all other dimensions. This is most frequently seen in figures depicting the x, y, and z dimensions in a graphical rendition of the three dimensions of space.

At the bottom in figure 10.1 is the "Hilbert space," a "space" where all six dimensions now intersect at a common point, the "origin."

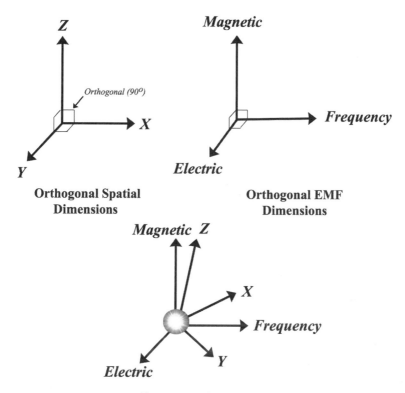

Fig. 10.1. A Hilbert space of six orthogonal dimensions

Understanding this superposition became key for Pribram in expressing his holonomic theory, which he referred to as "deep processing"; he stated that the "the holonomic theory uses vectors in Hilbert phase space to express covariance."[60]

Though six dimensions do appear around the same origin in the Hilbert space in figure 10.1, (*X, Y, Z,* Electric, Magnetic, Frequency), the dimension of *time* is missing. In 1946 Gabor published a new mathematical approach that solved the problem of applying the Fourier transform to a Hilbert space, by translating information from Hilbert dimensions into slices of time-based data; Gabor originally called his method the "windowed Fourier transform," but soon after publication it became known as the "Gabor function." Gabor had successfully devised a way to encode multiple "packets" of electromagnetic data and simultaneously transmit them through the trans-Atlantic cable, in both directions, to maximize transference rates and frequency content.[61] At each end of the cable were located electronic encoder/decoder circuit devices.

Pribram was delighted; from the Paris dinner with Gabor had emerged a feasible mechanism with which to model the two-way flow of memory imprinting and retrieval in the brain—Gabor's "windowed Fourier transform." Pribram related the process to that of the operation of a barcode system.

> Based on descriptions of the maps of receptive fields of cortical cells, I have proposed that the deep structure of our memory, as it is encoded in fine fibers in the brain, is much like a windowed Fourier transformation. The surface structure of memory, our retrieval and updating procedure, resembles what goes on at a checkout counter. It is only a step to conceive of a name as a barcode trigger identifying a purchase.[62]

In 1988, at age seventy, Pribram retired from his Stanford position as professor emeritus of psychophysiology, and relocated to Virginia to head the new Center for Brain Research and Informational Sciences (BRAINS) at Radford University, where he also began lecturing on cognitive neuroscience and computational neuroscience.[63]

Holoflux and the Frequency Domain

In evaluating evidence that he had collected from hundreds of experiments in over forty years of neurosurgical research at Yale, Harvard, and Stanford, Pribram observed that both visual sensory processing and audio sensory processing displayed holographic-like contour patternings among neuronal dendrites in the cerebral cortex. "In fact," he speculated, "the receptor mechanisms of the ear, the skin and probably even the nose and tongue work in a similar fashion."[64] With his new understanding of the Fourier transform and a working example of functional holography, Pribram pushed the envelope of his theory forward, though always supported by data.

For me, theory is data-based and, I have, whenever possible, obtained in my own laboratory at first-hand the data critical to theory.[65]

In contrast with the lack of success others were having in their efforts to establish the mechanism and location of memory engrams, Pribram put forth a theory that the brain mechanics of vision might be seen as holographic processes, projections onto the cortical surface from a frequency domain through the mechanism of frequency super-position and electromagnetic wave interference.[66] Pribram called this "the holonomic brain theory," and postulated the importance of the frequency domain.

> Essentially, the theory reads that the brain at one stage of processing performs its analyses in the frequency domain. . . .
> . . . [A] solid body of evidence has accumulated that the auditory, somatosensory, motor, and visual systems of the brain do in fact process, at one or several stages, input from the senses in the frequency domain.[67]

Pribram's theory holds that the mathematics of the Fourier transform operate within the brain, modulating electromagnetic fields of flux to create, store, replay, and process holograms within some as yet unidentified physiological context or substrate, but one that Pribram conjectures may be found within the fine-fibered dendritic webs of cerebral cortex regions.[68]

Pribram clearly distinguishes between observations made in the frequency domain and those made in space and time. While the ontological realization of flux in space-time can be conceptualized in the gyrations of three-dimensional electromagnetic waves, Pribram defines the ontological substrate of spectra in the frequency domain to be pure spectra or holoflux.

> The spectral domain is characteristically a *flux,* composed of oscillations, fluctuations, whereas interference patterns among waves

intersect to reinforce or cancel. Holograms are examples of spectra, that is, of a *holo-flux*.[69] (Emphasis in original.)

This holoflux is essentially the same concept as David Bohm's *holo-movement,* though in "Brain and Mathematics," Pribram takes exception to Bohm's use of the words *flow* and *movement,* holding that such words cannot be used to characterize dynamism in a dimension devoid of space or time axes:

> David Bohm (1973) had a concept similar to flux in mind, which he called holomovement. He felt that my use of the term "flux" had connotations for him that he did not want to buy into. I, on the other hand, felt holomovement to be vague in the sense of asking, "what is moving?"[70]

This issue is resolved in the model of a Hilbert space; the Hilbert space here is the superposition of the three orthogonal dimensions of space (*X, Y, Z*) with the three orthogonal electromagnetic field dimensions (see fig. 10.2) which then manifest in space-time as the movement of these superpositioned six-dimensional holoflux packets along the increasing dimension of time at the speed of light.

Within the frequency domain itself, the holoflux can be seen as neither static nor dynamic in the spatial and temporal sense, because the energy in the flux domain is understood (by definition) to be "outside of time" and "outside of space."

These conditions of the frequency domain correlate with David Bohm's concept of the implicate order, the enfolded, sub-quantum dimension of his ontological quantum theory.[71] While Bohm's theory is examined in detail in the next chapter, here a parallel concept can be visualized in Pribram's flow of holoflux energy out from a frequency domain into actualized phenomena in space and time:

> Only through their manifestations in space and time do we get to know of the existence of potentials such as those of energy, of

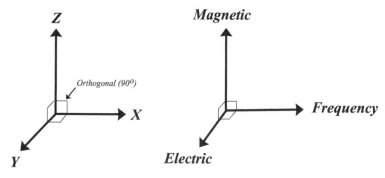

Spatial Field Coordinates   Electromagnetic Field Coordinates

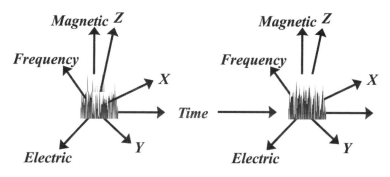

Holoflux Packets in the Time Dimension

Fig. 10.2. Flux packets moving through space-time

momentum, and of holographic processes. We can know the potential domain only by way of realization in space and time.[72]

Pribram regarded frequency as the direct mathematical link between a space-time electromagnetic domain and a transcendent flux domain, the mathematics of frequency bridging the two through a Fourier transform process, and he went so far as to say, "The frequency approach . . . is essentially Pythagorean."[73] At a San Francisco Zen Center physics and consciousness conference, Pribram was introduced to a conceptual diagram of the Fourier transform process (fig. 10.3) that perfectly encapsulated what he saw to be the function of the Fourier transform

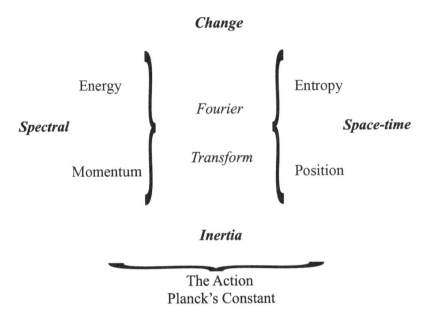

Fig. 10.3. Pribram's Fourier transform diagram

in linking a spectral (frequency) domain to a space-time domain via the transform's mathematics.[74]

Pribram first saw this diagram during a conference presentation given by the physicist Geoffrey F. Chew, a Berkeley theoretical particle physicist, who told Pribram that he had received it from his colleague at Berkeley, Henry Stapp, who said he himself received it directly from Dirac. Whatever the origin of the figure, Pribram chose to include the diagram in several future papers. In "Consciousness Reassessed," Pribram's caption to the figure reads, "The Fourier transform as the mediator between spectral and spacetime descriptions."[75] In *Brain and Being* Pribram captions the figure with "The wave/particle dichotomy is orthogonal to the above distinction."

In the diagram, the spectral domain is to the left and space-time to the right. The diagram can be seen as a key to Pribram's model and also posits that the Fourier transform process operates at a boundary dimension of Planck's constant, termed in the diagram "The Action: Planck's Constant." While Pribram himself never discusses what "The

Action: Planck's Constant" might imply for the diagram and his theory, the concept is perfectly congruent with David Bohm's discussion of the Planck length as the boundary between the implicate domain and the explicate domain (discussed in chapter 11 of this book). It is suggested that this transformation occurs at the Planck length of 1.616×10^{-35} m. This Fourier diagram, according to Pribram, implies that:

> matter can be seen as an "ex-formation," an externalized (extruded, palpable, compacted) form of flux. By contrast, thinking and its communication (minding) are the consequence of an internalized (neg-entropic) forming of flux, its "in-formation." My claim is that the basis function from which both matter and mind are "formed" is flux (measured as spectral density).[76]

An enhanced depiction of the spectral domain and the space-time domain is presented in figure 10.4, where electromagnetic fields and matter can be seen in the *space-time domain* at the right, and holoflux fields and frequency flux can be seen in the *spectral domain* at the left. Linking the two domains is the Fourier transform, shown in the center, that represents the continuous, bidirectional transformation of energy driven both

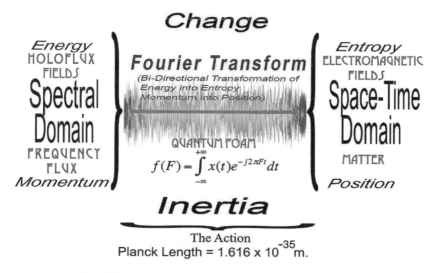

Fig. 10.4. Spectral domain and space-time domain

by change and inertia. The region separating the two at the Plank length boundary is known in quantum physics as quantum foam.

Bohm here comments on holograms and the spectral domain:

> Spectra are composed of interference patterns where fluctuations intersect to reinforce or cancel. Holograms are examples of the spectral domain. I have called this pre-space-time domain a potential reality because we navigate the actual experienced reality in space-time.[77]

How then might we model the dynamics of the process behind the transformation (or collapse) of holoflux packets from the spectral domain (Bohm's enfolded cosmos) into the space-time brain structure? In a 1997 paper published in the *Proceedings of Symposia in Applied Mathematics,* Pribram suggested the following answer:

> An answer to the questions as to how mind becomes organized by brain rests on our understanding of the lessons of quantum mechanics and especially of that aspect which encodes the spectral domain, the implicate order. Although engineers daily use the spectral domain in radar, crystallography and tomography—wherever image processing is important—cognitive neuroscientists are, as yet, only barely acquainted with the pervasive nature of this order. It is now necessary to make accessible, both by experiment and by theory, the rules for "tuning in" on the implicate domain so that this domain can become more generally understood and scientifically validated.[78]

Another model of the spectral-space-time domains can be seen in figure 10.5, which suggests that it is the Gabor function, operating in parallel with the Fourier transform, that describes mathematically the flow of holoflux packets moving back and forth simultaneously between the spectral frequency domain and the space-time domain. The figure indicates the probability of numerous mathematical "bridges" existing

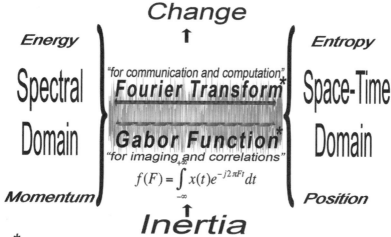

Fig. 10.5. *The Fourier transform and the Gabor function, the two processes linking the spectral frequency domain and space-time.*

between the space-time world and other string-theory dimensions such as the frequency domain.

An interesting theory—a proposal that provides a digital "clock" to describe the timing of this process, the movement between space-time and the spectral domain—can be seen in the "theory of laminated space-time," proposed by Dewey in 1985.[79]

This theory proposes that energy vibrates digitally between two domains at a sub-quantum dimensional level, alternating between cyclical transformations sequentially, like the ticks of a clock, between the spectral (frequency) domain and the space-time domain. The timing of such "ticks" as measured in the space-time domain can be calculated, and corresponds to the Wien calculated frequency derived from this smallest possible wavelength, the Planck distance itself: 1.616199×10^{-35} m. The frequency corresponding to such a wavelength would be at the limit of the frequency domain's extrusion into space-time; in other words, it must be the highest frequency (smallest wavelength) within the space-time domain. Dewey's theory visualizes the process of this flux extruding into space-time as a series of shells moving out at the speed of light, each shell a brane* separated from the next by a spatial gap equal to the Planck length, as described here:

> I believe the universe to be composed of *nothing but* shells of electromagnetic particles which the theory of Laminated Spacetime describes as laminae of spacetime.[80] (Emphasis in original.)

Laser-based holographic technology greatly simplifies the generation of a hologram by (1) using a laser-generated beam of photon energy (a single frequency), and (2) illuminating the object from two distinct fixed points in space (a single, fixed phase-angle). An interference pattern is created from the spherical waves of radiation incoming from the two fixed points in space, rippling at exactly the same frequency in space-time.

In nature, however, the situation is vastly richer in complexity: one can imagine radiant holoflux interactions processing in the space-time domain as a highly complex interaction of dynamic shells of every conceivable space-time radiation frequency, impinging from an infinity of phase angles, like inwardly directed radii aiming at a central point. In contrast with the human-generated holograms of a single frequency of electromagnetic flux and a single vantage point (phase angle), each point in space-time actually experiences an *entire frequency flux spectrum* impinging on a particular point in space-time. In nature, all frequencies of the spectrum and all incoming angles of approach must be considered in the process configuration of the holoflux as put forward by Pribram and Bohm.

That such a process would involve quantum-scale phenomena as well as superconductivity has been strongly suggested, not only by Karl Pribram, but by two of his colleagues:

> Mari Jibu and Kunio Yasui, an anesthesiologist and a physicist from Notre Dame Seishen University in Okayama, Japan, and I have sug-

---

*A brane can be pictured as a generalized membrane-like geometrical shape used in superstring theory to model relationships that may be outside of or partially outside of what is considered to be the normal dimensions of space.

gested that the membranes of the fine fibers, the media in which the receptive fields are mapped, may have quantum-scale properties. The membranes are made up of phospholipids, oscillating molecules that are arranged in parallel, like rows of gently waving poplar trees. The lipid, fatty water-repellent part makes up the middle, the trunks of the "trees," and the phosphorus water-seeking parts make up the inside and outside of the membrane. These characteristics suggest that water molecules become trapped and aligned in the phosphorus part of the membrane. Aligned water molecules can show super-liquidity and are thus super-conductive; that is, they act as if they had quantum-scale properties.[81]

In 1979, Karl Pribram, at that time at Stanford, met David Bohm, Fritjof Capra, and Brian Josephson at a conference in Cordoba, Spain, where the four presented papers.[82] At the time, Bohm was a professor of theoretical physics at London University; Capra, a theoretical physicist, was conducting research at the Lawrence Berkeley Laboratory; and Josephson, a theoretical professor from Oxford who had won the Nobel Prize in 1973 for his work on quantum tunneling and superconductivity (and who had become a serious student of transcendental meditation in 1971).[83]

During the conference, Pribram discovered that David Bohm's model of the implicate order and its projection, or extrusion, into space-time corresponded surprisingly well with his own holonomic theories, in particular where Bohm describes how the implicate unfolds into the explicate and the explicate enfolds into the implicate in a two-way process:

> The implicate order can be thought of as a ground beyond time, a totality, out of which each moment is projected into the explicate order. For every moment that is projected out into the explicate there would be another movement in which that moment would be injected or "introjected" back into the implicate order. If you have a large number of repetitions of this process, you'll start to build up a

fairly constant component to this series of projection and injection. That is, a fixed disposition would become established. The point is that, via this process, past forms would tend to be repeated or replicated in the present, and that is very similar to what Sheldrake calls a morphogenetic field and morphic resonance. Moreover, such a field would not be located anywhere. When it projects back into the totality (the implicate order), since no space and time are relevant there, all things of a similar nature might get connected together or resonate in totality. When the explicate order enfolds into the implicate order, which does not have any space, all places and all times are, we might say, merged, so that what happens in one place will interpenetrate what happens in another place.[84]

In 1984 Pribram and a colleague obtained laboratory proof that cells respond to specific bandwidths of frequencies, further support for his holonomic theories.

Together with an engineering student, Amand Sharafat (Pribram et al., 1984),[85] I performed an experiment in which we investigated whether neurons in the cat motor cortex were tuned to certain bandwidths of frequencies of passive movements of their forelimbs. Here, for once, we were testing a specific hypothesis, and the hypothesis was supported by our results. Certain cells in the motor cortex are responsive to the frequency.[86]

In a 1997 paper presented at a symposium for applied mathematics, Pribram offered a view even more congruent with Bohm's theories, hypothesizing that the mind-brain ontology is monistic; that a duality between mind and matter only *appears* to manifest, because information that can be measured is unfolded into observable space-time coordinates from an enfolded potential that lies in the timeless frequency domain.[87]

According to this view, another class of order lies behind the organization we ordinarily perceive. The ordinary order of appearances can be described in space-time coordinates. The other class of orders is constituted of fine-grain distributed organizations, which can be described as potential in the Aristotelian sense because only after "radical" transformation is their palpability in spatiotemporal terms realized. When the potential is actualized, information (the form within) becomes unfolded into its ordinary space-time manifestation; in the other direction, the transformation enfolds and distributes the information much as this is done by the holographic process.... Thus, on the one hand, there are enfolded potential orders; on the other, there are unfolded orders manifested in space-time.[88]

Such an unfolding of hidden patterns into space and time provides a mechanism in support of Rupert Sheldrake's theory of morphogenetic fields in which information fields are thought to unfold from within hidden dimensions into actual space-time phenomena.

But the model of mind/brain as a quantum mechanical process poses a new question. In 2002, Pribram presented a paper in Torino, Italy, in which he discussed the application of the Fourier basis of the holographic principle as a useful metaphor in describing the mind-brain relation with regard to perception.[89] In this paper he posed the following question:

Does this application indicate that the formalism of quantum physics applies more generally to other scales of inquiry? Alternatively, for brain function, at what scale do actual quantum physical processing take place? At what anatomical scale(s) do we find quantum coherence and at what scale does decoherence occur?[90]

Pribram himself discounted the possibility that electrical brain waves recorded by electrodes placed on the scalp might be significant carriers of cognitive information.

There is some considerable doubt whether "brain waves" as presently recorded form the substrate of any meaningful interference pattern organization for information processing, although they may indicate that such process is taking place. The wavelengths recorded are, of course, considerably longer than those of light waves and can therefore only be carriers of small amounts of information—though in the form of spatially interfering holographic patterns.[91]

While Pribram never proposed an answer to his question as to what scale the holonomic process occurs in human physiology, it is my thesis that the anatomical scale required for Fourier holography lies in the infrared wavelength region within which the human mammalian body operates, a wavelength that perfectly fits the average inner diameter of blood capillaries, which range from 8 to 10 microns and are found throughout the brain.[92] Infrared waves in space-time have a wavelength of approximately 10 microns, but the spectral frequencies associated with these waves, according to Pribram, are considered to be located within the non-space-time frequency domain. Thus waves and their equivalent frequency spectra appear on opposite sides of the Fourier equation, existing in different dimensions. Pribram said:

Waves occur in space-time. Spectra do not.[93]

Ontological Reality of the Frequency Domain

But is this frequency domain "real" in the same sense that science and most philosophers regard the dimensions of space and time? Is the enfolded spectral domain in which quantum mechanical mathematics works so well a "real" domain, or is it simply a mathematical abstraction?

This question has been at the heart of quantum physics since Erwin Schrödinger, often referred to as "the father of quantum mechanics," first described the wave function $\psi(x,t)$ in January 1926.[94] Prior to the discovery of the wave function, physicists were trying to understand the strange situation of experimental data that returned both wavelike and particle-like behavior.

Schrödinger was happy to dispense with particles altogether. He viewed the wavefunctions as the very real manifestations of a completely undulatory material world. In his description, particle-like behaviour was an illusion created by the overlapping and reinforcing of collections of "matter waves."[95]

However, the mathematician-turned-physicist Max Born soon radically reinterpreted the success of Schrödinger's wave function. In July 1926, just six months after Schrödinger's discovery, Born wrote a paper stating that:

> the wavefunctions represented the *probabilities* that the electron wave will be scattered in certain directions. . . . A more precise consideration shows that the probability is proportional to the square of [the wavefunction].[96]

Though Born's statistical calculations worked in quantum mechanical experimental predictions at the time, Einstein himself was not very happy with this probabilistic, statistical approach. In a letter to Born later that year (December 3, 1926), Einstein remarked:

> Quantum mechanics is certainly imposing. But an inner voice tells me that it is not yet the real thing. The theory says a lot, but does not really bring us any closer to the secret of the "old one." I, at any rate, am convinced that *He* is not playing at dice.[97]

Much later in the century, David Bohm, a young colleague and neighbor of Einstein's at Princeton, also adopted the realist view that the wave function directly describes a reality, not a set of probabilities. In developing his own quantum potential wave function (Q) in the 1980s, Bohm's primary assumption was that the wave function must be assumed to be real.

> The wavefunction is assumed to represent an objectively real field and not just a mathematical symbol. . . . We suppose that there is, beside the field, a particle represented mathematically by a set of coordinates. . . . We suppose that the particle is acted on not only by the classical potential . . . but also by an additional "quantum potential."[98]

The debate between the two approaches to the wave function has continued into the twenty-first century, with the realist side supporting what has come to be called the ψ-*ontic* model (holding that it is the "real state of affairs") versus the ψ-*epistemic* model group (which holds that the wave function should be regarded as a mathematical device only, a probability distribution).[99]

The debate has recently taken a turn in favor of the Bohmian realist approach; in early 2015, experimental proof supporting the ontological reality of the wave function was published in *Nature*, indicating that the quantum wave function may indeed be ontologically "real."[100] Experiments carried out at the University of Queensland consisted of repeatable measurements of a nonlocal wave function collapsing into a particle in space-time, yet the results failed to be predicted by probability distribution calculations. Single photons were manipulated in both horizontal and vertical polarizations, and their paths were controlled by an interferometer, while, according to the team, "every optical element in the experimental setup was carefully calibrated and characterized."[101] The paper, published in January 2015, is summarized as follows:

> Our results conclusively rule out the most compelling ψ-*epistemic* models. . . . This suggests that, if we want to hold on to objective reality, we should adopt the ψ-*ontic* viewpoint—which assigns objective reality to the wavefunction, but also has some intriguing implications such as non-locality or many worlds.

The authors also say that "The only alternative is to adopt more unorthodox concepts such as backwards-in-time causation, or to completely abandon any notion of objective reality."[102]

Pribram's Participatory Experiences as Data

Within the more than seven hundred papers and books published by Pribram during his lifetime there are almost no references to any personal knowledge or opinion regarding religion, meditative exercises, or psychotropic drug experience.[103] However, late in his career he did discuss such topics, and from these comments we may infer his own experience; such evidence can be found in interviews or panel discussions, but almost never in formal publication.

But in 1984 Pribram alludes to his own firsthand participatory experience of exploring consciousness through entheogens and meditation.

> Currently, the study of *consciousness* as central to the mind-brain problem has emerged from the explorations of altered and alternative states produced by drugs, meditation, and a variety of other techniques designed to promote psychological growth.[104]

An even stronger indication of firsthand participatory knowledge may be found in a remarkable paragraph in which Pribram describes an experience of "holoflux." His use of the phrases "we experience" and "we can experience" strongly implied direct knowledge of such states.

> Boundaries determine what is "without" and what is "within." This raises the issue as to whether the skin can really be considered a boundary between our self and the outside world. . . . Meditative exercises, drugs and dreams go further in dissolving these boundaries. First, we experience patterns rather than shapes and, if taken to the extreme, we can experience the loss of patterns as well: only a holoflux, "the white light" remains.[105]

There is also evidence of Pribram's association with the Transcendental Meditation movement. In 1977, a Stanford newspaper published an announcement of an upcoming presentation to be given by Karl Pribram and his Stanford colleague William Tiller at an event sponsored by local Transcendental Meditation organizations.[106] One of the primary teachings of the Transcendental Meditation movement, under the guidance of Maharishi Mahesh Yogi, is the practice of mantra, and it is possible that Pribram studied and practiced mantra himself.[107] Pribram specifically mentions the use of mantra in a 1991 publication, at the close of his book, in which he described experiences of an enfolded, spectral dimension in a somewhat cryptic final sentence:

> Perceptual experiences may on occasion reflect the spectral energy/ momentum potential more than they reflect space-time configurations. . . . Frontolimbic excitation can be induced by internal neurochemical stimulation [entheogens or hormones] or by external methods [yoga] such as concentrating on ambiguous (or otherwise meaningless) stimuli provided by a mantra, for example. When the spectral dimension dominates the production of a perception, space and time become enfolded in the experienced episode. Time evolution ceases and spatial boundaries disappear. . . . The boundary between mind and matter, as all other boundaries, becomes dissolved. More on this at a future occasion.[108]

It is easy to argue that Pribram is talking about his own participatory experience of the contemplative practice of mantra when he states "The boundary between mind and matter, as all other boundaries, becomes dissolved."[109] Pribram explained the experience of mantra stimulation in words that, as we shall see in chapter 11, are virtually identical to David Bohm's description of quantum dynamics ("space and time become enfolded"). Pribram described "perceptual experiences" as moving between "space-time configurations" and "spectral energy," though he failed to say anything beyond this about his altered perceptual experiences. Nor did he follow up on his promise of "More on this at a future occasion"; the rest of the book consists of a fifty-four-page technical appendix written by Kunio Yasue and Mari Jibu.[110]

More than twenty years after describing his experience of mantra in *Brain and Perception,* Pribram, in *The Form Within,* discusses his understanding of "spirit" in the context of his life's work.

> Spirit is ordinarily defined as being immaterial. . . . [And] thermodynamics is a scientific endeavor that is based on the utilization of forms of energy, not matter. Also, descriptions of holoflux, (the

quantum potential, zero-point energy) and quantum holography are devoid of any space-time structure. These endeavors are scientific and the patterns they investigate describe the patterns ordinarily probed under the rubric "spirit." There was a time when brain processes were described as mediated by "breath"—that is, spirit. Now we affirm that these "spirits" are electrical, and in the small-fibered web, they form electrical fields. And as we continue to explore the effects of magnetism and "soft photons," that is of heat, there is likely a great deal more we will discover about brain processing that affirms our spiritual nature.

We know that *Homo sapiens sapiens* has experienced the spiritual aspect of "being" since the dawn of our species. Science is a quest and, as I have tried to show, there is no reason scientists should continue to restrict that quest to be confined merely to the composition of matter.[111]

But a more complete example of Pribram's interest in both yoga and Zen, specifically in regard to his understanding of neurophysiology, can be found in a panel discussion held during a conference in Cordoba in 1979 called "Science and Consciousness," that was mentioned above.[112]

During a panel discussion held at the conference, Pribram provided a fascinating description of the difference between Zen and yoga mirrored in his own experience, as seen through the lens of his research in brain neurophysiology, and in this reply to a comment by Brian Josephson with regard to the spiritual dimension of meditation:

You are right on that point. The experiences of meditation are definitely of a spiritual nature, there is no doubt about that. Actually there are, roughly speaking, two types of procedure used in the East, Zen and Yoga, and we are going to see how they show up in neurophysiology. . . . What we have done in our laboratory is to study the observation of recuperative cycles in primary sensory systems. In carrying out this research, we have realized that it was in fact possible to manipulate the recuperative time of the system by stimulating either the frontal or posterior part of the brain. When the frontal part is stimulated, a much more rapid recovery is obtained—the channel acting as a synchronizer—and everything operates simultaneously. If, on the other hand, we stimulate the posterior part, we reduce the speed of the recovery of the system, but the channel is then of multiple type and carries much more information. I wonder, therefore, whether it is not this difference between the frontal and posterior parts of the brain that is operating in the various methods of meditation. That is, various techniques designed to induce modified states of consciousness, Zen appealing to the frontal part, and Yoga to the posterior.[113]

In an interview for *Psychology Today,* Pribram expanded on his belief that when approached with the understanding that a holographic system of consciousness is operating in the universe, certain otherwise unexplainable phenomena such as synchronicity, nonlocality, and paranormal phenomena could be explained. He said:

It isn't that the world of appearances is wrong; it isn't that there *aren't* objects out there, at one level of reality. It's that if you penetrate through and look at the universe with a holographic system, you arrive at a different view, a different reality. And that other reality can explain things that have hitherto remained inexplicable scientifically: paranormal phenomena and synchronicities, the apparently meaningful coincidence of events.[114]

In his autobiography published in 1998, Pribram discussed his affirmation that there lie other "classes of order" behind the conceptually ordering map of our world given to us by Euclidean Cartesian space-time coordinates and Newton's laws. Here can be seen, certainly in the phrases "enfolded potential orders" and "unfolded orders manifested in space-time," the influence and adoption of the ontological ideas of his friend and colleague, the quantum theorist David Bohm:

This other class of orders constitutes distributed organizations described as potential because of their impalpability until radical changes in appearance are realized in the transformational process. When a potential is realized, information (the form within) becomes unfolded into its ordinary space-time appearance; in the other direction, the transformation enfolds and distributes the information, as this is done by the holographic process. Because work is involved in transforming, descriptions in terms of energy are suitable, and as the form of information is what is transformed, descriptions in terms of entropy (and negentropy) are also suitable. Thus, on the one hand, there are enfolded potential orders; on the other, there are unfolded orders manifested in space-time.[115]

And on the closing page of his final work, published in his ninety-second year, Pribram ends with the following affirmation on the future scientific investigation of consciousness as it manifests in the domains of what is commonly called spirituality:

> Much of the research that I have reported here has dealt with forms, with patterns, that are, in themselves, not matter per se. These patterns can be considered the spiritual complements of matter. In this sense, spirit and spirituality now have status as topics ripe for scientific investigation.[116]

Pribram developed extensive laboratory data to support his paradigm that neuronal systems in the cerebral cortex—and in the sensory systems of vision, hearing, and smell—operate on holographic principles. His contention is that such activity is not primarily in and among the neurons themselves, but that the process manifests within an extended electromagnetic field among the fine-meshed dendritic fibers of the cerebral cortex. He found evidence to support his contention in the outer reaches of the cerebral hemisphere, where he mapped detectable holographic transformations that led him to the conclusion that there exists an ongoing "language" of transformation between space-time information and frequency-based information in the brain.[117]

In view of the serious nature of his discoveries during a lifelong search to understand the dynamic of memory and consciousness in the brain, it is refreshing to read Pribram's published answer to his own question of "what all this research is good for," expressed here at the age of ninety-four:

> There are more than 37,000 neuroscientists currently performing experiments that address the topics that have formed my scientific life and the chapters in this book. From them we can expect a torrent of research results that bear on the health of our bodies and our brains. But there is more we need to know. I am often asked what all this research is good for? My answer is the one Faraday gave when asked this question regarding his discoveries of the properties of electricity: "Someday you'll be able to tax it."[118]

While Pribram and his associates in California were trying to understand a holonomic Fourier transform paradigm of brain processing (from direct experimental evidence and firsthand observation), a complementary paradigm was emerging in London in the work of the theoretical physicist David Bohm, who began using concepts from quantum field theory and the Fourier transform to develop and support the cosmology of what he called the *implicate order*.[119]

Bohm's Conscious Holoflux in the Implicate Order

Strong support for Karl Pribram's holonomic theories relating brain and consciousness can be found in the quantum physics of the American physicist David Joseph Bohm (1917–1992), a professor emeritus of theoretical physics at Birkbeck College, University of London. Bohm's early research career began at the University of California in Berkeley, where he completed his dissertation in plasma physics in 1944 under Robert Oppenheimer at the Lawrence Radiation Laboratory.

Much as Pribram's was a search for a mind-brain process that was missing in mainstream research approaches, Bohm's search was focused on something that was missing in quantum theory: the relationship between matter and consciousness. Bohm derided physicists who seemed to show no interest in the *meaning* of the quantum world, those who used quantum mechanics merely as a mathematical tool for effectively predicting results in nuclear physics experiments. At the same time, Bohm perceived that reality lies beyond appearances, that it is the creative process of a whole, of a unity beyond theorizing, even given the repeatable appearances of scientific measurement. Bohm noted:

> The quantum jump or quantum leap is a creative process. . . . I called it the implicate order because it's the order of enfoldment that counts not the movement in a line. It manifests in the explicate. What we

thought was the essence is now the appearance. . . . Namely, that the particle which was thought to explain the reality is now seen as an appearance. The essence of the true being is unknown. Even the implicate order is merely a concept, so even that should turn out to be an appearance. But we say, by bringing in deeper, more penetrating appearances that we understand better, but we are never going to grasp the whole. Even a unified theory will only be an appearance.[1]

In his approach, Bohm stressed that the distinction between information and meaning is an important one, as did Karl Pribram (particularly in his *Languages of the Brain,* 1972). Unlike many physicists, whom he criticized for being information intoxicated, Bohm felt it of the utmost importance to search for meaning behind the information, and not to regard quantum mechanics simply as some exotic branch of calculation methodology. To understand the underlying ontology behind quantum mechanics, Bohm felt, was a key to understanding the relationship between matter and consciousness, and here Bohm criticized Niels Bohr, the founder of quantum mechanics, who had won the Nobel Prize in 1913 for his quantum theory in modeling the hydrogen atom:

> Bohr's approach is to say nothing can be said about quantum mechanics at all other than to use it is a calculator, but my approach is to give it another appearance, more meaning. In the mechanical order it is hard to get much meaning.[2]

In the middle of his career as a theoretical physicist, Bohm's search for the underlying meanings to quantum theory was enriched through an introduction to a contemplative approach to the mind and consciousness expressed in the ideas of Jidu Krishnamurti. In 1961, while a professor of physics at Bristol University, Bohm attended a conference in London to hear a series of Krishnamurti lectures on perception, a topic that, as a quantum physicist, greatly interested Bohm. During the prior year, Bohm had become interested in theories of consciousness and perception expressed in the writings of philosophers and mystics and had begun reading books on yoga, Buddhism, and the work of the mathematician P. D. Ouspensky, a follower of the mystic G. I. Gurdjieff.[3] Public knowledge of his new interest resulted in further loss of credibility among Bohm's critics in the United States. His colleague and biographer, the physicist F. David Peat, recounts:

> When his former colleagues in the United States learned of this change of interest, it caused them considerable distress. In the years that followed, some lamented that Bohm had gone "off the rails," that a great mind had been sidetracked, and the work of an exceptional physicist was being lost to science.[4]

Bohm, however, was completely serious in his search for an understanding of quantum theory, even though the quest had led him into these areas of philosophy, psychology, and mysticism. Bohm's driving interest can be seen in the first paragraph of *The Undivided Universe: An Ontological Interpretation of Quantum Theory*, completed in 1992, only weeks before he suffered a fatal heart attack. Here, he expresses his passion to understand the mysteries that continue to lie behind quantum theory, rather than regarding the theory simply as something applicable:

> The formalism of the quantum theory leads to results that agree with experiment with great accuracy and covers an extremely wide range of phenomena. As yet there are no experimental indications of any domain in which it might break down. Nevertheless, there still remain a number of basic questions concerning its fundamental significance which are obscure and confused. Thus for example one of the leading physicists of our time, M. Gell-Mann, has said "Quantum mechanics, that mysterious, confusing discipline, which none of us really understands but which we know how to use."[5]

To understand Bohm's approach to quantum theory, it is useful to examine the development of his revolutionary ideas in the context of the complexity of his life. Born in Pennsylvania in 1917, Bohm took an early interest in science, having become an avid reader of science fiction by the age of seven. After graduating in physics and receiving the mathematics prize from the University of Pennsylvania, he accepted a fellowship to enter graduate studies at Caltech. Within a year he found himself dissatisfied with the seemingly exclusive focus on problem solving at Caltech, a focus that seemed to discount Bohm's passion for seeking an understanding of what must be underlying ontological realities, favoring instead the development of mathematical models and their manipulation.[6] In 1941 Bohm met with J. Robert Oppenheimer at the University of California, Berkeley, having heard that, in addition to being a brilliant theoretical physicist, the thirty-seven-year-old Oppenheimer encouraged wide-ranging intellectual discussion among his grad students and postdoctoral researchers. Bohm soon after accepted a fellowship offer from Oppenheimer to study at Berkeley, and in 1941 Bohm moved from Los Angeles to begin graduate work in plasma research.[7]

After a year of intense collaboration with other physicists at the laboratory, often working more than sixty hours a week, Bohm gave his first presentation of the ideas he had thus far developed to model the complex nature of plasma, but early in the presentation, as he began to try to convey his new ideas to Oppenheimer and the rest of his committee, something unexpected occurred.

> A naturally shy person, as he began to speak he nonetheless felt that everything was going extremely well. Soon he had the sensation that he was going beyond physics into something almost mystical, to the point where he felt himself in direct contact with everyone in the room. He was convinced that each individual consciousness had been transcended so that his audience was also sharing this experience.[8]

This intense feeling was overwhelming, leading immediately to a deep depression, and Bohm took a leave of absence, during which he was unable to work or study for almost an entire year.[9]

Even more problematical for Bohm during the first year of work on his dissertation under Oppenheimer was his growing interest in several activist antiwar groups, including the Committee for Peace Mobilization, the Campus Committee to Fight Conscription, and the Young Communist League, and "it was noted that Bohm had been involved in organizing activities for the Communist party and had distributed copies of Earl Browder's *Victory—and After*."[10] These associations and activities were later to haunt him.[11]

The Communist Party in the United States had peaked at about 30,000 members in 1941, having grown steadily during the Great Depression due in part to the rapid growth of labor unions but also because Communism was seen as a clear enemy of fascism.[12] In November 1942, Bohm joined the Communist Party in Berkeley, but membership was not particularly exciting or eventful, as Bohm later described to the historian Martin Sherwin during an interview: "The meetings were interminable, discussing all these boring attempts to stir up things on the campus which didn't amount to much."[13]

Back at Berkeley in 1943, Bohm completed his doctoral research project, an effort to develop a mathematical theory with which to model the dynamics of plasmas, a poorly understood phenomenon that greatly intrigued Bohm.

> As he studied the plasmas he became struck by their extraordinary nature. They began to take on, for him, the qualities of living beings. When physicists studied a plasma by introducing an electrical probe, it would generate a charged sheath around the probe and neutralize its effects. It was as if the plasma were protecting itself and preserving its internal status.[14]

Bohm completed his project, and the results were considered by Oppenheimer to be spectacular; the calculations that Bohm developed in his thesis were able to accurately model the behavior of uranium fluoride plasma in an electric arc and directly led to an elegant technique for separating uranium-235 from uranium-238, a critical step in Oppenheimer's effort toward building a nuclear bomb.[15]

Unfortunately, shortly before the publication of his dissertation, Bohm's previous political activities caught up with him. It was suddenly apparent that his affiliation with Communism made it impossible for him to obtain a security clearance, while paradoxically the importance of his own dissertation for the war effort led to it being considered highly classified:

> The scattering calculations (of collisions of protons and deuterons) that he had completed proved useful to the Manhattan Project and were immediately classified. But without security clearance, Bohm was denied access to his own work; not only would he be barred from defending his thesis, he was not even allowed to publish his own thesis.[16]

Oppenheimer was accordingly forced to petition the University of California regents to rule on an exception to academic policy in order to approve Bohm's doctoral dissertation without allowing it to be published. The regents assented; Bohm was awarded his doctorate and permitted to remain working at the Lawrence Laboratory, where he continued to focus his intense intellect upon the behavior of plasma flow and the mathematics of flux movement.* Here in an interview, Bohm describes his early interests and work with Oppenheimer during the period 1943–46:

> When I worked at the Lawrence Laboratory, after taking my Ph.D., I became very interested in the electron plasma. This is a dense gas of electrons that exhibits radically different behavior from the other, normal states of matter and it was a key to much of the work the laboratory was doing at the time. My insights sprang from the perception that the plasma is a highly organized system, which behaves as a whole. Indeed, in some respects, it's almost like a living being. I was fascinated with the question of how such organized collective

---

*Plasmas constitute over ninety-nine percent of the matter of the universe—most stars and interstellar gases exist in this fourth state of matter. Peat, *Infinite Potential,* 65.

behavior could go along with the almost complete freedom of movement of individual electrons.[17]

Unfortunately, Bohm's early flirtation with Communism made the
suppression of his dissertation only the first of what would eventually
be a series of challenges to his academic career. Nevertheless, in 1947
the young physicist was hired as an assistant professor by Princeton
University. During the relocation to New Jersey, he found a room
near campus and soon met his neighbor, another Princeton professor,
the fifty-seven-year-old Albert Einstein—who, like Bohm, objected to
quantum mechanics for its "lack of an objective description."[18] Bohm's
clarity on this topic was no doubt helped by the many discussions he
had with Einstein in his days at Princeton.[19]

During his time at Princeton, Bohm also continued his research on
the mathematics of plasma dynamics, while giving classes and public
lectures on quantum mechanics, but he refused to accept the majority
view which was, "and still is," in the words of his colleague, B. J. Hiley
"that the precise nature of the conceptual changes is not important. All
that was needed was to work with the self-consistent mathematical formalism, which, in some mysterious way, correctly predicts the numerical
results of actual experiments."[20]

After lecturing on the subject for three years at Princeton, Bohm
wrote a definitive textbook in which the physical aspects of the mathematics were emphasized.

Bohm worked furiously in his spare time on this major textbook; it
was intended to be a full interpretation of quantum theory, grounded
both in mathematics and conceptual clarifications, which he hoped
would resolve major unanswered problems within the quantum theory.[21] He also began working on a reinterpretation of quantum theory
in a paper of his own, which he called the "hidden variable theory." His
textbook was published in 1951 and the paper in 1952, but in October
1951 Bohm fled the United States for Brazil, his reputation having been
seriously affected by the politics of McCarthyism, and himself fearful of
being jailed for contempt of Congress.[22]

In late 1949, while working on the final chapters of his book, Bohm had been served with a summons, a subpoena ordering him to appear before Senator Joseph McCarthy at the House Un-American Activities Committee. At the hearing, Bohm was asked to identify which of his previous numerous colleagues at Berkeley had been interested in Communism. Not wishing to incriminate his friends and colleagues, Bohm repeatedly had his attorney plead his "right to silence" under the Fifth Amendment. Notwithstanding, on December 4, 1950, Bohm was arrested at his home for contempt of Congress, and though he made bail and was released, the administration at Princeton University peremptorily suspended him from "all teaching and other duties" for the duration of the trial.[23]

The publicity associated with the McCarthy hearings soon led to Bohm's dismissal from his position at Princeton, and his subsequent inability to find employment in the United States. With letters of reference from Einstein and Oppenheimer, Bohm was offered a position in the physics department of the University of São Paulo, the largest university in Brazil, then in the throes of development and expansion, and seeking to attract a prominent quantum physicist from a mainstream American university.[24] Bohm decided to accept the position and prepared to make a hasty departure for Brazil, a day described here by his biographer:

> On the October day in 1951 when Bohm left the United States, thunderstorms and hurricane-force winds swept across New Jersey and New York. The flooded streets made it difficult for him to reach the airport. . . . On board the aircraft while taxiing to take-off, he heard an announcement that the plane would return to the terminal because of an irregularity in the passport of one of the passengers. Already highly nervous, Bohm wondered if he was going to be arrested. The problem, however, concerned another passenger, who was removed from the flight.[25]

In December 1951, two months after his arrival in Brazil, the U.S. consulate in São Paulo confiscated Bohm's passport, effectively stripping him of his U.S. citizenship, and making it impossible for him to leave Brazil other than to return to the United States.[26]

Undeterred, with his passion for learning undiminished, Bohm continued to work, and he was soon sufficiently fluent in self-taught Portuguese to lecture at the University of São Paulo.[27] He was especially encouraged by favorable peer reviews of his recent U.S. publication of *Quantum Theory,* a 646-page textbook interpreting quantum theory, the first paragraph of which begins to emphasize the importance of familiarity with Fourier analysis:

> Modern quantum theory is unusual in two respects. First, it embodies a set of physical ideas that differ completely with much of our everyday experience, and also with most experiments in physics on a macroscopic scale. Second, the mathematical apparatus needed to apply this theory to even the simplest example is much less familiar. . . . It seems impossible, however, to develop quantum concepts extensively without *Fourier analysis.* It is, therefore, presupposed that the reader is moderately familiar with *Fourier analysis.*[28]

THEORY OF HIDDEN VARIABLES

In 1951, the publication of Bohm's textbook *Quantum Theory* set off a storm of criticism in the physics community. The negative reaction centered around Bohm's criticism of the popular Copenhagen approach to calculations in quantum physics. In his book, Bohm states, "Perhaps there are hidden variables that really control the exact time and place of a transfer of a quantum, and we simply haven't found them yet."[29] Bohm believed that physicists should focus on discovering these "hidden variables" that would not only increase the accuracy of quantum calculations but would also offer a more accurate interpretation of the mechanisms in play at the extremely small spatial and temporal dimensions being explored by quantum particle experiments. However this idea of the existence of yet-to-be-discovered hidden variables, though fully supported by Einstein, was seen to run counter to the prevailing acceptance of the popular Copenhagen interpretation of quantum physics.

In 1925 in Copenhagen, Niels Bohr and two of his young students, Heisenberg and Pauli, had initiated a series of formal and informal meetings and conferences that led to the development of what was later to be called the "Copenhagen interpretation" of quantum mechanics, a conjectural descriptive explanation of what the working mathematical equations seemed to imply.[30] This interpretation, heavily dependent upon the use of statistics and the mathematics of probability theory, was able for the first time to succesfully model the observations of nuclear experiments that had previously been difficult if not impossible to predict.

Over the ensuing twenty years, the majority of physicists had come to accept the Copenhagen approach, primarily because the statistical probability methods developed by proponents of the theory were able to match the data observed closer than any other approach. Physicists using the new method viewed Bohm's hidden variable intepretation of quantum phenomena as being almost heretical, a direct challenge to the accepted interpretation. Yet from Bohm's point of view it was the Copenhagen approach that was in error, with its heavy reliance on probability mathematics and the lack of any concerted attempt to truly understand what was occurring among individual nuclear particles at quantum dimensions.[31]

Yet Albert Einstein, Bohm's former neighbor, friend, and mentor, was himself in agreement with Bohm. Einstein is quoted here in a 1926 letter to Max Born, where he comments on the recently published Copenhagen interpretation, expressing special concern regarding the excessive reliance on probability calculations in quantum mechanics:

> Quantum mechanics is certainly imposing. But an inner voice tells me that it is not yet the real thing. The theory says a lot, but does not really bring us any closer to the secret of the "old one." I, at any rate, am convinced that He does not throw dice.[32]

According to the Copenhagen interpretation, quantum events are indeterminate and discontinuous, and therefore no individual physical events are predictable at quantum scales of matter. Thus probability mathematics had become the only effective tool for predicting experimental outcomes, and the numerous discrepancies between calculations and observed data were thought to be statistical outliers.

Bohm argued that no processes within the universe can be attributed to purely random statistical activity. He passionately believed that there must be an underlying order and comprehensive connectivity to the cosmos, a wholeness not predicted by mere probability theory.[33] He was astounded that physicists were willing to have given up a deeper search to understand what was really occurring in the cosmos at quantum levels.

Statistical quantum calculations, while they offered a way to predict experimental outcomes, treated particle actions collectively in a similar way as temperature readings measure the collective effect of billions of gas molecules. In neither case can individual particle motion be mapped or predicted in their actual scalar regions. Nowhere are real dimensions being examined; only statistical averages are measured.

While his textbook on quantum theory was generally well received and subsequently used worldwide in undergraduate courses on quantum mechanics for its clarity of language, analogy, and supporting calculus, his concept of hidden variables was attacked almost universally by physicists as being incompatible with the prevailing Copenhagen interpretation.[34] Bohm's rejection by the physics community also a political side, fueled by his alleged communist affiliations and his flight from the country to take up residence in Brazil.[35]

At best, Bohm's criticism of the Copenhagen theory was ignored, though some went so far as to accuse him of being a Trotskyite and a traitor. One physicist termed Bohm's work "juvenile deviation," and another called Bohm "a public nuisance."[36] The strong peer reaction against Bohm's hypothesis led his own one-time supervisor, mentor, and hero, Robert Oppenheimer, to gather a meeting of physicists at Berkeley in 1953 with the objective of disproving Bohm's theory; the meeting closed with Oppenheimer being heard to say, "If we cannot disprove Bohm, we must continue to ignore him."[37]

Yet Bohm's publications in support of hidden variables display his early fascination with exploring the realities occurring at the greatest depths of scale in the physical cosmos, far below the normal range at which even quantum mechanics is applied, down to distances at the Planck length (approximately 10^{-33} cm), a scale at which "classical notions such as causality or distance between events cannot be expected to be applicable."[38] (The Planck constant is discussed in detail in elsewhere in this book.)

MOTION OF "PARTICLES" IN SPACE-TIME

But Bohm was undeterred by the widespread criticism and continued to search for new ways of interpreting quantum processes. In an example of his own intellectual efforts to supplement the statistical blindness of the Copenhagen interpretation, Bohm speculates that, rather than manifesting as a solid, continuous particle in space-time, "the proton takes the form of a wave that collapses inward from all space," like a whirlpool in water.[39]

Similarly, in a conclusion that is contrary to the conventional assumption that electrons and protons are well-defined particles, Bohm describes the apparent motion of protons and electrons as

> a continuous process of inward collapse and outward expansion. Therefore, every elementary particle collapses inward from the whole of space. In fact, each elementary particle is a manifestation of the whole universe.[40]

FIRST CONCEPTION
OF THE IMPLICATE ORDER

In 1955, after five years in Brazil, Bohm accepted an offer to teach physics at the Israel Institute of Technology in Haifa. There he met his future wife, Saral, an artist. In 1957 Bohm left Israel with his wife to take up a position at Bristol University in southern England. In London, that same year, Bohm presented a more mature version of his hidden variable theory, which he had first begun to develop in *Quantum Theory*.

In London, Bohm introduced the idea of processes occurring at sub-quantum levels considerably smaller in dimension than those regions being explored in experiments dealing with atomic particles such as electrons and protons. This eventually led to Bohm's conceptualization of the implicate order, a consideration that arose through exploration of the possible ontological reality of regions far below the quantum dimensions being explored by his contemporary colleagues.

During his second year in England, Bohm presented a series of lectures at London University detailing his hidden-variable theory; the lectures were attended by a young doctoral student in physics, John Bell, who had become interested in mathematical approaches to the non-locality problem in quantum mechanics. Bell, encouraged by Bohm's theories, went on to develop a mathematical proof of nonlocality, a phenomenon that has since been verified several times in rigorous experiment.[41] It is of interest to note that Bell said of Bohm's theory, "No one can understand this theory until he is willing to see psi as a real objective field rather than just a probability amplitude."[42]

Bohm did not limit his intellectual pursuit exclusively to physics. During his three years at Bristol University, he began to read widely in areas of speculative philosophy, and soon became acquainted with the process philosophy of Alfred North Whitehead, the Cambridge mathematician turned Harvard philosopher. One evening, according to Bohm, while reading Whitehead's *Process and Reality,* he experienced what seemed to be an epiphany, a visualization of infinity in the image of a large number of silvered spherical mirrors, each one reflecting all of the others, a cosmos composed of an infinity of reflections, and of reflections of reflections: "Every atom was reflecting in this way, and the infinity of these reflections was reflected in each thing; each was an infinite reflection of the whole."[43] The influence of this image can be found twenty years later in Bohm's understanding of what he had by then come to call "the implicate order." The image of mirrors reflecting the whole is echoed in *Wholeness and the Implicate Order* in the following passage, which describes Bohm's concept of the holomovement:

> In certain ways this notion is similar to Leibniz's idea of monads, each of which "mirrors" the whole in its own way, some in great detail and others rather vaguely. The difference is that Leibniz's monads had a permanent existence, whereas our basic elements are only moments and are thus not permanent.[44]

KRISHNAMURTI AND MEDITATION

It was also while at Bristol University that Bohm first became acquainted with the philosopher Jiddu Krishnamurti. In the Bristol public library, Bohm's wife, Saral, discovered a book in the philosophy section discussing the topics of perception and thought, and brought it home as of possible interest. Bohm was immediately fascinated by what Krishnamurti had to say:

> My first acquaintance with Krishnamurti's work was in 1959 when I read his book *First and Last Freedom*. What particularly aroused my interest was deep insight into the question of the observer and the observed. . . . I felt that it was urgent for me to talk with Krishnamurti directly and personally as soon as possible. And when I first met him on one of his visits to London, I was struck by the great ease of communication with him, which was made possible by the intense energy with which he listened and by the freedom from self-protective reservations and barriers with which he responded to what I had to say . . . it was in essence of the same quality as that which I had met in contacts with other scientists with whom there had been a very close meeting of minds. And here, I think especially of Einstein who showed a similar intensity and absence of barrier in a number of discussions that took place between him and me. After this, I began to meet Krishnamurti regularly and to discuss with him whenever he came to London.[45]

In 1961, Bohm left Bristol University to accept the offer of chair of theoretical physics offered to him by J. D. Bernal, the head of the physics department (and a dedicated Marxist) at Birkbeck College, University of London. In that same year Bohm, for the first time, arranged a private conversation with Krishnamurti in London. The two continued their dialogues, at first privately, and then eventually in public venues, before audiences in London, Switzerland, and later in Ojai, California.[46]

In Switzerland in 1965, the first public recordings were made of a series of dialogues between Krishnamurti and Bohm. Undoubtedly Bohm's previous reading experience of Whitehead, Hegel, Ouspensky, and Indian philosophy had prepared him well for these flowing dialogues with Krishnamurti, and likely influenced his own conceptualizations. In addition to published books containing transcripts of many of these dialogues, numerous video and audio recordings have been released; a recent YouTube search on "Krishnamurti" and "Bohm" pulled up 32,000 results.[47]

It was in 1967 that Bohm and his wife, at the urging of Krishnamurti, became vegetarians and took up the daily practice of meditation. Bohm was particularly interested in Krishnamurti's teaching on the process of "dying to thought" in which the physical brain no longer gives energy to the movement of thought process in the brain.[48] According to Krishnamurti, it is this incessant conditioned mental thought process that masks and conceals the silence within which the less-conditioned consciousness process might be perceived, and within which new modes of "nonverbal thought" might operate. Bohm here describes his own understanding of Krishnamurti's teaching on the process of meditation:

> Krishnamurti has observed that the very act of meditation will, in itself, bring order to the activity of thought without the intervention of will, choice, decision, or any other action of the "thinker." As such order comes, the noise and chaos which are the usual background of our consciousness die out, and the mind becomes generally silent. . . .
>
> In this silence, Krishnamurti says that something new and

creative happens, something that cannot be conveyed in words, but that is of extraordinary significance for the whole of life. So he does not attempt to communicate this verbally, but rather, he asks of those who are interested that they explore the question of meditation directly for themselves.[49]

It is easy to imagine how Bohm's exceptional, trained capability (as a theoretical physicist) for focus on abstractions served to reinforce his growing capabilities in the practice of formless meditation. Bohm soon established a daily period in the early morning during which he would walk slowly in the park or countryside while watching the movement of his thoughts, not allowing himself to become distracted or "caught up" in their content; this practice continued throughout his life.[50]

THE IMPLICATE ORDER

It is of interest to note that within two years of beginning his daily meditation walk, Bohm conceptualized a significantly new idea, the "implicate order," which ontologically strengthened his hidden-variables theory. By 1969 the subjects of topology, nonlocality, and pre-space had come to the forefront of discussion within the physics department at the University of London, and as his colleague, physicist B. J. Hiley, recalls, Bohm had a breakthrough in his understanding: "Suddenly, a new idea emerged from Bohm, apparently entirely out of the blue . . . Bohm called it the *implicate order*."[51]

Bohm identified this implicate order as being the source of the hidden, sub-quantum variables that he hypothesized were providing the causality underlying the operation of quantum mechanics, and he began an effort to model the effect of the implicate order mathematically.[52] In 1925, Werner Heisenberg had taken a similar view as described here by the mathematician Robert Crease:

Inside the atom, he declared, not only do particles and electron orbits have no meaning, but neither do even such basic classical properties as position, momentum, velocity, and space and time. And because our imaginations require a space-time container, this atomic world cannot be easily pictured.[53]

But Heisenberg's approach fell by the wayside when the Copenhagen approach proved successful in predictive calculations of nuclear particle trajectories using probabilities. Decades later, Bohm pursued a similar idea, and in 1980 published *Wholeness and the Implicate Order*. The book revealed both the mathematics of, and a mature conceptual model for, his proposed implicate order, a model based not on "things" considered as objects or restricted solely to phenomena in a Cartesian space-time order, but rather a model based on a lens-like flowing of simultaneous enfolding and unfolding dimensions between two orders, an implicate order and an explicate order. Bohm explained:

> There is the germ of a new notion of order here. This order is not to be understood solely in terms of a regular arrangement of *objects*. . . . Rather, a *total order* is contained, in some *implicit* sense, in each region of space and time.
>
> Now, the word "implicit" is based on the verb "to implicate." This means, "to fold inward.". . . . So we may be led to explore the notion that in some sense each region contains a total structure "enfolded" within it.[54]

Bohm went so far as to describe the implicate order as the ground within which the entire universe is enfolded at each and every "point" in space-time, as the Finnish philosopher Paavo Pylkkänen, a former student and friend of Bohm's, explained clearly:

> Just think of all the atoms and particles that constitute your body. We are used to thinking about them as tiny little things that just passively sit there. But quantum field theory, as interpreted by Bohm, suggests otherwise. There is a sense in which each particle in

your body enfolds information about the whole universe. . . . There is also a sense in which information about each particle in your body is enfolded throughout the universe.[55]

However, Bohm's focus of interest clearly ranged beyond the conventional boundaries of physics into theories of mind, thought, and consciousness. It is easy to conclude that Bohm's dialogue with Krishnamurti influenced the expansion of this focus, bringing to the forefront for Bohm issues of thinking and mind. But with his deep understanding of quantum theory, Bohm was able to see a direct connection between thought, consciousness, and the implicate order, as can be discerned in his description of the thinking process, recorded in a 1990 interview:

And that's how the thinking process goes, it's enfolded in your consciousness, it unfolds to a certain thought, folds back, and then the next thought appears, different; a series of thoughts not too different seems to be continuous.[56]

In imagining this process as an "enfoldment," we are led to the obvious next question: "Enfoldment into what?"

And Bohm's non-Cartesian answer, then, is enfoldment *into something within,* enfoldment into the implicate order.

How then might this be conceptualized? Imagine the universe at the lowest possible spatial range. Moving to ever-smaller dimensions, to the very bottom of the dimensional scale, we encounter the end of space, according to accepted quantum theory, at a limiting length below which length has no meaning.[57] Thus this implicate order, located at the center, everywhere, can be seen as the ground, base, or center out of which dynamically springs the space-time continuum itself, the explicate order.

THE SUB-QUANTUM ORDER

Bohm applied the term "sub-quantum order" to that order of physics that he viewed as expressing the underlying causal reality *from which* quantum mechanics operates, calling this approach "going beyond the quantum theory."[58] While quantum mechanical theory works well for predicting the path of nuclear particles in dimensional ranges around 10^{-15} meter, the theory places a heavy insistence on pure probability considerations, and this randomness had always bothered Bohm. As early as 1952, in *Quantum Theory,* Bohm stated:

> We have come to the point of view that the wave function is an abstraction, providing a mathematical reflection of certain aspects of reality, but not a one-to-one mapping.[59]

He further argues that the ontological cause is to be discovered at lower levels, below quantum mechanical dimensions, and that "quantum theory is inconsistent with the assumption of hidden causal variables" governing processes at the lowest, sub-quantum levels.[60] At the end of the introduction to his 1993 book, Bohm predicted the failure of the "current laws of physics" at the Planck length:

> The idea is that there will be a stochastic sub-quantum and sub-relativistic level in which the current laws of physics will fail. This will probably first be encountered near the Planck length of 10^{-33} cm. . . .
>
> These ideas are connected with our ontological interpretation by means of a model of a particle as a sequence of incoming and outgoing waves, with successive waves very close to each other. . . .
>
> One of the main new ideas implied by this approach is that the geometry and the dynamics have to be in the same framework, i.e., that of the implicate order.[61]

This leads us to the observation that there exist three sets of framework-dependent mathematical models, applicable in three ranges: (1) Newtonian mechanics, operating at human dimensions, in the 10^0 m range; (2) quantum mechanics, operating at nuclear particle dimensions, in the 10^{-15} m range; and (3) Bohm's "hidden variables," operating at the boundary of space-time, in the sub-quantum 10^{-35} m range. Here Bohm reiterates an observation he had previously made regarding the important significance of the dimension 1.616×10^{-33} cm, the Planck length, and designated with the symbol ℓ_p in quantum theoretical calculations.* In *Wholeness and the Implicate Order*, Bohm, discussing the calculation of what is called "the zero-point energy" for points in space, provides another explanation for the significance of this 10^{-33} cm distance:

> We come to a certain length at which the measurement of space and time becomes totally indefinable. Beyond this, the whole notion of space and time as we know it would fade out, into something that is at present unspecifiable. . . .
>
> When this length is estimated it turns out to be about 10^{-33} cm. This is much shorter than anything thus far probed in physical experiments (which have gone down to about 10^{-17} cm or so). If one computes the amount of energy that would be in one cubic centimetre of space, with this shortest possible wavelength, it turns out to be very far beyond the total energy of all the matter in the known universe.[62]

It is here then, in the region of the Planck length at 10^{-33} cm, that Bohm predicts that there will be found *a boundary* separating an outer, *explicate order* from an inner, *implicate order*. There will also be seen gaps of, at minimum, 10^{-33} cm between each and every concentric shell that might be surrounding the central area, a spherical locus of Planck-length diameter ℓ_p. This is in accord with the founding quantum theory of Max Planck, first published in 1900, in which he proposed that a photon could have only distinct, fixed energy states, separated by inte-

---

*The Planck length of 10^{-33} cm was first discussed by the German physicist Max Planck, the 1918 Nobel Prize winning originator of quantum mechanics, and is derived from three values: (1) the speed of light in a vacuum; (2) the gravitational constant; and (3) the Planck constant, h, which is required to calculate quantum changes of wavelength as a function of temperature. Patrick Bruskiewich, *Max Planck and Black-Body Radiation*.

gers, which he termed "quanta."[63] Bohm used such quantum theoretical considerations to point out a fallacy still held by many: the classical Cartesian assumption that space is continuous. He argued:

> What of the order between two points in space? The Cartesian order holds that space is continuous. Between any two points, no matter how close they lie, occur an infinite of other points. Between any two neighboring points in this infinity lies another infinity and so on.
>
> This notion of continuity is not compatible with the order of quantum theory. . . . Thus the physicist John Wheeler has suggested that, at very short distances, continuous space begins to break up into a foam-like structure. Thus the "order between" two points moves from the order of continuity to an order of a discontinuous foam.[64]

According to Bohm, at the ultimate bottom level of these subdivided infinities, between two points in space, like a bumping post at the termination of a railroad track, will be found a cosmologically fixed boundary at the Planck length of 10^{-33} cm, beyond which no further subdivision is meaningfully possible. From this tiny region, where nothing can be smaller than 10^{-33} cm, here at the very bottom of scalar space, the universe expands outward to reach a diameter currently estimated to be 10^{+29} cm, and even now its expansion continues, accelerating!

Viewed another way, to use the depths of the ocean as an analogy, Bohm's sub-quantum mechanics can be viewed as being at the bottom of a dimensional ocean, with a floor significantly below the depths of the region mapped and explored by the mathematics of quantum mechanics. In the image in figure 11.1 can be seen three regions along a vertical depth-of-scale axis. On the same vertical axis can be ranges within which operate (1) classical Newtonian physics, (2) quantum physics, and (3) Bohmian physics, each operating within distinct ranges and separated by over 10^{15} orders of magnitude. In a real sense, Bohm was plumbing this depth of dimensional physics far below the

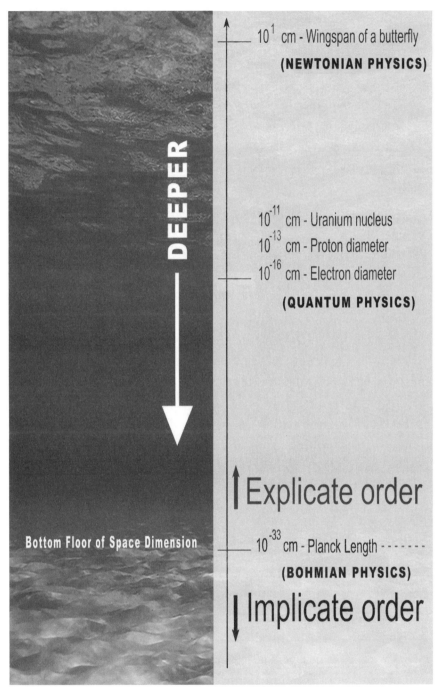

Fig. 11.1. Sub-quantum ocean-floor analogy. Data from Benenson, Harris, Stocker, and Holger, Handbook of Physics.

level at which conventional quantum theory is applied, at depths of scale considerably below those of the dimensions of a monarch butterfly wingspan, a uranium atom nucleus, a proton, or a calculated electron (photon) diameter.

Bohm comments on the depths of this range that:

> It is interesting to note that between the shortest distance now measurable in modern physics (10^{-16} cm) and the shortest distance in which current notions of space-time probably have meaning (10^{-33} cm), there is a vast range of scale in which an immense amount of yet undiscovered structure could be contained. Indeed this range is roughly equal to that which exists between our own size and that of the elementary particles.[65]

Note that quantum mechanics is applicable in a range only halfway down between the scale of the human biosphere and the depths of space-time at the Planck length. The mathematical models (and operational physics) that work in one range (for example, Newtonian mechanics as it operates within the human body parts) are, in general, not applicable within the other ranges (such as the operational physics of quantum mechanics working in electron and proton ranges).

At the absolute bottom of the figure's ocean floor lies the Planck length of 10^{-33} cm, above which the explicate order manifests in increasingly larger ranges of scale until the dimensional length of a butterfly (of about 1 cm) is reached, floating on the surface of the explicate order's ocean depth of scale. Of course, a more inclusive scale would expand upward to include the size of the universe, with a diameter of 10^{26} meters, and the human dimensional range would then be seen to lie approximately halfway between these two limits, the size of the universe (10^{26} m) and the Planck length (10^{-35} m).[66] Such a complete scale range, spanning the entire cosmos, is depicted in figure 11.2.

Another foundation upon which Bohm's model of the universe grew can be seen in his vision of an endless infinity of ordered fields, described here:

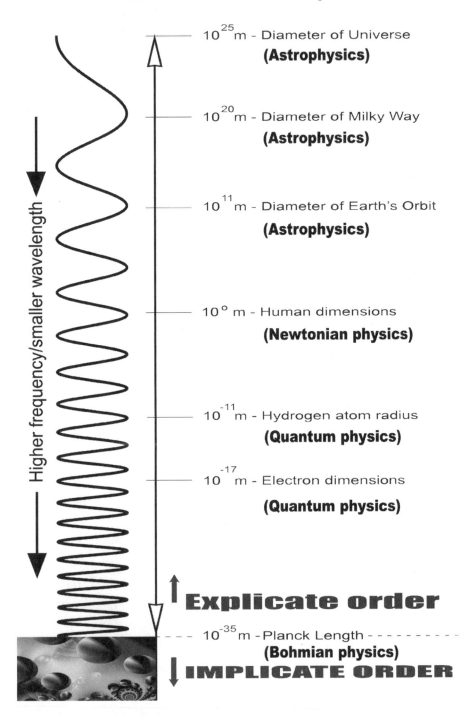

Fig. 11.2. Spectral domain and space-time domain

We may suppose that the universe, which includes the whole of existence, contains not only all the fields that are now known, but also an indefinitely large set of further fields that are unknown and indeed may never be known in their totality. Recalling that the essential qualities of fields exist only in their movement we propose to call this ground the *holo-movement*. It follows that ultimately everything in the explicate order of common experience arises from the holomovement. Whatever persists with a constant form is sustained as the unfoldment of a recurrent and stable pattern, which is constantly being renewed by enfoldment, and constantly being dissolved by unfoldment. When the renewal ceases the form vanishes.[67]

Fields need not exist only within space-time. Einstein's theory of general relativity posits ten fields to describe the movement of gravity in four dimensions.[68] As early as 1919 a German mathematician, Theodor Kaluza, sent Einstein a paper proposing an extremely small fifth dimension in which additional frequency and phase fields could provide a solution to resolve Einstein's struggle to resolve the connection between gravity and electromagnetism.[69] In 1926 the Swedish physicist Oskar Klein, "drawing on quantum mechanics, calculated the size of this compact dimension, arriving at a number that was tiny indeed—around 10^{-30} cm in circumference."[70] The theory became known as the Kaluza-Klein theory, offering the potential of extra fields in an additional dimension as a promising approach to resolving Einstein's search to connect gravity and electromagnetism. Einstein wrote to Kaluza, saying he liked the idea "enormously" and in fact continued working with the theory for the next twenty years; ultimately, however, the Kaluza-Klein theory was discarded because of its prediction of a particle so small that it could not be proven to exist using any foreseeable technology.[71]

But by the same token it has also been impossible to *disprove* a cosmological reality existing at such small dimensions, and it is here, at the limiting space-time scale of 10^{-33} cm, that Bohm hypothesizes an implicate order.[72] In figure 11.3, Pribram's diagrammatic concept of the Fourier transform, discussed previously, is shown with Bohm's implicate

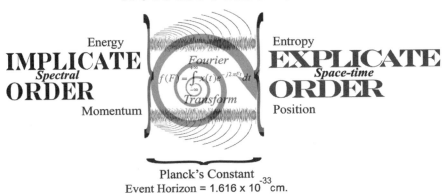

Fig. 11.3. The holodynamic process between the implicate and the explicate orders

order to the left, in the spectral domain, and Bohm's explicate order to the right, in the space-time domain.

At the center of the diagram, what Bohm calls a "holodynamic process" links the two orders in the mathematical relationship of a two-way Fourier transform. Bohm also refers to this process as "holomovement," a continuous fractal infolding and unfolding of spectral energy flowing between an implicate order and an explicate order. Bohm viewed the universe as one whole ("uni-verse") consisting of these two primary orders and multiple dimensions operating continuously under the law of "holonomy."

> The implicate order has its ground in the holomovement which is vast, rich, and in a state of unending flux of enfoldment and unfoldment, with laws most of which are only vaguely known, and which may even be ultimately unknowable in their totality. . . . Nevertheless, . . . the overall law (holonomy) may be assumed to be such that in a certain sub-order, within the whole set of the implicate order, there is a totality of forms that have an approximate kind

of recurrence, stability, and separability. Evidently these forms are capable of appearing as the relatively solid, tangible, and stable elements that make up our "manifest world."[73]

HOLOMOVEMENT AND HOLOFLUX

In 1978 Bohm discussed these concepts with remarkable clarity during a Harvard conference on "Science and Mysticism: Exploring the New Realities." After his presentation, which he called "The Implicate Order: The Holodynamic Model of the Universe," Bohm was interviewed by Renée Weber for *ReVision* magazine, and in that interview he discusses the difference between holography and the holomovement, and introduces the term "holoflux," a term suggested by Pribram.

WEBER: Could we begin by clarifying the difference between the holomovement, the holograph, and the implicate order?

BOHM: Holomovement is a combination of a Greek and Latin word and a similar word would be holokinesis or, still better, *holoflux*, because "movement" implies motion from place to place, whereas flux does not. So the *holoflux* includes the ultimately flowing nature of what is, and of that which forms therein. The holograph, on the other hand, is merely a static recording of movement, like a photograph: an abstraction from the holomovement. We therefore cannot regard the holograph as anything very basic, since it is merely a way of displaying the holomovement, which latter is, however, the ground of everything, of all that is. The implicate order is the one in which the holomovement takes place, an order that both enfolds and unfolds. Things are unfolded in the implicate order, and that order cannot be entirely expressed in an explicate fashion. Therefore, in this approach, we are not able to go beyond the holomovement or the *holoflux* (the Greek word might be *holorhesis*, I suppose) although that does not imply that this is the end of the matter.[74]

In a theory congruent with Pribram's, Bohm hypothesizes that consciousness must operate dynamically in a holonomic fashion, driven by a quantum potential wave, and that the information guiding motion in space-time must originate from an other order, the implicate order, which lies outside of the commonly perceived explicate order of the space-time domain.[75] From early in his career, Bohm had tried to visualize the motion of quantum "particles," not moving in linear sequential tracks as viewed in a cloud chamber, but as oscillating in and out of space-time.[76]

Bohm, in a 1990 interview recorded for Dutch television, not only describes this movement or "holomovement" as superseding the so-called particle phenomena of quantum mechanics, but in doing so, emphasizes the reality of the whole and the continuum of mind and matter, while discussing the general implications of this for perception.

> Now, I saw that you could understand the quantum mechanics in terms of that process. That instead of saying an electron, for example, is a particle just moving along, you could think that there is a wave coming in, enfolding, or it's really unfolding at a point, it's enfolded in the whole universe. Then it folds back. Then another wave comes in, at a slightly different point. You get a series of points that are very close together so we imagine they're a particle, right? But, because of that wave nature, from which it comes, you understand, the wave/particle nature, that is, it's a wave.[77]

Support for this view is found in an interpretation of holodynamics put forth by a consciousness researcher at UC–Irvine, Gordon Globus, who describes Bohm's holodynamic process as follows:

> There are two primary phases of this holodynamics according to Bohm: *implication* and *explication*. . . . Implication is the "enfolding" of world to the whole and explication is the cotemporaneous "unfolding" of world from the whole. Each moment of unfolding/enfolding has a brief duration. . . . The world is explicate order continually unfolded from implicate order, rather than explicate order persisting.[78]

And what then might be the temporal rate of such an oscillation or "brief duration" of unfolding of the world in space-time? Here again it is the Planck constant that sets the limiting boundary condition. The Planck second, or "Planck time," calculated to be 5.44×10^{-44} seconds, is the smallest conceivable time interval consistent with quantum theory, and below this interval time has no meaning. If indeed time is granulated at such a limit, then the cosmos may be created, destroyed, and recreated a staggering number of times per "human second." In the limiting case, space-time reality can be seen to emerge from an implicate order into an explicate order, from holoflux frequencies into space-time electromagnetic fields. This would occur at a clock cycle of 5.44×10^{-44} seconds, only to collapse out of space-time and back into the implicate order in alternate intervals between each of these sub-quantum clock cycles. Such a cyclic pattern of unfolding potential accords well with Bohm's description of holomovement in a 1990 paper where he wrote:

All things found in the unfolded, explicate order emerge from the holomovement in which they are enfolded as *potentialities,* and ultimately they fall back into it. They endure only for some time, and while they last, their existence is sustained in a constant process of unfoldment and re-enfoldment, which gives rise to their relatively stable and independent forms in the explicate order.[79]

MEANING, FORM, AND INFORMATION

In developing his appreciation for the ontological and cosmological implications of quantum theory, Bohm placed great importance in maintaining a clear distinction regarding three terms: meaning, form, and information.

He describes the essential significance of form as being the conveyor and shipping container of embedded meaning.

What is essential for a form to constitute information is that it shall have a *meaning*. . . . The form in the radio wave thus literally "informs" the energy in the receiver . . . this form is eventually *trans-formed* (which means "form carried across") into related forms of sound and light.[80]

How then is the meaning unpacked from the shipping container? How is information related to meaning? Bohm says that for information to become meaning requires, specifically, what Bohm terms "active information."[81]

> The basic idea of active information is that a *form,* having very little energy, enters into and directs a much greater energy. This notion of an original energy form acting to "inform," or put form into, a much larger energy has significant applications in many areas beyond quantum theory.[82]

For Bohm, active information is the state in which a receiving energy is informed by the *form* of a transmitted energy, the receiving energy is "in-formed." Here he gives as an example of a radio wave of electromagnetic energy being "in-formed":

> In the radio wave, the form is initially inactive, but as the form enters into the electrical energy of the receiver, we may say, that the information becomes active. In general, this information is only potentially active in the radio wave, but it becomes actually active only when and where there is a receiver which can respond to it with its "own energy."[83]

Bohm goes on to say that the operation of active information can be detected in nature outside of the human context and can be seen, for example, in the action of RNA as it decodes information locked in the form of DNA. He states:

> It is assumed that the DNA molecule constitutes a code (i.e., a language), and that the RNA molecules "read" this code, and are thus in effect "informed" as to what kind of proteins they are to make.[84]

Finally, Bohm identifies the *activity* of the energy in the receiving entity as the *meaning* (i.e., the active information flow *is* the meaning).

> I would like to suggest then that the activity, virtual or actual, in the energy and in the soma *is* the meaning of the information, rather than to say that the information affects an entity called the mind, which in turn operates somehow on the matter of the body.[85]

What Bohm is implying here is that perhaps there is, in actuality, no "thing" that can be called mind, that there is no "entity called the mind," but that, rather, it is the *active information* itself, sourced in the implicate domain, that is in-forming the region of the explicit domain directly. Bohm summarizes his ideas:

> The thinking process unfolds certain explicate thoughts, then folds back into the implicate, and then the next thought appears, the entire process forming a series of thoughts, which, seeming not too different, appear to be flowing in a continuous stream.[86]

ACTIVE INFORMATION AND THE QUANTUM POTENTIAL

To visualize "active information," imagine that radiating waves of information-encoded energy emerge from the implicate domain at the center of each Plank-length diameter "point" or "holosphere" in the universe (but outside of space-time). Picture the waves radiating outward into space as in expanding shells.

Active information, like conceptual thought, does not need to be of great magnitude to be the effective cause of relatively large orders of magnitude of effect in the explicate domain. An example given by Bohm is the action of a tiny electrical signal that guides the movement of a large ship, airplane, or missile in flight. Here he provides a common example of how, even in the explicate world, a source of active information comprising relatively minute quantities of energy can effectively influence a receiver operating at considerably higher energy levels:

As an example, let us take a radio wave, whose form carries information representing either sound or pictures. The radio wave itself has very little energy. The receiver, however, has a much greater energy (e.g., from the power source). The structure of the radio is such that the form carried by the radio wave is imposed on the much greater energy of the receiver.[87]

Here Bohm claims that it is not the magnitude of the energy itself that makes active information so highly effective, but *its ability to modulate* and thus influence comparatively huge sources of energy in space-time. Bohm developed his mathematics of active information by deriving a potential function directly from the Schrödinger equation in quantum mechanics and designating it as Q, the "quantum potential."[88]

As time went on, Bohm emphasized the role played by the quantum potential. The quantum potential—whose influence depends on its overall form and not on its strength—is totally unlike anything previously postulated in physics.[89]

In order to prove that there is *real* causation acting in quantum mechanics, rather than accepting the commonly held theory that it is all probability and stochastic process, Bohm proposed that a quantum potential (Q) also acts upon quantum particles such as electrons and protons, and states that this Q function

expresses the activity of a new kind of implicate order. This implicate order is immensely more subtle than that of the original field, as well as more inclusive, in the sense that not only is the actual activity of the whole field enfolded in it, but also all its potentialities, along with the principles determining which of these shall become actual.[90]

Bohm was eventually able to discover a precise mathematical expression for his quantum potential function, Q, by deriving it from proven models of particle motion. The equation is given in figure 11.4.[91]

$$Q = \frac{-\hbar^2 \nabla^2 |\psi|^2}{2m |\psi|^2}$$

Fig. 11.4. Equation of the quantum potential

In Bohm's equation of the quantum potential (Q) of active information, the function ψ is the quantum field or "wave function" derived from Schrödinger's equation, $\hbar$ is Planck's constant, and m is the mass of the electron or "particle."[92] The symbol ∇ is called a "curl," and this symbol indicates an infinitesimal rotation of multi-dimensional coordinates (usually three or more) around a common origin, in order to obtain the differential motion of the wave in space-time. Bohm here points out what appears to be of special importance:

> What is mathematically significant in the above equation is that this wave function is found in both the numerator and the denominator. . . .
>
> The fact that ψ is contained both in the numerator and the denominator for Q means that Q is unchanged when ψ is multiplied by an arbitrary constant. In other words, the quantum potential Q is *independent of the strength, or intensity,* of the quantum field but *depends only on its form.* This is a particularly surprising result.[93]

Of great significance for Bohm is that fact that Q, the quantum potential, is seen to be independent of strength, or signal-energy magnitude. This provides support for his insistence on causality by implying that there is a formal cause, independent of magnitude, below the postulated randomness that is otherwise implied by the probabilistic calculations of quantum mechanics, and here Bohm concludes:

> In the causal interpretation, the electron moves under its own energy, but the information in the *form* of the quantum wave directs the energy of the electron.[94]

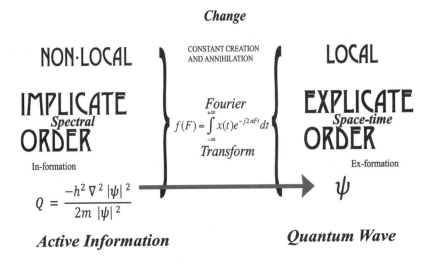

Fig. 11.5. Active information and the quantum wave

This can be visualized in figure 11.5, in which the function Q, sourced in the implicate order, molds or in-forms the quantum wave ψ in the explicate order. Here the metaphor of waves influencing the course of a ship is applicable.

In fact, a "pilot wave theory" similar to Bohm's active information model was proposed by de Broglie in 1927, though his idea was immediately criticized by the skeptical Wolfgang Pauli for being untestable.[95] In consequence, de Broglie abandoned his suggestion in favor of probability theory, but some years later Bohm brought up the idea again when he published, in 1952, "A Suggested Interpretation of the Quantum Theory in Terms of 'Hidden Variables.'"[96]

In the figure, the "Active Information" function can be seen to be guiding the "Quantum Wave" function. Bohm here provides another example of *form* as active information in everyday human experience:

> It is clear, of course, that the notion of active information also applies directly to human experience. For example, when the form of a road sign is apprehended in the brain and nervous system, the form is immediately active as meaning.[97]

But not all information is active, and Bohm refers to information that is not active as *virtual information,* "the activity of meaning may be only virtual, rather than actual. Virtual activity is more than a mere potentiality . . . it is a kind of suspended action."[98] Until it is made explicate as active information, this virtual information exists only in the implicate domain.

Indeed, Bohm's logic leads him to the conclusion that consciousness—at least of the non-active kind ("non-minding" as Karl Pribram might have said)—is of, or resides "within," the implicate order (though, of course, the word *within* has no clear meaning for the spaceless, timeless implicate order). While Bohm views the seat of consciousness as residing primarily within the implicate order, he sees its extensions into the explicate order in "human experience" (thought, taste, love, and so on), as newly evolved ways for consciousness to experience.

> In some sense, consciousness (which we take to include thought, feeling, desire, will, etc.) is to be comprehended in terms of the implicate order, along with reality as a whole. . . .
>
> . . . The actual "substance" of consciousness can be understood in terms of the notion that the implicate order is also its primary and immediate actuality.[99]

Bohm goes on to point out that some forms of information *from within* the implicate order are perceived, or can be perceived, by modes of consciousness in the explicate order: "Evidently this order is *active* in the sense that it continually flows into emotional, physical, and other responses." And here he provides music as an example: "In listening to music, *one is therefore directly perceiving an implicate order.*"[100] But it is not only in listening to music that consciousness resonates in the implicate order, but also in ordinary, everyday experience, as Bohm says:

> A great deal of our difficulty comes from the fact that we accept the idea that not only matter, but all of our experience as well, is

in the explicate order, and then suddenly we want to connect this up with consciousness, which is of a totally different order ... [the implicate order] consider the nature of ordinary, everyday experience. I say that it is totally misunderstood, that it is actually part of the implicate order ... in that order [the implicate order] everything contacts everything else and thus there is no intrinsic reason why the paranormal should be impossible.[101]

In a 1978 interview at the Krishnamurti center in Ojai, by which time Bohm had been practicing meditation for over a decade, Bohm commented on distinctions between different modes of consciousness, and how it may be possible to experience the implicate order as a mode of consciousness that is timeless:

QUESTION: When mystics use the visualization of light they don't use it only as a metaphor, to them it seems to be a reality. Have they tapped into matter and energy at a level where time is absent?

BOHM: It may well be. That's one way of looking at it. As I've suggested the mind has two-dimensional and three-dimensional modes of operation. It may be able to operate directly in the depths of the implicate order where this timeless state is the primary actuality. Then we could see the ordinary actuality as a secondary structure that emerges as an overtone on the primary structure. . . . The ordinary consciousness is one kind of music, and the other kind of consciousness is the other kind of music.[102]

THE UNIVERSE AS A
MIRROR OBSERVING ITSELF

Above all, Bohm insists, the universe as one single process, one enormous wholeness that is everywhere interconnected in complex and often unimaginable ways. Though our own recently evolved explicate modes of space-time consciousness may not yet be able to "see" in other dimensions, consciousness and matter do form a continuum, an interconnected whole, as Bohm says in the final words of his last book, using the metaphor of a mirror.

> At no stage is there a break in this process. . . . There is no need, therefore, to regard the observer as basically separate from what he sees, nor to reduce him to an epiphenomenon of the objective process. Indeed, the notion of separateness is an abstraction and an approximation valid for only certain limited purposes. More broadly one could say that through the human being, *the universe is making a mirror to observe itself.* . . .
>
> . . . All proposals are points of departure for exploration. Eventually some of them may be developed so far that we may take them as working hypotheses.[103]

Here it may be useful to examine the conception of dualism versus monism. In figure 11.6, Cartesian dualism, on the left, contrasts with three positions of monism; Bohm's "neutral monism" can be seen in the lower right on the diagram, where matter and mind are both shown as derivative (both are in Bohm's explicate order of space-time); while the fundamental "3rd substance" would be Bohm's implicate order.

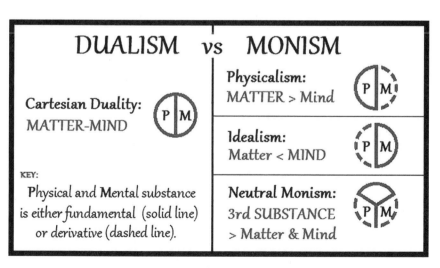

Fig. 11.6. Dualism versus monism.
Graphic by Dewynne (2012), modified.

In an interview videotaped in Amsterdam in September 1990 by the Dutch Public Television Network, Bohm discussed the phenomenon of the sense of self, that sense that individuals have of being "I," and stated clearly that this sense of self is a *product* of thought, and not the real situation. Rather, he pointed to the implicate order as being the source of deeper reality, as being the true "I," "the me" that we all assume to be so very unique. Here, Krishnamurti's influence is apparent!

BOHM: Remember, thought is conditioned reflex at a very high subtle level. It just goes by itself, but it has in it the thought that thought is being produced by a center, which it calls "me." And all the feelings, which should belong to that center, are thrown onto consciousness as if from "me," right?

INTERVIEWER: And our society reinforces that.

BOHM: Everybody says the same thing, like everybody sees the same rainbow, everybody sees the same "self," whether it's there or not. In fact, it becomes all-important, the concept is regarded as central and supremely important. All sorts of powerful feelings will arise if it's questioned. You see, now, it all goes on by itself. . . and, you see . . . there's a deeper being, I say, which can . . . which is that being which may be able to reveal itself an . . . rather than being a fixed being . . . it's deep in the implicate order . . . in the infinite. . . .

INTERVIEWER: . . . So, thought creates "the me," rather than "me" creating the thought?

BOHM: Yes. If you don't see that happening, you will treat that as real and give it apparent reality. The whole being will take actions on that basis which seems to be coming from the center.[104]

QUANTUM MECHANICS AND THE COSMOLOGY OF CONSCIOUSNESS

Bohm's interest, like Pribram's, also lay in trying to understand and map consciousness and its role in cosmology, an area outside of the normal range of inquiry in both their respective professional careers. Bohm was forthright in his inclusion of consciousness as an important aspect of his quantum cosmology. According to Bohm, there is a two-phase reciprocal movement, or holomovement, at the boundary of (between) the implicate order and the explicate order,[105] and in a 1978 interview, he stated unequivocally, "Let me propose that consciousness is basically in the implicate order."[106]

In the last chapter of his final book, Bohm reinforces his belief that quantum theory and consciousness are linked by the implicate order.

> Several physicists have already suggested that quantum mechanics and consciousness are closely related and that the understanding of the quantum formalism requires that ultimately we bring in consciousness in some role or other. . . . The intuition that consciousness and quantum theory are in some sense related seems to be a good one. . . .
>
>   Our proposal in this regard is that the basic relationship of quantum theory and consciousness is that they have the implicate order in common.[107]

BOHM'S WAVES COMING INTO AND GOING OUT OF A POINT

Bohm easily grasped the geometry of quantum phenomenon. When other physicists discussed "quantum jumps" of energy, Bohm was able to perceive an ontologically feasible process. Here in an interview with Bill Angelos, he describes the reality as waves coming in to a point and waves coming out of a point, for all points in the holoplenum:

ANGELOS: Could we . . . Again, the term "quantum" itself has its base in?

BOHM: Well, the "quantum" . . . That's one of the features of "quantum.". . . The quantum has its base in the fact that energy is transferred in discrete jumps or "quanta" rather than continuously.

ANGELOS: I see.

BOHM: Now, you can see that some sort of quantum appears here . . . the wave comes to a point, then there is a jump to another point. See one thing—according to quantum theory—was that the electron could go from one state to another without passing in between. Now you said: That is an utter mystery, right? But you see, if the wave comes in to this point . . . then it spreads out . . . it could come in to another point. So, therefore, it needn't look so mysterious.[108]

For a more nonverbal approach to understanding Bohm's implicate/ explicate universe we now explore two visual metaphors: the implicate order as a micro black hole, and the yin-yang symbol as mirroring the implicate/explicate process.

IMPLICATE ORDER AS A QUANTUM BLACK HOLE

It is appropriate here to use the image of a quantum black hole as a visual metaphor for realizing the topology of the implicate order.

Micro black holes, which have also been called quantum mechanical black holes, quantum black holes, or mini black holes, are hypothetical tiny black holes. . . . It is possible that such quantum primordial black holes were created in the high-density environment of the early Universe (or Big Bang).[109]

Visualizing the implicate order as a micro black hole, we can perhaps view its boundary as a spherical event-horizon shell, marking the limits of an "external," explicate order and the outer limits of an "internal," implicate order. Below the surface of such a sphere, of diameter equal to the Planck length, lies a transcendental implicate order, while outside the quantum black hole begins a universe of the explicate order, replete with time and space.

It must be noted that the conventional definition of a point is a mathematical one: it has no diameter at all, or is conceptualized as a sort of sphere with an infinitely small diameter. But in a cosmological understanding of the point, considering that below the Planck length there is no space as we know it, the closest approximation to a point in space-time would seem to be a micro black hole of Planck length diameter.

YIN-YANG SYMBOL AS A HOLONOMIC PROCESS

Bohm's cotemporaneous enfolding/unfolding process can be visually captured in the yin-yang symbol (fig. 11.7), attributed historically to Chinese Taoist sages of the third century BCE.[110]

*Fig. 11.7. Implicate/explicate orders as yin-yang.
This is the Taoist yin-yang symbol, with black
representing yin and white representing yang. It is a
symbol that reflects the inescapably intertwined duality
of all things in nature, a common theme in Taoism.
Graphic by Alkari.*

Fig. 11.8. Niels Bohr and his coat of arms.
Left, photograph by Bain; right, graphic by Fulvio314.

In the yin-yang symbol, one side can be taken to represent a timeless, spaceless implicate order, and the other side can be seen as the expressed space-time explicate order. And yet each one is also at the heart of the other (designated by the dots in the two regions of the symbol).

It is of interest to note that the physicist Niels Bohr, famous for his visionary conception of electrons moving in fixed orbits around the nucleus of an atom, selected this Taoist symbol for his personal seal to adorn his "coat of arms" on the occasion of receiving the Royal Danish Award for Physics (fig. 11.8).[111]

That an ancient Taoist symbol might capture so well the essence of Bohm's primary cosmological process speaks well for the powers of human consciousness. The Taoist shamans as early as 400 BCE seem to have been able to observe the same cosmic processes that David Bohm was able to perceive in the late twentieth century, a continuous process of enfolding and unfolding the universe between two primary domains.

12

Joye's Sub-Quantum Holoflux Theory of Consciousness

Perhaps the most widely debated issue in consciousness research can be found encapsulated in the phrase "the hard problem of consciousness," first articulated by the Australian cognitive scientist David Chalmers in a 1995 essay. In his paper, Chalmers focuses upon consciousness as *experience*. Chalmers tells us that the hard problem of consciousness is that of finding the link between the rich inner life displayed in the mind, a product of a "whir of information processing," and the actual experience of that display.

> The really hard problem of consciousness is the problem of experience. When we think and perceive, there is a whir of information processing, but there is also a subjective aspect. . . .
>
> . . . Why should physical processing give rise to a rich inner life at all? It seems objectively unreasonable that it should, and yet it does.
>
> If any problem qualifies as the problem of consciousness, it is this one.[1]

Now, a quarter of a century later, researchers have yet to come up with any plausible theory to solve the problem. Donald Hoffman, who earned his Ph.D. at MIT in the area of computational psychology, addresses the issue in his 2019 book, *The Case against Reality* where he writes:

> We have no scientific theories that explain how brain activity—or computer activity, or any other kind of physical activity—could cause, or be, or somehow give rise to, conscious experience. We don't even have one idea that's remotely plausible. . . . Our utter failure leads some to call this the "hard problem" of consciousness, or simply a "mystery."[2]

Hoffman argues that conscious beings have not evolved to perceive the world as it actually is but have evolved to perceive the world in a way that maximizes survival. Borrowing images from his mathematical model of consciousness, Hoffman has us try to visualize our mind as it operates through myriad parallel program subroutines that take in and process sensory data, organize it, filter it, and generate a display that is appropriate for the *experiencer*, that subject or entity who observes the display. Hoffman frequently uses a metaphor: that we experience the mind as a computer desktop display. Our *experiencing consciousness* is separate from this display, and it is *not* the same as the mind. The objects that we perceive in time and space are filtered, simplified, and edited before being combined and projected out onto our "inner display."

Both Chalmers and Hoffman agree in their supposition that consciousness and the mind are different things. To them, consciousness is not the mind, it is different. It is the direct *subjective experience* of the activities of the mind. The mind itself is more like a higher level sensory organ that acts more as an electronic computer to collect, integrate, edit, format, and then serve up a resultant display for viewing by our "pure consciousness," resulting in what we call "our experience" of the inner display.

Nevertheless, the contention that consciousness and the mind are distinctly separate phenomena runs counter to the dominant hypotheses of material science. Neurophysicists assert that consciousness arises through the activity of neurons in the brain operating much like a computer, offering sensory input that is logically manipulated by internal "mental software."

But Chalmers does not believe that software can generate the directly felt experiential sensations that include the sweetness of sugar, the joy of seeing a butterfly, the sensation of awe while viewing galaxies at night, or the feeling of being in love. Such uniquely distinct "experiential feelings" or "qualia" seem far beyond the logical operations of even the most complex of software routines. He suggests that consciousness may be a primary category of the universe, *perhaps transcending both space and time,* and strongly disagrees with the neurological computer model of consciousness, holding that consciousness as direct "awareness" is something categorically different than operations within the human brain, a something that *uses* the brain to extend itself into space-time.

Like the scientific materialist bias of epiphenomenalism, other assumptions also restrict the range of contemporary approaches to consciousness research, and may be similarly misleading, for example, (*a*) the assumption that the word *consciousness* is limited specifically to "human consciousness" of the waking individual, (*b*) the assumption that consciousness must have a biological basis, and (*c*) the assumption that consciousness is a phenomenon exclusive to the space-time continuum.

But the larger scientific community continues to believe that the brain, an organ of meat and nerves, generates consciousness from nothing, from some as yet unknown complex activity of neurons and glial cells. Beginning with this tacit assumption, researchers focus almost exclusively upon an exploration of the hardware of the brain. To some extent, the assumption that the brain manufactures consciousness is fostered by an approach to science that limits itself to measurements that can be observed in space-time. An example of this assumption, that epiphenomenalism is widespread in the scientific community, is supported by Gerald Edelman, an American biologist who won the 1972 Nobel Prize in Physiology, and neuroscientist Giulio Tononi in the conclusion to their 2002 book, *A Universe of Consciousness.* There they state:

Consciousness, while special, arose as a result of evolutionary innovations in the morphology of the brain and body. The mind arises from the body and its development; it is embodied and therefore part of nature. . . . We have argued throughout this book that consciousness arises from certain arrangements in the material order of the brain.[3]

Yet there has been little progress in identifying neurons or even larger brain structures as plausible *sources* of consciousness. Major research efforts that are currently underway focus on creating a map of the brain's neuronal wiring (i.e., the interconnection of neurons in the brain). This is truly a daunting task given that there are about 85 billion neurons and 85 billion glial cells within the adult human brain.[4]

We believe that the observed neuronal activity within the brain is *not* the source and home of consciousness. The theory expressed in this chapter takes the opposite view: that the human mind, mental cognition, and the operational processes of the brain all arise *from* consciousness, that the mind and consciousness are *not* the same thing. That which is being sought to resolve the hard problem of consciousness, does *not* arise from neurons within the brain. We must look elsewhere.

Nevertheless, pervasive neuron-centric researchers continue to make serious attempts to produce functional maps of consciousness by looking within various brain regions through the use of new imaging technologies such as PET (positron emission tomography) and MRI (magnetic resonance imaging). These devices allow neurophysiologists to watch brain regions light up and to correlate them with specific categories of the host's momentary experience (e.g., emotions, diseases, drugs, the effects of injuries, and so on).

A much smaller group of scientists have begun to seek consciousness at the quantum level, sourced in dimensions far below the scale of neurons, glial cells, and macro structures of the brain. Among these are Hameroff and Penrose (see chapter 8) who focus upon quantum activities within microtubules, and William Tiller (see chapter 6) the former Stanford professor and expert on crystallography who has since become focused on consciousness at quantum levels.

This chapter offers an additional theory to support the proposition that consciousness manifests at *sub-quantum dimensions,* far below the ocean of atomic "particles." The sub-quantum holoflux proposal is supported by electromagnetic theory and a geometry of consciousness explored by the neurophysiologist Karl Pribram and the quantum physicist David Bohm.[5]

The table below presents three different levels of scale at which consciousness may be sourced. Almost all contemporary research seeking the source of consciousness is being conducted in level 1, within the region of cellular structures in the brain at a scalar depth of 10^{-3} meter. Far deeper are the unknown intervening depths that reach down to the floor of space at 10^{-35} meter, below which space does not exist.

TABLE 2. THREE SCALAR LEVELS THAT MAY BE A SOURCE OF CONSCIOUSNESS

Region of Exploration	Objects of Consideration	Scalar Range
1. Macro	Neurons and neuroglial cells; physiology of the brain	10^{-3} meter
2. Quantum	Atomic particles/waves	10^{-15} meter
3. Sub-Quantum	Planck length phenomena; the quantum-vacuum; the holoflux field zero-point energy	10^{-35} meter

The basic assertion in this chapter is that while consciousness may be clearly *acting* through structures within the first two levels, the macro and quantum, it is the sub-quantum region that is the source and substrate of consciousness. Thus the holoflux theory of consciousness proposes consciousness as an active awareness that projects space-time from within Bohm's implicate order, acting from beneath a spatial depth of 10^{-35} meter.

As noted in chapter 11, the concept of the holoflux field began with Bohm's concept of holomovment that he conceptualized as a cyclical flow of information-laden energy between the two domains he called the implicate order and the explicate order (space-time). He often referred to this flow as a "folding" and "unfolding" of information between space-time and the implicate order. Pribram suggested that holoflux might be a more appropriate term than "holomovment," as movement implies motion in space. Figure 12.1 models the cyclic unfolding of holoflux from within the implicate order outward into space-time. Though containing no space or time, the implicate order is thought to consist of seven "rolled-up" dimensions predicted by quantum physics. From within the implicate order at the left of the figure information unfolds into the space-time order at the right. Information emerges as the electromagnetic energy that forms the structures we call material objects (galaxies, stars, and zebras) within our familiar and observable universe.

But the process is also a two-way cybernetic loop. Information recording events in the space-time universe flows back from space-time *into* the implicate order; space-time information is continuously pulled in and stored in a timeless eternity, affecting and modifying the next cycle of projections into an unfolding, evolving universe.

This holoflux theory is in full accord with the injunction that Chalmers made in the following passage, that any new theory should

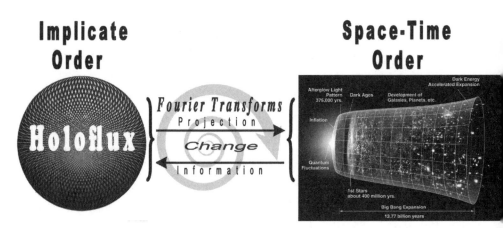

Fig. 12.1. Projecting holoflux from implicate order into space-time

be "the simplest possible theory that explains the data." As he writes in his essay "An Outline of a Theory of Consciousnes":

It is not too soon to begin work on a theory. We are already in a position to understand certain key facts about the relationship between physical processes and experience and about the regularities that connect them. . . .

. . . Finally, the fact that we are searching for a *fundamental* theory means that we can appeal to nonempirical constraints such as simplicity, homogeneity, and the like in developing a theory. We must seek to systematize the information we have, to extend it as far as possible by careful analysis, and then to make the inference to the simplest possible theory that explains the data while remaining a plausible candidate to be part of the fundamental furniture of the world.[6]

Chalmers challenges us to search for a new theory of consciousness for which perhaps a new methodology may be appropriate. Here we have approached consciousness through a *synairesis*. The philosopher Jean Gebser here defines the term *syneresis* in *The Ever-Present Origin,* his magnum opus on the structure of consciousness:

Syneresis comes from the Greek *synaireo,* meaning "to synthesize, collect," notably in the sense of "everything being seized or grasped on all sides, particularly by the mind or spirit"; . . . synairesis is an integral act of completion "encompassing all sides" and perceiving aperspectivally.[7]

The holoflux theory of consciousness emerges as a synairesis of the eight perspectives displayed in Figure 12.2 (p. 178). The figure offers a visual diagram of consciousness approached from eight categorically distinct perspectives. Using this multi-domained approach, new connections have been identified from which a new theory has emerged.

The combined work of Pribram and Bohm also exhibits elements of a synairesis. After many years of research and study, and having begun

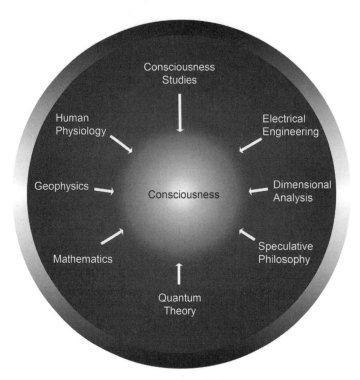

Fig. 12.2. Consciousness approached through a synairesis

to collaborate after meeting in 1974 when both were at the peak of their careers, Karl Pribram and David Bohm shared doubts that consciousness or even memory could be generated by neurons or quantum mechanical processes within the brain. Instead, as Bohm stated in a 1978 interview, "consciousness is basically *in* the implicate order."[8]

The holoflux theory of consciousness that I am presenting here can be thought of as a geometry of consciousness. The concept of the holoflux is supported by quantum physics and the mathematics of the Fourier transform, an equation that, as discussed above, states that energy signals manifesting as electromagnetic waves in the space-time domain are equivalent to information manifesting as pure frequencies in the frequency domain. This mathematical relationship has been proven extremely useful in many fields, and is widely used by electrical engineers in the design of electromagnetic devices. The frequency domain is what David Bohm terms the implicate order, and what electrical engineers using the Fourier transform call the frequency domain.

Holoflux theory is also in agreement with panpsychism, a philosophical school that assumes that consciousness is the substrate of everything. However, the holoflux theory goes further by explaining how consciousness within space-time has origins outside of space-time. Holoflux exists in a transcendental dimension, outside of (or beyond) space and time. Yet it maintains a continuous direct link to space-time through resonance. More specifically, holoflux energy is understood to be the primal consciousness underlying and projecting everything in our space-time universe, but manifesting as a continuously transforming flow of energy between that which exists in the space-time domain and a spaceless, timeless domain of pure cognition, or energy flux.

To express the interconnectedness of this energy flux, spanning a wholeness that embraces both space-time phenomena as well as transcendent phenomena, we use the term *holoflux,* from the root term *holism,* defined here as: "The fundamental interconnectedness of all phenomena, and within this fundamental interconnectedness not only is each entity, relationship, experience and phenomenon a whole, in its own right, but all wholes are held together by a great unifying force."[9]

The boundaries between the immanent and the transcendent are omnipresent and everywhere interpenetrating. Holoflux can be described as energy within the transcendent domain encoded with both information and meaning, resonating between the explicate domain of space-time and the nonspatial, nontemporal transcendent domain that David Bohm termed the *implicate order.* In the space-time domain, holoflux consciousness manifests in what we call the electromagnetic field.

The electromagnetic holoflux theory of consciousness rests upon two fundamental paradigms: Karl Pribram's holonomic brain theory and David Bohm's ontological interpretation of quantum theory.[10] Their theories have been shown to be congruent, supported and knit together by established principles of electrical communication engineering. The holoflux theory of consciousness proposed here is based upon the following nine propositions:

- **A Centered Cosmos:** In agreement with the theory of general relativity, the holoflux theory is founded upon the paradoxical concept that the center of the universe is not located in one particular point in space. In order for the laws (and calculations) of general relativity to hold true, physicists consider the universe to be centered everywhere, at each and every point within the spatial expanse of the cosmos.

- **Holoflux:** Pribram and Bohm agreed to use the term "holoflux" to denote the dark energy of the implicate order, an energy that Bohm believed to be consciousness itself. Sourced within the implicate order, this holoflux is active beyond the dimensions of space and time, and can be visualized as a dynamic multidimensional flux of holographic patterns composed of pure frequency information filling the implicate order. Projected from out of the implicate order, this holoflux transforms into objects and events in the space-time universe through operations of the Fourier transform. Bohm originally called this process "holomovement," however Pribram convinced him that using "movement" as part of the term was misleading, as movement is defined only in terms of changes in location within the three dimensions of space.[11]

- **Quantum Black Holes:** Quantum black holes, also called primordial black holes by Stephen Hawking, are spherical regions in space that have the smallest possible spatial diameter, the Planck length or 10^{-35}m. Also called micro black holes, the interior of these regions lie outside of space as they are within what Bohm terms the implicate order, a region of dimensions that are outside of the dimensions of space and time. In 1975 Hawking published a paper showing that these quantum black holes emit what is now termed "Hawking radiation." It had been assumed previously by Einstein in his Theory of General Relativity that absolutely nothing could escape from a black hole, that information flowing into the black hole would be lost to the universe of space-time. They may also be referred to as "Planck holospheres" or "Planck isospheres."

- **The Holoplenum:** An invariant *holoplenum* of close-packed holospheres or *Planck isospheres*,* underlying and from which is projected the explicate order; the holoplenum fills a continuum of nested isospheres, like a nesting of Russian dolls, everywhere in the physical universe from the center of each position in space-time outward; the concept had been intuited by Leibniz in his theory of monads.[12] Each holospheric shell is encoded with information specific to the unique wavelength (diameter) of the particular shell.

- **Resonance:** The term *resonance* (from Latin, *resonantia,* "to echo") originated in the field of acoustics. The resonance discussed here is that conjectured to exist between holoflux in the implicate order and objects and processes within the space-time order. Through holoflux resonance, the Fourier transform links information-encoded holoflux energy with electromagnetic energy in space-time in order to project the universe of things and events that we perceive in space and time. Holoflux resonance occurs everywhere between the implicate order and isospheres of the explicate order that exist as spherical shells projected from individual quantum black holes.

- **Cyclic Process:** An infolding/unfolding of energy-information shells cycles continuously at a rate of 10^{44} Hz between the implicate order and the explicate order; this energy-information manifests as electromagnetic waves within space-time and as patterned holoflux frequencies within the implicate order.

- **A Cosmic Clock:** Currently accepted in physics is that fact that the smallest unit of time possible, the smallest "tick" of the universe in time, is the Planck time constant, a value of 5.39106×10^{44} Hz. A cosmic clock in the cosmos can be pictured as a square wave, a Planck-time clock. During each of these cosmic clock cycles, the space-time universe is projected out from within the implicate order as a vast electromagnetic field pattern only

---

*A key concept developed by Teilhard de Chardin in his essay "Centrology" is the concept of an *isosphere,* which he defines as "surfaces of equal centro-complexity." Information is encoded on the surface of these spheres.

to immediately collapse back into the implicate order as purely holonomic energy-information. Thus the cosmos is digital with respect to the time dimension.

- **Bohm's Quantum-Potential Function:** Bohm's theory proposed what he called the quantum-potential function, Q, that acts at extremely small, sub-quantum dimensions. The quantum-potential "nudges" particles in external space-time into a new configuration, much as a tugboat nudges a large ocean liner. Thus a relatively small pressure projection from the implicate order has significant effects on evoking changes in the much larger scaled objects of space-time.

- **A Fourier Lens:** The Fourier-type mathematical transform can be seen to act as a lens through which the implicate "views" or "cognizes" the explicate order of space-time; this Fourier lensing is the process by which the implicate order observes, retrieves, and projects information generated within the explicate order.

These nine propositions are elaborated in the following discussion. A diagram that summarizes and integrates these propositions is presented in figure 12.3. Major concepts of five contemporary philosophers

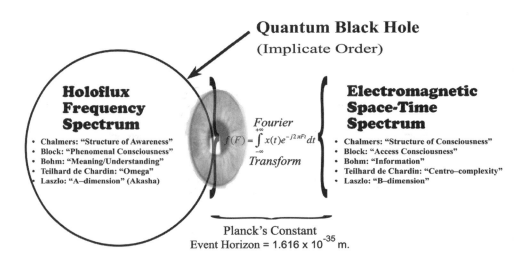

Fig. 12.3. Solving the hard problem of consciousness

of consciousness are contextually positioned. In the figure, the following concepts are identified:

- David Chalmers' "structure of awareness" is posited to be synonymous with the implicate order, and his "structure of consciousness" accordingly is shown within the explicate order.[13]
- Ned Block's "A-consciousness" lies in the implicate order, and his "B-consciousness" in the explicate order.[14]
- David Bohm's "meaning" lies in the implicate order, and his "information" in the explicate order.[15]
- Pierre Teilhard de Chardin's "Omega" lies in the implicate order, and his "centro-complexity" in the explicate order.[16]
- Laszlo's "A-dimension" lies in the implicate order, and his "B-dimension" lies in the explicate order.[17]

COSMOLOGICAL PROCESS AS PLASMA DISPLAY

The holonomic process underlying what David Bohm terms "the Whole" operates through means of a plenum of quantum black holes at the very bottom of our spatial universe. These micro black holes, or Planck-diameter holospheres, are located spatially at the center, everywhere throughout our universe. Surrounding and radiating outward from each central tiny holosphere throughout space, like nested Russian dolls, are surrounding spherical shells of quantum potential, infinitely thin information-encoded shells of information-energy, each separated from an inner shell by the radial distance of one Planck length. These isospheric shells of Bohmian quantum potential extend out to the diameter of the universe itself.

Thus, it is possible to visualize an almost infinite series of nested isospheric shells of dynamic information storage, spread out at discrete quantum radii from their respective central micro black holes. Within these black holes (Plank-diameter holospheres), exists the spaceless, timeless region of transcendental holoflux, a region identified by ancient sages in India as the *akasha,* a region in which all informaion and knowledge exists eternally, reaped from the world of space-time.

The intersection of these innumerable holospheric shells of information-energy is a projection of the holoflux, the *akasha,* into space-time. The cumulative effect of this projection, as viewed by human physicists observing from significantly higher scalar dimensions, is described as "matter." The phenomenon can be understood as a *process of projected creation,* an omnipresent, ongoing holographic extrusion of information *from within* the implicate order *into* the explicate order. This explains the various structures of the cosmos (galactic clusters, stars, etc.), the complex unfoldings *into* space-time, that are perceived by the human eye and mind to exist in our three-dimensional time-based cosmos, though they are actually holographic projections *from within* the implicate order, projecting from the center outward.

Another way of visualizing the projected illusion of space-time reality from the holoplenum is by expanding upon the metaphor of a flat-panel plasma display (such as the one you may be viewing as you read this).

Consider the human visual threshold for detecting separate images, which lies somewhere between 10 to 12 images per second; the industry standard in the motion-picture industry is 24 frames per second.[18] This standard ensures that the presentation of a sequence of projected images will appears to a human viewer as smooth and continuous motion.

By contrast, if the entire universe flashes in and out of existence at a clock-cycle rate limited only by the Planck-time constant of 5.3×10^{-44} seconds, equivalent to a "frame" rate of almost 10^{44} "frames per second," the cosmos would *appear* to be smooth and continuous in all respects even to an electron, and certainly to any human observer of the cosmos.

The approximate image resolution of a "holoplenum display" obtained by dividing one inch by the Planck length, yields a maximum resolution of 1.584×10^{34} *holopixels* per inch (a *holopixel* is the smallest possible bit of information possible to record or read in spatial dimensions). At such hyperfine resolution, even a Higgs boson in the 10^{-17} m dimensional range would appear to be moving smoothly through space.

HOLONOMIC STORAGE:
THE BEKENSTEIN BOUND

This radical new holoflux model of consciousness projecting the universe is supported by the mathematics of David Bohm. In *Wholeness and the Implicate Order,* Bohm articulated and developed a "quantum potential" function that projects the explicate space-time universe out from within an enfolded sub-quantum implicate order.[19] Bohm's quantum-potential function is almost identical to the de Broglie "pilot wave" theory of 1927. Both are based upon the conviction that there exist "hidden variables" in sub-quantum regions that are not currently accessible to observational exploration. Modern quantum mechanics deals primarily with particles around the size of protons and neutrons, both of which are physically in the range of 10^{-15} m in diameter. Even smaller are photons (electrons) at 10^{-18} m in diameter. Going even deeper we find the "sub-quantum regions," those mysterious, incredibly small depths of space that shrink down toward the floor of space at the bottom limit of 10^{-35} m.

To investigate the interaction of fundamental particles in a nuclear physics experiment requires enormous amounts of power. The velocity of the particles in an accelerator device must be brought up to speeds approaching that of light itself. Ironically, the smaller the particle being investigated, the higher energy that is required. The most powerful contemporary instrument in quantum research, the CERN Large Hadron Collider, uses enough power during one experiment to light the city of Philadelphia, yet is only able to measure particle sizes down to 10^{-19} m in diameter. The proposed hidden sub-quantum effects, or hidden variables, are thought to occur at scales far below 10^{-19} m, closer to the very bottom of the ocean of space at Planck length dimensions. Technologies do not yet exist to generate the enormous amounts of energy that would be required to begin to explore sub-quantum regions and thus there remains vast unknown oceans of possible sub-quantum particles and regions of the natural world that are completely out of reach of current physics experiments.

The de Broglie pilot-wave theory and Bohm's quantum potential are mathematical attempts to map these assumed "hidden" sub-quantum dimensions and their effects that are thought to be issuing from within the implicate order to create a region of "hidden variable" activity far below the observational capabilities of contemporary material science. It is not impossible that at some future date our human technology will develop to the point of offering the ability to view, explore, and interact with these sub-quantum realities, but for now we must rely on mathematical models that support the facts that we do know.

Mathematics supports a cybernetic processing of information, simultaneously being cycled from the space-time world and enfolded into the non-dual frequency domain, where the accumulating information may be processing nonlocally within the implicate order. Driven then by the implicate order, a pilot wave of quantum potential would be seen to "nudge" the current space-time configurations into altered, slightly new configurations, much as a small tugboat might influence an enormous freighter. If the cosmos operates at its maximum possible clock cycle, as discussed previously, this pilot wave might be seen to operate at the extreme clock cycle rate of the Planck time constant, or 10^{44} Hz. The implications of the Planck time constant are that the universe cycles in and out of existence 10^{44} times per second, with every cycle making ever so small changes in the configuration of the cosmos, while during the half of the cycle in which the universe flashes out of existence, the total information collected within the implicate order is superimposed and recalculations occur, in a process mirrored in the newly emerging human parallel computing technologies.

Regarded as a cybernetic process, the sequence of information feedback and action at the rate of 10^{44} Hz can be metaphorically imaged in the alchemical Ouroboros, the classical symbol for consciousness, depicted as a snake in a circular configuration eating (or chasing) its own tail. This process can be viewed as the cyclic transfer of information coming in (from the tail) and the resulting action after digestion (by the head). A cybernetic feedback loop requires new data, information, as input. Where then might data be accumulated and retrieved in space-time at these most fundamental sub-quantum levels, in a

Bohmian holonomic universe consisting topologically of the distributed plenum of micro black holes, each surrounded by a series of nested quantum isospheres?

One possibility is to consider the information storage potential of an isosphere encoded with granular "bits" of data. In 1970, Jacob D. Bekenstein, then a graduate student working under John Archibald Wheeler (who coined the term "black hole") proposed a novel idea. Bekenstein proposed that there must be an absolute maximum amount of information that can be stored in a finite region of space, and that the Planck constants in quantum theory can be used to determine this limit.[20] Twenty years later, Bekenstein's theory was extended by Leonard Susskind into what is called the *holographic principle,* which describes how information within any volume of space can be encoded on a boundary of the region.[21] A description of this configuration is presented here by Wheeler himself, as first related to him by Bekenstein:

> One unit of entropy (information), one unit of randomness, one unit of disorder, Bekenstein explained to me, must be associated with a bit of area of this order of magnitude (a Planck length square). . . . Thus one unit of entropy is associated with each 1.04×10^{-69} square meters of the horizon of a black hole.[22]

This proposed upper limit to the information that can be contained upon the surface of a specific, finite volume of space has come to be known as the "Bekenstein bound."[23] This can be visualized as a spherical shell (think of a Ping-Pong ball) with information bits, or "qubits," stored on the bounding surface of a sphere. According to Bekensteins's calculations, the surface of the sphere can hold all of the information within the bounded volume as encoded information. The larger the sphere, the more information that can be stored on the spherical surface. Thus we can imagine that an entire universe, bounded by a spherical shell, might potentially store *all information* within that universe upon the spherical shell's surface area.

This same topological approach to data storage can be applied to human physiology. Using a well-known biological structure as an example, it is possible to calculate the maximum memory storage capacity of an isosphere the size of a single erythrocyte, the ubiquitous red blood cell found throughout the human body. Using Wheeler's approach to determine the number of Bekensteinian equivalent data bits (qubits) on the surface of an isosphere, and using the average diameter of a typical human erythrocyte of 8.1 microns, (or 8.1×10^{-5} m), the maximum possible storage capacity on the surface of a single red blood cell can be calculated.[24] To obtain this limiting number of bits, the surface area on a spherical shell 8.1 microns in diameter must be divided by 1.04×10^{-69} square meter (which is the Bekenstein unit of entropy, or approximately the square of the Planck length of 1.616199×10^{-35}). The surface area of this erythrocyte-bisected sphere according to this calculation is $4\pi r^2$ or $4\pi(8.1 \times 10^{-5})^2$ $= 4\pi(6.561 \times 10^{-9}) = 8.24 \times 10^{-9}$ square meter. Dividing this by the qubit area of 1.04×10^{-69} square meter yields an estimated maximum storage capacity of 8×10^{60} qubits of storage space for potential information encoding. This is an extremely large data storage capacity, considerably larger than, by contrast, the entire projected capability of the National Security Agency's Utah Data Center, which has been designed, when completed, to have a maximum data storage capacity of twelve exabytes or 12×10^{18} bytes.

UNFOLDING THE IMPLICATE INTO SPACE-TIME

The basic topology of the holoflux hypothesis has now been delineated. The real understanding of quantum physics that Bohm sought emerges in this model of a sub-quantum, omnipresent holoplenum of Planck holospheres (micro black holes), each enclosing a transcendent region of nonspatial, nontemporal dimensions termed by Bohm "the implicate order."[25]

What are the implications of this model for human consciousness, cognitively operational at temporal and spatial scales vastly larger than those found at these sub-quantum Planck boundaries?

To answer this question we must first complete the Pribram-Bohm cosmological topology of consciousness, and to do this the concept of isospheres, shells within shells, must be considered. Moving outwardly, radially, from the interior bounding event horizon at each central Planck holosphere, can be identified isospheric shells of the implicate order, extruding into space at exact Planck-length (quantum) intervals.

This series of concentric shells, each one separated from the next by one Planck length, are isospherical loci of the implicate order (see fig. 12.4); they extrude into space and they intersect in space with other shells bounding other Planck holospheres in the space-time holoplenum. It is the cumulative effect of the intersections of these innumerable (virtually infinite) isospheric shells that projects the three-dimensional "objects" (that we call electrons, protons, atoms, and zebras, perhaps) at much higher scales, all cast holographically into three-dimensional

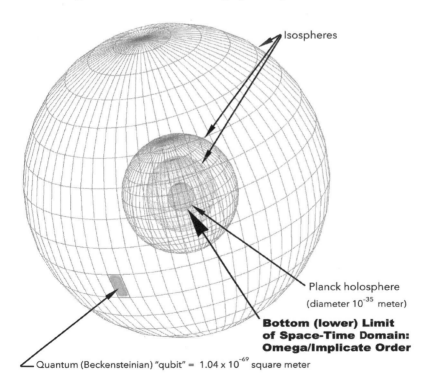

Fig. 12.4. Topological model of isospheres
surrounding a Planck holosphere

space and time from within the implicate order through resonance.

Each isospheric shell, as Bekenstein determined, has a potentially enormous storage capacity in qubits of information encoded on the event horizon bounding each shell, depending only upon the radius of the shell from its central Planck holosphere.[26] Accessible simultaneously in both the implicate order and the explicate order, such encoded information provides the data to guide evolving forms as they project into the explicate via the pilot wave mathematics of Bohm's "many-dimensioned quantum potential."[27] As part of this process, in-formation becomes ex-formation as the implicate order unfurls into the explicate. The plasmoid forms appearing in space-time as electromagnetic flux energy are mirrored by and resonate within the implicate order as the dark energy of frequency-phase holoflux.

Within this cosmic geometry of the Pribram-Bohm hypothesis can be identified a framework for omnipresent two-way portals, potential bridges between the explicate and the implicate. Here, the deep consciousness of the universe flows in a cyclic, cybernetic—perhaps fractal—movement in time and space, moving through an endless, bidirectional process: consciousness seems to be dancing with itself in a graceful ballet of eternal transformation.

How then does this topology support human consciousness, thought, and perception in space-time? How can electromagnetic-frequency plasma in space-time resonate with holoflux plasma in the implicate order? First of all, the energies must be within the same frequency range in order for maximum interactive resonance to occur. Where the frequencies overlap as they superimpose and interpenetrate one another, resonance occurs.

The term *resonance* (from Latin *resonantia*, "echo," and *resonare*, "resound") originated in the field of musical acoustics. Resonance is seen when objects or complex signal systems exhibit remarkable frequency sensitivity to specific external (incoming) frequency waves; perfect resonance occurs where the input frequency and the natural frequency are identical.[28] This principle of resonance governs all cybernetic feedback loops, and is a key factor in the design of antennas in electromagnetic transmitting and receiving systems. The goal of a receiving antenna design is to construct an antenna that is highly resonant to a specific narrow frequency range of electromagnetic radiation; when the input frequency and the natural frequency of the antenna coincide, resonance occurs resulting in energy (and information) being transferred into the antenna. The simplest and most common antenna is designed to be physically half the size of the incoming wavelength because the signal, visualized as a sine wave, has a maximum detectable change in amplitude as measured between its peak at the top of the sine wave, and its trough at the bottom of the sine wave.

This same half-wavelength effect governs the design of network communication waveguides applied to fiber optics in the internet, where the antenna is the fiber channel itself acting as a waveguide. The waveguide is highly efficient for two reasons: first, as its name implies, the waveguide guides the electromagnetic wave within its channel with maximum efficiency; and second, it shields the signal in the channel from external electromagnetic waves. The inner diameter of the hollow waveguide is designed to be equal to exactly half the wavelength of the electromagnetic energy signal shielded by and flowing through the waveguide channel.

Waveguides have been used for over a century both commercially and in research to channel and guide vibrating energy of specific limited frequency ranges; the fiber-optic networks hosting the global internet operate on this principle, channeling electromagnetic radiation at fixed laser frequencies.[29] It was discovered late in the nineteenth century that circular metallic tubes, or hollow metal ducts similar to air-conditioning and ventilation ducts but much smaller, could be used to channel and guide either sound vibrations in air, or electromagnetic energy in air or vacuum. Without the waveguide, the vibrational energy field is transmitted in all directions, visualized as magnetic lines or arrows emerging from a point at the center of an expanding sphere. This energy disperses outwardly, the magnetic vectored arrowheads pushing out on the inside of an infinitely expanding sphere. A waveguide, however, constrains the magnetic component of the wave front of vibrating energy to one specific linear direction, in parallel with the center of the waveguide, and thus, conceptually, the confined wave itself loses very little power while it propagates along the central axis of the waveguide, like a stream of water emerging from the pinprick of a large, taut, water balloon.[30]

The most common type of fiber-optic cable used in the internet has a core diameter of 8–10 micrometers and is designed for use in the near infrared.[31] The electromagnetic signal wavelength that runs through the global fiber-optic network is powered by highly efficient carbon dioxide lasers, and has a wavelength of 10 micrometers. Coincidentally (or not?), the average human blood-capillary diameter is also 10 microns, and blood capillaries are at all times full of carbon dioxide.

Dimensional analysis and a cursory examination of human physiology would immediately suggest two candidates for waveguide systems within the human body: (*a*) the blood capillary system, and (*b*) the microtubule system. The corresponding resonant frequency for electromagnetic waves using such waveguides corresponds to wavelengths matching the inner diameter of these structures. For blood-system capillaries, this corresponds to radiation with a wavelength of 9.3 to 10.0 microns, the average inner diameter of a capillary. For microtubules, the radiation wavelength would be found in a range of 40 nanometers, the inner diameter of the microtubule waveguides. Figure 12.5 depicts the location of each of these potential waveguide frequency bands within a wider region of the electromagnetic spectrum.

That our blood might act as an electromagnetic plasma within the capillary system should not be surprising—the opening page in a textbook on plasma physics reads, "It has often been said that 99% of the matter in the universe is in the plasma state."[32]

The circulatory system can be seen as a magnetic plasma composed primarily of ionized red blood cells (erythrocytes) and water molecules, flowing together in complex vortices of blood plasma around every cell and through every capillary of the body.[33] Each erythrocyte is a flexible, annular, biconcave disk shaped like a doughnut (in geometry, a torus), having a thin webbed center where the hole in a doughnut would be

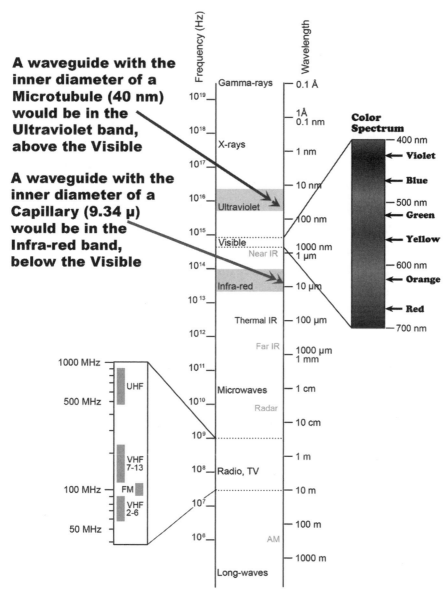

*Fig. 12.5. Microtubules and capillaries as waveguides
shown in a diagram in comparison to other types of waves*

located. The typical outside diameter of a red blood cell is approximately
9 microns, close to the infrared wavelength of 9.6 microns generated
by the human body.[34] The adult human body contains approximately

6 grams of iron, of which 60 percent is stored throughout the 10^{12} erythrocytes, each of which contains approximately 270 million atoms of ionic iron embedded within transparent hemoglobin in a toroidal locus.[35] Thus each erythrocyte, replete with iron ions embedded in hemoglobin, creates, in effect, an ionized iron toroid.[36]

Recent studies have also discovered neuronal generation of electromagnetic energy in the near infrared region of the spectrum centered around 10 microns. Radiation emission was repeatedly measured emanating from live crab neurons in extremely narrow, discrete spectral bands within the frequency range corresponding to a spectral region from 10.5 to 6.5 microns.[37]

The implications of this model are considerable: there may exist in nature a unique resonant frequency for each individual human being. It is useful here to step through a topological analysis of the possible functions of a human red blood cell—given its geometry—as a locus of consciousness, and the possible use of the erythrocyte as a locus of memory storage at human biological scales. If, as previously conjectured, the red blood cell has an ideal diameter to resonate electromagnetic radiation in its ferrite-embedded ring at the human infrared wavelength of 10 microns, then it is reasonable to ask if this configuration could accommodate a single unique isospheric frequency (wavelength) for each of the currently 7 billion living humans on the planet. In other words, does this geometry allow for the possibility of each human being to also have a single unique frequency within the infrared electromagnetic radiation that resonates within the human cardiovascular waveguide system? Figure 12.6 outlines the topological feasibility of this approach.

Assuming each unique frequency would match its radially unique isosphere, each separated by only one Planck length, figure 12.6 suggests how 7 billion unique isospheres, each of quantum discrete frequency, might be nested within the spherical geometry of a typical human red blood cell (in the image, a multiple of 7 billion times the Planck length of approximately 10^{-35} m results in an estimated shell thickness of 10^{-26} m). This supports the feasibility that each living human being might represent a distinct, unique set of holospheric frequencies,

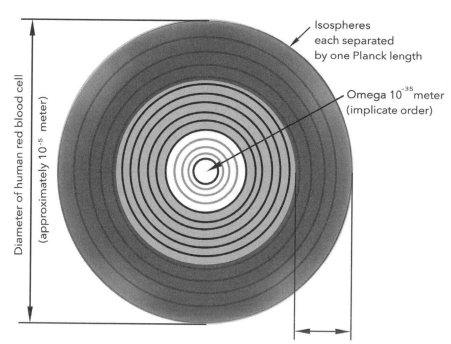

Isospheres
each separated
by one Planck length

Omega 10^{-35} meter
(implicate order)

Diameter of human red blood cell
(approximately 10^{-5} meter)

7 billion human isospheres separated by 1 Planck length in a 10^{-26} meter range
(not to scale)

Fig. 12.6. Isospheric capacity of a single erythrocyte

detectable by other human blood cells through the mechanism of resonance within the implicate order about which each is centered. Such a unique frequency signature for each conscious human being could provide channels for direct communication "heart to heart" via the phenomenon of resonance, nonlocality, and superposition of information signals in the frequency domain (the implicate order).

EXPLICATE AND IMPLICATE CONSCIOUSNESS IN ALIGNMENT WITH AXIAL AND TANGENTIAL CONSCIOUSNESS

According to the two highly trained, professional, methodologically introspective explorers of consciousness, Teilhard de Chardin and

Rudolf Steiner, there are *two primary modes* of consciousness. In the last page of his essay "The Activation of Human Energy," Teilhard de Chardin states, "there are two different energies—one axial, increasing, and irreversible, and the other peripheral or tangential, constant, and reversible: and these two energies are linked together in 'arrangement.'"[38] Likewise, during his discussion of a human physiology of consciousness, Rudolf Steiner provides a description, replete with diagrams, of how "nerve-activity" must be seen to be at right angles to the alignment of the "blood-activity" in consciousness.[39] In the Pribram-Bohm hypothesis these two primary modes of consciousness are characterized rather generally as *implicate* consciousness and *explicate* consciousness.

Teilhard de Chardin goes further and links the axial component of consciousness to the process of crossing "a certain *critical point of centration,*"[40] thus thermodynamically heating up consciousness while moving radially inward to resonate with ever-smaller radial wavelengths. De Chardin also occasionally refers to radial consciousness as "soul" and "spirit" in his essays (perhaps to satisfy superiors in his religious order), and he also describes this radial component of energy as "a new dimensional zone" that brings with it "new properties."[41] Teilhard describes how increasing centration along the radial component leads to increasing states of complexity-consciousness that result in "being mentally ultra-humanized by self-compression."[42] Congruently, Steiner and Teilhard de Chardin both agree that these modes of awareness can be seen to operate orthogonally to one another, each in their own domain, and thus they both refer to consciousness as operating in two modes: a *tangential* consciousness and an *axial* consciousness. It is of interest to note that Steiner says that one of these primary modes, what he calls the *radial mode* of consciousness, operates *within the blood system.*[43]

The holoflux hypothesis posits that human consciousness—what is normally experienced as awareness by humans who are not sleeping or in a coma—is tangential consciousness, as it manifests, in accordance with Pribram's research,[44] in the resonance of electromagnetic plasma fields swirling in space-time within the fabric-like dendritic neuronal regions of the cerebral cortex. This is the "consciousness" examined in experiments conducted by Benjamin Libet, whose research revealed that human awareness of an "intention to act" *lagged behind* the actual EEG measured "readiness potential" by an average of 200 milliseconds.[45] This evidence supports the currently widely held view among neurophysiologists that consciousness is an epiphenomenon of neuronal activity. This epiphenomenal view is correct only if one mode of consciousness is being considered, what Teilhard and Steiner would call the tangential mode of human cognitive mental consciousness, which interfaces most generally with the neuronal synaptic activity of the nervous system throughout the human body.

The actual situation is more complex in the Pribram-Bohm holoflux model, in which two modes of consciousness function in a cybernetic process depicted by the diagrams in figures 12.2 and 12.3, where the Teilhard/Steiner axial consciousness is seen to "peer out from" the transcendent implicate order on the left *into* the explicate space-time order on the right while simultaneously projecting the explicate configuration itself. The tangential mode of consciousness in the space-time explicate domain lags, temporally, behind the axial, due to its operational requirement of comparing slices of mnemonic information storage in

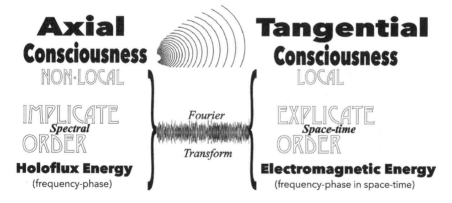

Fig. 12.7. Axial consciousness and tangential consciousness.
Axial consciousness is seen to "peer out from" the transcendent implicate
order on the left into the explicate space-time order on the right while
simultaneously projecting the explicate configuration itself.

the time stream. Given the various operating cycles of physiological systems with the human body, this lag is measured to be an average of 200 milliseconds *after* cognition by the more immediate, axial, implicate consciousness.

This timing is in accordance with Libet's experimental data,[46] and Bohm used the phenomenon to draw a distinction between thought and a more primary mode of consciousness that is "before thought," the mode of consciousness that dwells in the present moment:

> To dwell in the present moment requires not dwelling in thought, because thought takes duration and is a slow process. We start to find a need, not to deny thought, but to find the part of the experience which unfolds prior to thought.[47]

13

Quantum Brain Dynamics and Neuroanatomy

NEUROANATOMY AND NEUROANATOMICAL CONCEPTS

Before considering the quantum brain dynamics (QBD) theory in detail, a brief review of neuroanatomical terms and concepts will provide a context for a critical examination of the theory. A typical neuron cell consists of a single nucleus, a single axon, and multiple dendrites, as can be seen in the image on the left of figure 13.1 on the following page.

All cells have a nucleus, but the neuron has two types of neuronal fiber extrusions: a single, usually relatively long axon, which is long in comparison to the second type, the dendrite branches, which are many and complexly bifurcated.[1] The longest axons in the body belong to the sciatic nerves that run from the brain down through the spine and end in the big toe. Axons are also known as "nerve fibers," and most neurological research focuses on these fibers since they carry the relatively large "nerve impulse" electrical spikes that are easily measured. The numerous dendrites, on the other hand, resemble finely bifurcating tree branches gathered in dense felt-like regions.

The thick-layered dendritic region of Purkinje neurons can be seen to the right in figure 13.1, where a typical section of the cerebral cortex is depicted. Surprisingly thin, the entire cortex, at its thickest, is only

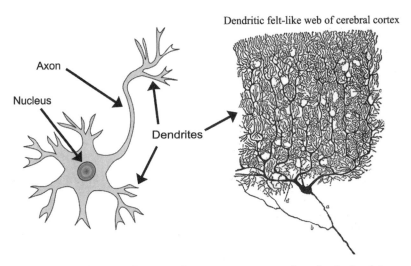

Fig. 13.1. Left, typical neuron having one axon and multiple dendrites, and right, Purkinje neuron—one of the largest neurons in the brain with an intricately elaborate dendritic arbor. Graphic on left by Jonathan Haas; graphic on right by Santiago Ramon y Cajal.

2 millimeters in depth, about the thickness of four human hairs placed side by side.[2]

Details of a 2 mm thick cerebral cortex slice can be seen in figure 13.2. To the left of the figure axis can be seen four stacked human hair cross-sections, emphasizing the thinness of the cerebral cortex. The main drawing (to the right of the axis) depicts the four outer layers of the thin cerebral cortex: from left to right, the first region shows a single sensory nerve fiber, the middle region reveals the interlinked systems of fibers and pyramidal cells, and the right-most region of the figure indicates fiber bundle types.[3]

Due to extremely intricate folding and refolding, the cortex alone occupies fully 88 percent of the human brain mass.[4] Within this cortex region can be found three distinct types of cells: neurons, glial cells, and blood capillary cells.

The major focus of scientific research is upon the 86 billion neuron cells in the human brain; glial cells and capillary cells are dismissed as having no role in cognition or consciousness. Since their discovery in

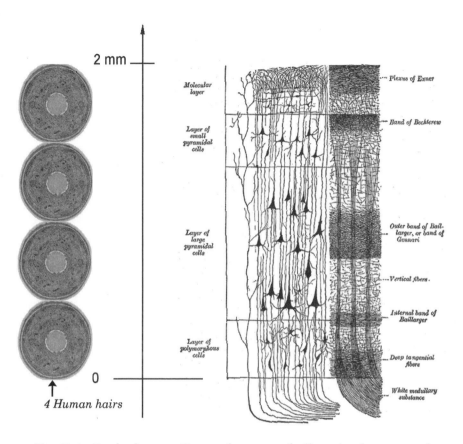

Fig. 13.2. Cerebral cortex. Center, the groups of cells; right, the systems of fibers of the cerebral cortex. At the far left of the figure a sensory nerve fiber is shown. Cell body layers are labeled on the left, and fiber layers are labeled on the right. Graphic by Henry Gray, Gray's Anatomy, *1918.*

1856, glial cells have been tacitly dismissed in the widespread agreement that they have evolved primarily for mechanical purposes, acting in supportive, structural roles (the word *glia* in Greek, γλοία, means "glue"). Glial cells do not conduct electrical impulses as neurons do, even though glial cells wrap around neuron axons to form myelin sheaths and thus are capable of modulating the speed and strength in the neural conduction of electrical impulses passing through these glial "wraps." Likewise, any possible function of the blood capillary cell system in consciousness has also been dismissed; it is assumed that the function of the circulatory system is fully understood, and not involved in thought or conscious sensation.[5]

QBD: HIROOMI UMEZAWA

The field of quantum brain dynamics (QBD) shows great promise in providing an answer to the so-called hard problem of determining just where and how within the human brain consciousness links directly to the senses, to memory, and to cognitive processes.

The Japanese quantum physicist Hiroomi Umezawa (1924–1995) obtained his Ph.D. in Japan in 1952 and was subsequently recognized as one of the most eminent quantum-field theorists of the twentieth century.[6] Midway through his career he became one of the first physicists of his generation to focus his attention upon the role of quantum theory in the operation of various aspects of consciousness experienced in the human. Umezawa eventually developed a quantum-field theoretical approach to memory.[7] His work provides an alternative to the dominant conception in neuroscience that assumes consciousness and the mind to be phenomena that are the product of neuronal firing within vast networks of nerve fiber in the brain.

Umezawa developed a quantum theory of the brain that suggests that it is the quantum dynamics of a spatially distributed charge formation within the cerebral cortex that is the fundamental source of thought and memory. He proposed that this distributed charge field acts as a single coherent agent, operating far below the scalar region of individual neurons, and that this dynamic electromagnetic charge field is located primarily within the region of the cerebral cortex; he called it the *cortical field*.[8] He was convinced that this distributed field influences the neuronal system through direct electromagnetic resonance, exchanging information with individual neurons that are active throughout the cerebrum.

Umezawa's hypothesis offered a radically new vision of how consciousness within the brain may be operating. Instead of viewing consciousness as a single process, he saw the possibility that the mechanism involves the integration of two quite separate dimensional regions operating at different depths of scale but directly interacting through frequency resonance within the cerebral cortex. As early as 1979 Umezawa published a paper with his colleagues, Stuart and Takahashi, proposing a mechanism of human memory and consciousness, consistent with quantum field theory. They called the new model of consciousness quantum brain dynamics (QBD), and they hypothesized that there exists a unified quantum electromagnetic region that is operational throughout the volume of the cerebral cortex, Umezawa's previously identified "cortical field" region.[9]

JIBU AND YASUE

Mari Jibu and Kunio Yasue, two brain researchers at Notre Dame Seishin University, Okayama, following closely upon the work of Umezawa, agreed that research into the physics and neurophysiology of consciousness was focusing too exclusively upon the macroscopic regions of the brain and ignoring quantum considerations. They noted that the focus of much brain research on mapping the "wiring" of the vast and complex neuronal network in the brain received the lion's share of research attention and funding. This macroscopic approach put great emphasis on recording and trying to interpret electrical signals of relatively low frequency, commonly known as "brain waves," or EEG (electroencephalogram) signals. Jibu and Yasue believed that such an approach can only reveal information regarding muscle control, organ-system regulation, and wiring of the various sensory systems. Though valuable in itself, such information, they held, will not result in any significant understanding of higher consciousness and cognitive mental activities.

Following the death of Umezawa in 1995, Jibu and Yasue continued his work to explore operational cognitive consciousness in several unconventional regions: (*a*) in the distributed macro region of the human circulatory system's bloodstream, and (*b*) in sub-quantum regions far below the scale of the neuron and glial cells that fill the cerebral cortex.

Consciousness within the Ionized Human Bloodstream

Jibu and Yasue explore the possibility that consciousness may be manifested within the electromagnetic ionized totality of the flowing human bloodstream as a single conscious "entity." They suggest that life itself can be seen to be the equivalent of "the unity of water" in the human body, or as "a single molecule" resonant within the human blood system. They state:

> All H_2O molecules bound together in a QBD vacuum domain form a single, extensive molecule of water in a macroscopic domain. That is, water throughout the entire region of the cerebral cortex is thought to be composed of many macroscopic water molecules whose sizes are all comparable to the coherence length of the QBD vacuum, that is, about 50 microns. This remarkable feature of water in living matter might provide us with quantum field theoretical support for the idea that life is nothing but the unity of water as a single molecule in living matter.[10]

A further implication of quantum brain dynamics supports the model of a locus of consciousness beyond that of the nervous system and brain. This runs counter to the widespread assumption that consciousness is simply an epiphenomenon of brain activity. The supporting pattern can be found in the QBD manifestation of a "single, extensive molecule of water,"[11] dipolar in geometry like an antenna, generating a complex magnetic field through the circulation of hydrogen ions and carbon dioxide in warm blood plasma.

In such a model, the entire blood system within the human body can be considered to act as an extensively polarized "super cell" of nonlocal electromagnetic plasma energy, which can then be differentiated from the neuronal brain body of consciousness, itself generated by sequential electrical-impulse-driven patterns flowing in the nervous system. Moving charges generate magnetic fields, and ionized human blood flow is no exception: flowing blood plasma results in creation of a magnetic field, and this is in accord with the conjecture of QBD.[12]

Consciousness within Sub-Quantum Regions

Jibu and Yasue also proposed that an understanding of consciousness and memory would be forthcoming only through rigorous investigation of quantum electrodynamical field configurations.

> Each brain cell is enfolded within a common field of macroscopic condensation of evanescent photons and all the physico-chemical processes taking part in the stratified society of brain cells are subject to the control and unification by quantum electrodynamics. Unity of consciousness thus arises from the existence of the global field of condensed evanescent photons overlapping the whole brain tissue in the cranium.[13]

Their work pointed to activity of an electromagnetic field in a region thousands of times below the size of individual nerve cells. They adopted Umezawa's concept of the cortical field as being fundamental to consciousness and cognitive activity, and they focused upon developing the mathematics to justify their hypothesis that consciousness is to be found in the quantum effects of photons, biophotons, and electromagnetic field activity in a plasma charge field within the cerebral cortex.

DIMENSIONAL LEVELS
OF NEUROSCIENCE RESEARCH

Modern brain researchers conduct experiments with a primary focus on neurons; there are about 100 billion of these neurons in the brain, ranging in size from 10^{-4} m to 10^{-6} m in diameter. By contrast, QBD researchers examine regions in the human brain at dimensional levels that are a million times below the size of individual neurons, in the scalar range of water molecules. The size of a liquid water molecule is approximately 10^{-12} m, almost a million times smaller than a neuron and much shorter than wavelengths of visible light. At this quantum scale water is "invisible" to the human eye.

Quantum brain dynamics as developed by Jibu and Yasue is a focus upon a phenomenon first discovered by Umezawa, that the electromagnetic polarization of billions of water molecules in the brain creates what is called "the cortical field." Working with Karl Pribram they continued to expand Umezawa's pioneering work to develop a fully unified quantum theory of brain dynamics. They further elaborated their theory in a fifty-four-page appendix for Pribram's book that provided a mathematical basis to support Pribram's work on the neurodynamics of perception and memory in his 1991 book *Brain and Perception: Holonomy and Structure in Figural Processing*.[14]

Yet in a third region far below neurons water molecules lies a third region many magnitudes smaller even than an electron, the sub-quantum region at the very bottom of space near the Planck length limit of 10^{-35} meter.

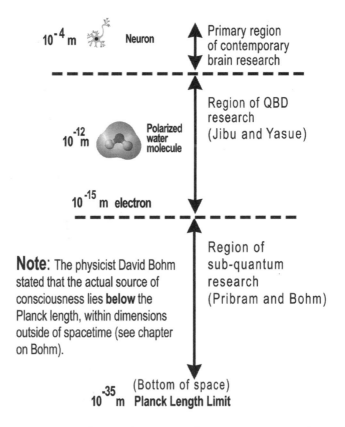

Fig. 13.3. The three scalar ranges of consciousness research

HUMAN CONSCIOUSNESS AS
A SINGLE RESONANT WATER DIPOLE

Extending Umezawa's theory of QBD, Jibu and Yasue advanced the notion that it is through dynamic resonance (spin) that polarized dipole water molecules throughout the bloodstream produce the activity, in effect, of *a single resonant water dipole,* a single "macromolecule" of consciousness operating within the bodies of all living, water-based creatures.

Such a macromolecular-dipole not only provides an exceptional information highway for electromagnetic fields at the macro level but exhibits the properties of a unified plasma field. It is useful here to clarify the definition of plasma:

A state of matter in which a significant portion of the particles are ionized. Plasmas are by far the most common phase of matter in the universe, both by mass and by volume. All stars are made of plasma, and interstellar space is filled with plasma. Common forms of plasma include lightning, St. Elmo's fire, the polar aurorae, the solar wind, neon signs, and plasma displays in modern home television.[15]

Within this polarized, nonlocal, H_2O quantum field is embedded an electromagnetic field described here by Jibu and Yasue:

There are two basic fields in QBD: the water rotational field and the electromagnetic field. The two must be described simultaneously by quantum-field theory because they interact with each other. The water rotational field extends over the whole assembly of brain cells and manifests an overall domain structure in which the whole region occupied by water is divided into many domains. In other words, they are bound to each other quite strongly by a quantum theoretical nonlocal coherence.[16]

In 1995, building upon their earlier paradigm, Jibu and Yasue published the mathematics to support their theory that points to an "energy quanta of the water rotational field extending to the whole assembly of brain cells, and photons, that is, energy quanta of the electromagnetic field."[17] Their theory focuses upon the nonlocal quantum field that is generated within the human circulatory system, embedded in an electromagnetic field manifesting throughout the contiguous ionized, blood-plasma system.

They explain the mechanism whereby this low-level cortical electromagnetic field communicates with the much larger dimensioned neurons by pointing out how there is a sandwich structure on each side of the membranes that enclose neurons. This sandwich structure consists of two layers of ionized water molecules that can be observed on both sides of the neuronal cell membrane, providing what is called a Josephson junction that can operate without dissipation from thermal losses, effectively exhibiting superconductivity.

JOSEPHSON JUNCTIONS

"Josephson junctions" are named after Brian David Josephson (b. 1940), who predicted in 1962 that pairs of superconducting electrons could "tunnel" right through the nonsuperconducting barrier while moving from one superconductor to another. A year later, an experiment conducted at Bell Labs verified Josephson's predictions, and Josephson subsequently was awarded the Nobel Prize for Physics in 1973 for having predicted the effect. It was also discovered that a slight difference in the voltage gradient between the two superconducting sheets results in an electromagnetic oscillation in the ionized layers on either side of the junction. These oscillations vary their wavelengths with minute changes in the voltage gradient, and offer a possible mechanism for encoding information within the ionized plasma layers of H_2O adjacent to the cell membrane wall.

A Josephson junction is defined in physics formally as consisting of two superconducting ionic plasma layers, separated by a nonsuperconducting layer that allows electrons to cross through the insulating barrier. In the case of the neuron, the insulating barrier is the cell-

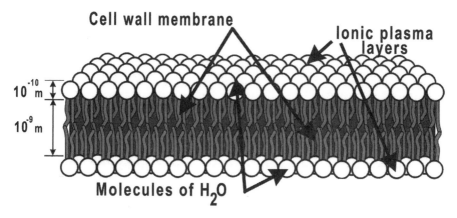

Fig. 13.4. Josephson junction of a neuron's membrane

wall membrane itself (fig.13.4). According to Josephson's theory these regions have the ability to operate in a superconductive mode so that any information stored within the field configuration are stable and do not degrade with temperature fluctuation.

The fact that neuronal cell wall membranes provide a distributed ionic electromagnetic field within these two regions (on either side of the cell membrane) and having discovered that dynamic electromagnetic-voltage gradients can directly alter the frequency characteristics of small regions of the distributed ionic plasma layers leads to the conclusion that there could very well exist holographically structured layers surrounding each neuron's membrane with dynamic information content, perhaps even the memory engrams Pribram was hoping to find. One other way of viewing the sandwich structure of the neuron's membrane is to compare it with a capacitor in electrical circuits. Congruent with the definition of a Josephson junction, a capacitor consists of two conducting plates separated by a thin insulator. In electronics, capacitors are used to allow high-frequency information to pass, while blocking low frequencies.

In the early 1970s Josephson took up Transcendental Meditation (TM) and turned his attention to issues outside the boundaries of mainstream science. He set up a research program to explore the relationship between quantum mechanics and consciousness. In 1980 he and V. S. Ramachandran published their edited proceedings of a 1978 interdisciplinary symposium on consciousness at Cambridge under the title *Consciousness and the Physical World*.[18] Josephson's work subsequently became an object of criticism among fellow scientists as had happened to the work of other scientists (e.g., Tiller and Sheldrake) who had begun to explore consciousness, psi, and traditional ways of introspectively studying consciousness through direct experience.

But the work of the physicist Herbert Fröhlich (1905–1991) further clarified the possible dynamics of an electromagnetic field within the "sandwich structure" of the neuron's membrane. Fröhlich proposed a theory in which biomolecules within this sandwich structure resonate as standing waves in a superconducting mode at a frequency between 10^{11} and 10^{12} hertz, and called this the "Fröhlich frequency."[19] This frequency range lies within the infrared light region, precisely the peak thermal-energy frequency of the human body. It is the distributed electrical change within these membranes surrounding the nerve cells, resonating within the infrared region, that receives and transmits electromagnetic patterns from and to the lower-level cortical field. In fact Jibu and Yasue relate this interaction to the processing of memory and consciousness.

> It is astonishing that water which has been tacitly assumed to play only a trivial role, is now highlighted as the central material constituent participating in the fundamental physical phenomena that evoke highly advanced brain activities, such as memory and consciousness.[20]

They go on to state that, owing to the amazing resonance of rotating water molecules in their ionic state, the entire planet Earth may exhibit a single consciousness involving the dynamic resonance of every water molecule in the planet.

> All the oxygen and hydrogen atoms in water are thought to be bonded to each other by hydrogen bonding. The totality of water on the planet Earth could be considered one huge water molecule.[21]

Jibu and Yasue point out that their theory of quantum brain dynamics supports the idea that life itself can be seen to be equivalent to "the unity of water" in the human body, or as "a single molecule" in the human blood system.

> All H_2O molecules bound together in a QBD vacuum domain form a single, extensive molecule of water in a macroscopic domain. That is, water throughout the entire region of the cerebral cortex is thought to be composed of many macroscopic water molecules whose sizes are all comparable to the coherence length of the QBD vacuum, that is, about 50 microns. This remarkable feature of water in living matter might provide us with quantum field theoretical support for the idea that life is nothing but the unity of water as a single molecule in living matter.[22]

Quantum brain dynamics supports the model of a locus of consciousness beyond that of the nervous system and brain. The supporting pattern can be found in the QBD manifestation of a "single extensive molecule of water," dipolar in geometry like an antenna, generating a complex magnetic field through the circulation of hydrogen ions in blood plasma.

In such a model, the blood system of the human body can be seen as an extensively polarized "super cell" of nonlocal electromagnetic plasma energy, which can then be differentiated from the neuronal brain body of consciousness, itself generated by sequential electrical patterns flowing as pulses in the nervous system pathways.

Moving charges generate magnetic fields, and ionized human blood flow is no exception: flowing blood plasma results in creation of a magnetic field, and this is in accord the conjecture of QBD.[23] The circulatory system can be seen as a magnetic plasma composed primarily of ionized red blood cells (referred to as erythrocytes) and water molecules, flowing together in complex vortices of blood plasma around every cell and through every capillary of the body.[24] Each erythrocyte is a flexible, annular, biconcave disk shaped like a doughnut (in geometry, a torus),

Fig. 13.5. Red blood cell or erythrocyte.
Graphic by Svdmolen.

having a thin webbed center in the region where the hole in a pastry doughnut would be found (fig. 13.5).

This concept of a distributed magnetic field throughout the circulatory system is supported by the experimental neurophysiologist Giuseppe Vitiello, who writes that consciousness manifests in the activity of dipole wave quanta resonating with the external and internal environments.[25] This distributed magnetic field is greatly facilitated by the approximately six grams of iron within the human body, of which 60 percent is located in the 10^{12} red blood cells. Each single erythrocyte contains approximately 270 million atoms of ionic iron embedded within transparent hemoglobin.

All of these research efforts are using quantum theory to explore consciousness. QBD theorists focus attention upon the nonlocal quantum field that is generated within the human circulatory system. This single, distributed field, is embedded within the electromagnetic field that is generated by innumerable resonating dipole water molecules. Both the local electromagnetic field and the nonlocal quantum field, to the extent that they are able to maintain resonance with one another, exchange two-way information via the Fourier transform. Both fields share the frequency spectrums generated as the ionized blood plasma circulates throughout the entire human body.

14

Past and Present Varieties of Electromagnetic Brain Stimulation

This chapter presents a broad view of contemporary approaches to electromagnetic brain stimulation devices. In the first recorded incident of electromagnetic stimulation, Luigi Galvani (1737–1798), the pioneer of "animal electricity," discovered in his kitchen in 1771 that frogs' legs twitch when electricity is passed through their muscles (fig. 14.1). Galvani called this phenomenon *bioelectricity*. From this early observation of the single twitching of a living organism has evolved the subject of electrophysiology, and various direct applications of electricity to human subjects.

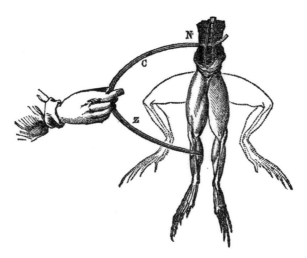

Fig. 14.1. Galvani's frog legs experiment.

In 1801, Giovanni Aldini (Galvani's nephew and an avid student of "animal magnetism" or mesmerism) discovered that applying two low-voltage electrodes of electricity to each side of the head of an adult seemed to improve the mood of those patients suffering from "melancholy." Aldini was also among the first to have experimented with passing an electric current through a human corpse. In a well-documented incident, Aldini applied electricity to the corpse of the recently executed prisoner George Foster.*

On the first application of the process to the face, the jaws of the deceased criminal began to quiver, and the adjoining muscles were horribly contorted, and one eye was actually opened. In the subsequent part of the process the right hand was raised and clenched, and the legs and thighs were set in motion.[1]

The stunning spectacle gained much notoriety, and the idea of "galvanizing a corpse" (fig. 14.2) came into public discussion, triggering a debate on whether science should try to raise the dead back to life. It must be noted that by 1846 the term "mesmerism," also referred to as "galvanism," had been replaced by "electricity."

Twenty-two years earlier, in 1779, Franz Mesmer had introduced the theory of "animal magnetism," the hypothesis that there is an invisible and natural magnetic force that flows within all living things and that with sufficient training and practice, this force can be detected and manipulated to heal and strengthen various regions of the human body. Animal magnetism (also known as "Mesmerism") instantly became a medical specialty taught in medical schools for the next seventy-five years. Physicians specializing in the treatment soon became known as "magnetizers," rather than mesmerists. Hundreds of books were written about it between 1776 and 1925, but today it is entirely dismissed by medical science.[2]

---

*Foster had been found guilty of murdering his wife and child by drowning. He was hanged at Newgate prison in 1803 and shortly afterward his body was taken to the laboratory by Galvani's nephew, Giovanni Aldini.

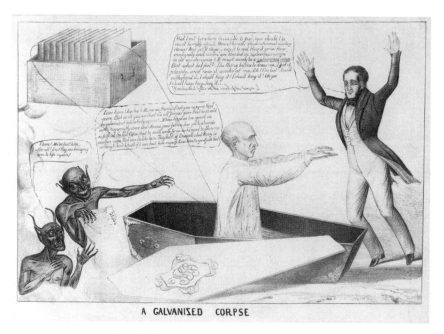

Fig. 14.2. Raising the dead by galvanizing a corpse.

The sensational application of electricity for raising the dead became a central theme of Mary Wollstonecraft Shelley's famous novel (fig. 14.3) *Frankenstein: Or, The Modern Prometheus.* In her book, electricity was channeled from a lightning source and harnessed to energize and breathe life into Frankenstein's monster, activating a previously dead brain.

Fig. 14.3. Frankenstein's monster. Boris Karloff in Bride of Frankenstein, *1945.*

CAPITAL PUNISHMENT
AND ELECTROMAGNETISM

One of the first documented applications of electricity to a human subject was the effort to provide a more "humane implementation" of capital punishment. Slightly more than a century after Galvani's discovery that electricity affected frogs' legs, a dentist in New York, Alfred Southwick (1826–1898), distressed by the media outcry over a series of botched executions by hanging, put forth the idea of a possibly "humane alternative" to capital punishment through use of electricity. In 1881, Southwick read the account of a drunk man dying instantly after touching the poles of an electrical generator. Southwick subsequently wrote to Thomas Edison, asking him which approach might be more effective, the use of direct current (DC), used by the Edison Electric Company, or through application of a newer electrical source, alternating current (AC), then being marketed by the Pittsburgh entrepreneur George Westinghouse (1846–1914). Edison replied that he wanted nothing to do with the issue, as he was involved in efforts to abolish capital punishment.

Secretly, the shrewd Edison realized that associating execution with the Westinghouse electrical system would make Edison's DC appear safer in the public eye by way of contrast; Edison went so far as to contract with another engineer to design, construct, and donate the first AC electric chair for the prison at Auburn, where New York executions were carried out. Westinghouse refused to sell one of his AC generators for the project, and the generator was procured surreptitiously via a vendor from Brazil. Meanwhile, Edison launched a public campaign, touting DC electrical systems as inherently safe, compared to the lethality of AC systems. Westinghouse countered by hiring an expensive legal team to defend one William Kemmler, said to be a violent drunk who had been convicted of murdering his wife with an ax. The case wound its way up to the Supreme Court, but to no avail: Kemmler was sentenced to death.

The initial test of the new electric chair, which by then had been nicknamed "Old Sparky," occurred in Auburn on August 6, 1890. At 6:38 a.m. the switch was thrown, which connected the prison's

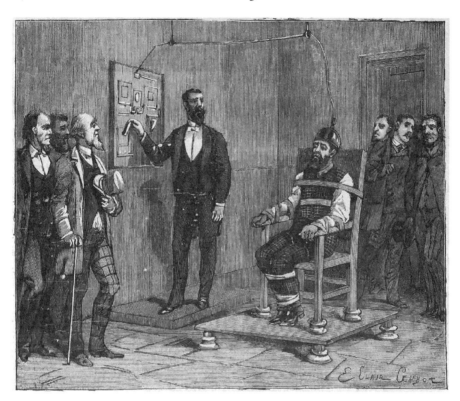

Fig. 14.4. First execution by electricity,
Auburn Prison, 1890.

AC electrical generator directly to a metal skullcap and the metal floor
upon which the metal chair rested (fig. 14.4) Immediately 1,000 volts
of AC began to flow through Kemmler, throwing his entire body into
massive shuddering and twitching. After seventeen seconds the breaker
system blew, but by then the three doctors and seventeen witnesses all
assumed that Kemmler was dead.

However, as the three physicians approached the body to certify
death, to their great astonishment Kemmler began rapidly breathing,
twisting against the burnt leather straps, and making strange noises!

The warden ordered that the electric circuit be reset and power
restored so that the execution procedure could be resumed. This time,
the full output voltage of 2,000 volts was applied, and the circuit held
for a full sixty seconds before failing. Kemmler's hair caught fire, and

the strong smells and sights caused half the crowd of witnesses to flee the room, while three of the witnesses fainted. Over eight minutes elapsed before the attending physicians were able to officially certify that the inmate had expired.

The press came up with a new name for the procedure: "electrocution"—a combination of "electricity" and "execution." Nevertheless, Edison's final push to discredit Westinghouse and his AC system introduced a popular new euphemism for execution by electricity, that of "being Westinghoused." George Westinghouse himself commented during an interview, "They would have done better using an axe."[3]

APPROACHES TO ELECTROMAGNETIC THERAPY

After the first execution by electricity, almost fifty years passed before medical science began to investigate the possible uses of electricity in therapeutic settings. Since then, the number of distinct approaches to electromagnetic therapy can be seen to have fallen into two broad categories: the electrical approach and the magnetic approach.

The electrical approach involves applying a voltage via two electrodes in order to direct the flow of an electrical current through the patient (table 3). The magnetic approach uses electromagnetic pulses produced by the energizing of electromagnetic coils (table 4).

TABLE 3. SIX ELECTROMAGNETIC APPROACHES TO BRAIN STIMULATION

Abbreviation	Description
ECT	Electroconvulsive Therapy
tDCS	Transcranial Direct Current Stimulation
tACS	Transcranial Alternating Current Stimulation
tPCS	Transcranial Pulsed Current Stimulation
tRNS	Transcranial Random Noise Stimulation
DBS	Deep Brain Stimulation

It should be noted that all of these applications have been developed through trial and error, and most are not sanctioned by the American Medical Association.

TABLE 4. TWO MAGNETIC APPROACHES TO BRAIN STIMULATION

Abbreviation	Description
TMS	Transcranial Magnetic Stimulation
CMS	Circumcerebral Magnetic Stimulation (Persinger's "God helmet")

The underlying mechanisms of interaction between these electromagnetic sources on the brain, nervous system, and state of mental consciousness are not well understood.

ELECTROCONVULSIVE THERAPY (ECT)

First introduced in psychiatric work in 1938, electroconvulsive therapy (ECT), popularly known as "shock treatment," has continued as a form of sanctioned medical treatment up through the present day.

In the early 1930s biomedical researchers noticed that the introduction of a strong electrical current to the brain of primates through electrodes placed on the scalp resulted in immediately observable "epileptic type" activity. In 1938, after several years of research recording the effects of various electrical charges on primate nervous systems, electrical currents were clinically applied to a human patient.

In the therapy, seizures are induced in patients in order to provide relief from various mental disorders, generally mentioned as chronic depression and bipolar disorders. In typical commercial devices (fig. 14.5), the electrical stimulus used in ECT is about 800 milliamps and can be up to several hundred watts. The current flows for between one and six seconds. Electrode placement can be seen in figure 14.6 on the next page.

ECT is usually administered every other day over a period of three to four weeks. While it is considered the "treatment of choice" for

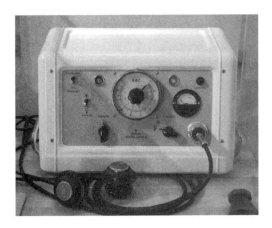

Fig. 14.5. "Konvulsator III" electroshock device (1938).

depressions resistant to multiple trials of antidepressant medications or depressive episodes with psychotic features, its use has been declining for several decades primarily due to the expense associated with inpatient treatment and the widespread lack of insurance coverage.

In 1961, Ernest Hemingway received ECT at the Mayo Clinic. Shortly after, he committed suicide, and was quoted by his biographer as having said:

> Well, what is the sense of ruining my head and erasing my memory, which is my capital, and putting me out of business? It was a brilliant cure, but we lost the patient.[4]

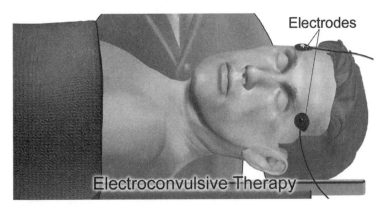

Fig. 14.6. Electrode placement during "shock treatment."

TRANSCRANIAL DIRECT CURRENT STIMULATION (TDCS)

Known by the abbreviation tDCS, transcranial direct current stimulation is a noninvasive procedure that operates through applying a constant low-voltage direct current (DC) of approximately 1.0 milliamp flowing through the human scalp between two electrodes. (See waveform in fig. 14.7, where a single waveform is depicted, showing that current has a fast rise time, reaches a steady level for close to 30 seconds, and then quickly drops to zero again, similar in shape to a pulse waveform.)

In early experiments with tDCS, low power was applied for short time periods, typically 1 milliamp for thirty seconds. When no adverse effects were observed, power limits were increased to a typical maximum limit of 2 milliamps for thirty minutes; however, recently available commercial devices are designed to deliver power up to a 4 milliamps maximum. A typical session of tDCS in 2018 lasts for thirty minutes, during which the current is increased in steps from 0.5 milliamp to 1.0 milliamp.

The placement of the two electrodes appears to be significant in the evocation of specific therapeutic benefits. Table 5 presents a series of typical configurations of positive (+) electrode (the anode) and negative (−) electrode (the cathode). Originally developed in an

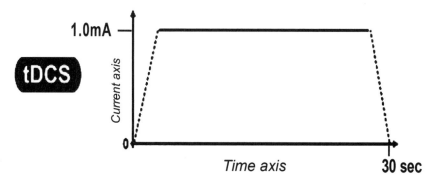

Fig. 14.7. Transcranial direct current stimulation (tDCS) waveform, which applies a constant voltage over time.

attempt to help patients with brain injuries or major depression, the placement of electrodes has been claimed to result in various different effects on patients.[5]

While the mechanism of interaction between the externally introduced voltage-differential/current and the electromagnetic flux in the brain is largely unknown, what is known is that in tDCS there are two different directions of current, either anodal voltage (V+) stimulation or cathodal (V−) stimulation. Each has been observed to cause markedly different effects, resulting in the following clinical model:

1. In cathodal stimulation (V−) an excess of electrons flows through the electrode into the area of the scalp contacting the electrode, *decreasing* the neuronal excitability of the adjacent area within the cerebral cortex, just below the bone of the skull.

2. Converseley, anodal stimulation (V+) *attracts* electrons to the area *increasing* neuronal activity in the adjacent area.

Following this model, physicians select a treatment of cathodal stimulation for patients exhibiting symptoms of hyperactivity, placing the cathodal electrode above the indicated area of the brain. For patients with chronic depression, the therapeutic approach is to place anodal electrodes in an effort to increase neuronal activity.

It has also been determined that neuronal activity is induced in repetitive TMS by using a higher frequency, and decreased neuronal activity is induced by using a lower frequency.

In 2014 a European study of small randomized clinical trials of tDCS found them effective in alleviating symptoms of major depression, and subsequently tDCS was approved for major depressive disorder (MDD) within the European Union. However, a 2015 review of results from hundreds of tDCS experiments found no statistically conclusive evidence to support any net cognitive effect, positive or negative, of single-session tDCS in healthy populations, and there was no evidence that tDCS is useful for cognitive enhancement.

TABLE 5.
tDCS ELECTRODE PLACEMENTS.[6]

Claimed Therapeutic Benefit	Placement of Anodal Electrode (V−)	Placement of Cathodal Electrode (V+)
Improved attention	Suprarobital (left or right forehead)	Opposite shoulder
Reduction in addiction craving	Right DLPFC (dorsolateral prefrontal cortex)	Left DLPFC
Chronic pain	Opposite side of head from body pain location	Opposite prefrontal cortex
Increased awareness	Right mastoid (behind ear)	Right DLPFC (dorsolateral prefrontal cortex)
Accelerated learning	Right temple	Left shoulder
Depression and anxiety	Left DLPFC	Right supraorbital (forehead)
Improved insight	Right temporal	Left temporal
Enhanced mathematical abilities	Right parietal	Left parietal
Improved pitch perception	Temporal	Opposite shoulder

Many tDCS devices have the capability of allowing the current to be "ramped up" gradually until the necessary current is reached. This initially decreases the amount of stimulation effects felt by the person receiving tDCS. After the stimulation is initiated, the current continues for the amount of time set on the device until shut off.

As of early 2020 more than two dozen commercial tDCS devices are currently available; six of these are listed in table 6.

TABLE 6.
COMMERCIALLY AVAILABLE tDCS DEVICES.*

Name of tDCS Device	Listed Prices (US$)	Maximum Output Current
"The Brain Stimulator v3.0"	$130–$190	1.0 mA
tDCS TransCranial Stimulation Kit	$398	2.0 mA
"Focus v3"	$299	2.0 mA
tDCS devices on eBay	$34	2.0 mA
"Halo Sport"	$499	2.2 mA
"GoFlo 4"	$244	4.0 mA

*As of July 2019.

Adverse effects of tDCS have been reported when treating those with epilepsy. A daily treatment of 4.0 mA for sixty minutes over a period of two weeks has been found to cause skin irritation, dizziness, nausea, and headaches.[7]

TRANSCRANIAL AC STIMULATION (TACS)

Also known as cranial electrotherapy stimulation (CES), transcranial alternating current stimulation (tACS) devices apply an oscillating current waveform derived from a pure sinusoidal waveform that can be seen in figure 14.8.

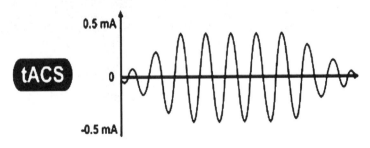

Fig. 14.8. Transcranial alternating current stimulation (tACS) waveform, which oscillates over time.

Electrodes are often placed on the ear lobes and temples, occasionally in the occipital region. Stimulation of approximately 1 milliamp has shown to reach the thalamic area at a radius of 13.3 millimeters and induce changes in the electroencephalogram, including increases in alpha-wave power with corresponding decreases in delta and beta frequencies. However, there is as yet no clinical evidence of effectiveness for relief of acute depression, as has been claimed by manufacturers of such devices.[8]

TRANSCRANIAL PULSED CURRENT STIMULATION (TPCS)

Transcranial pulsed current stimulation (tPCS) applies pulses of electric current of up to 2 milliamps at a pulse repetition rate of from 1 to 5 pulses per second. Application of tPCS has been shown to increase the interhemispheric coherence of brain oscillatory activity, in frontotemporal regions, and seems to enhance functional connectivity across neural networks. A time domain graph of a pulse can be seen in figure 14.9.

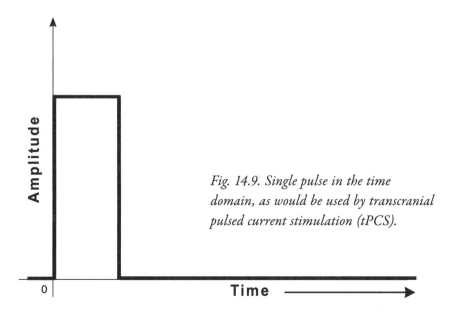

Fig. 14.9. Single pulse in the time domain, as would be used by transcranial pulsed current stimulation (tPCS).

Laboratory results indicate that the technique improves response time in decision-making, for example, in those taking a multiple choice test; however, no increase in accuracy was observed.[9]

TRANSCRANIAL RANDOM NOISE STIMULATION (TRNS)

While tDCS uses a constant current intensity, transcranial random noise stimulation (tRNS) generates an oscillating current of waveforms derived from a random noise generator (fig. 14.10).

While laboratory data shows that tRNS *does* specifically increase gamma oscillation in the human auditory cortex, as in all previous studies of transcranial electromagnetic stimulation, the researchers profess that the physiological mechanisms "are not completely understood." Perhaps of more importance, no behavioral consequences of tRNS were observed.[10]

TRANSCRANIAL MAGNETIC STIMULATION (TMS)

While tDCS, tRNS, tACS, and tPCS treatments require electrodes to be pasted directly to the scalp in order to pass an electrical current through regions of the head, transcranial magnetic stimulation (TMS) is quite different. In TMS there are no electrical contacts touching the

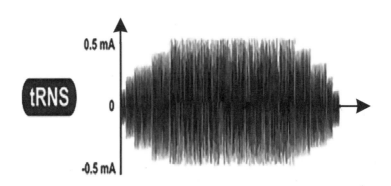

Fig. 14.10 Transcranial random noise stimulation (tRNS) waveform. Notice the variation compared with other waveforms.

scalp. Instead, the devices used are small magnetic coils that generate magnetic pulses at various locations above the scalp, such that the magnetic field induced reaches up to several centimeters within the cranium. As in tDCS, the mechanisms of interaction with the brain are poorly understood.

During treatment with TMS, patients are required to sit in specially designed chairs, with the patient's chin resting on rigid positioning frames and a brace keeping the forehead in a steady position during treatment. The magnetic coils are placed such that they hover just a few centimeters above the scalp. When energized, the coils emit magnetic pulses that reach into the scalp. Theoretically, the magnetic pulses produce an electric current in the nearby neurons within the brain through the process of electromagnetic induction.

TMS can only penetrate just a few centimeters into the outer cortex of the brain, and the magnetic field rapidly declines the farther away the machine is positioned from the scalp. Due to the large size of the magnetic coils, targeting very specific areas of the brain is quite difficult, and the patient needs to remain completely still, unlike tDCS, where the electrodes used to incite stimulation are secured directly against the scalp using a headband or positioning strap, allowing the individual to move about if they desire to do so. In general, TMS is only used within clinical settings owing to the complex nature of the technology and the need for precise positioning.

DEEP BRAIN STIMULATION (DBS)

Deep brain stimulation (DBS) differs from all other brain stimulation techniques previously discussed, in that DBS is an *invasive* stimulation technique. Invasive brain stimulation involves a preliminary procedure to surgically implant parts of the stimulation device into the patient's brain (fig. 14.11). During the procedure, the patient is fully sedated while the device's electrodes are secured to the area of interest within the brain. Additionally, the wires connecting the electrodes to the device, and sometimes the device itself, are implanted underneath the skin's surface.

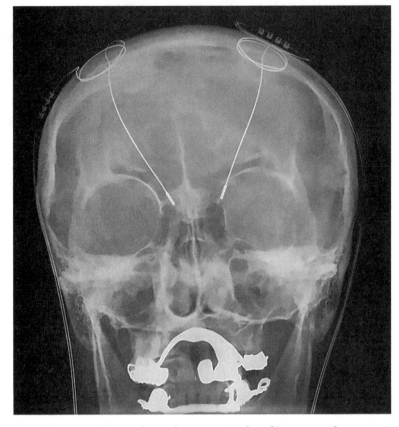

Fig. 14.11 Electrode implantation in deep brain stimulation

As in all contemporary forms of electromagnetic brain stimulation, "its underlying principles and mechanisms are still not clear; the exact mechanism is not known."[11]

CIRCUMCEREBRAL MAGNETIC STIMULATION (CMS)

The Canadian American neuroscientist Michael Persinger (1945–2018) developed a circumcerebral magnetic stimulation device—popularly known as the "God helmet"—to explore consciousness through studying what he believed to be the bicameral human mind in which each hemisphere of the human brain is viewed as an independent, though usually cooperative, conscious entity (agent of consciousness), and that the left-hemispherical personality normally dominates the right-hemispherical personality. Persinger, who published over five hundred technical articles in scientific journals and authored seven books, was a professor of psychology at Laurentian University in Ontario for forty-seven years prior to his death in 2018. His primary areas of research were exploring electromagnetic field effects upon biological organisms in general, though his primary focus was the human brain.

Persinger, as director of Laurentian University's Neuroscience Department, tasked one of his department researchers, Stanley Koren (1943–2014), to develop a prototype "helmet" as a means of testing his own "bicameral mind" brain theory. Persinger's theory rested largely upon the interdisciplinary ideas of Julian Jaynes (1920–1997).

In 1976, Jaynes published *The Origin of Consciousness in the Breakdown of the Bicameral Mind,* in which he articulated the belief that the two hemispheres of the brain are fundamentally two separate "selves."[12] According to Jaynes, who found support for his idea through a great range of interdisciplinary material, prior to about 1000 BCE human consciousness operated quite differently than it does in modern humans. The dominant left hemisphere received "suggestions" from the right hemisphere through auditory verbal hallucinations, and individuals in many instances assumed that the "voice" was that of God. Jaynes put forth evidence indicating that around 1800 BCE a major change began to occur in the functional operation of the human brain as it shifted from this bicameral mode to what we now refer to as "consciousness." In modern times the left hemisphere of the brain generally dominates awareness and is experienced as the primary waking sense of self due in large part to increased integration of language and thought. While his theory was initially well received, particularly by the general public (the first edition of his book sold out quickly), neurophysiological researchers found it difficult to assess the validity of his theory through use of clinical methods, and eventually the theory became a target of widespread criticism and was shelved. However, interest in the theory was revived during the late 1990s with the radical improvement in brain imaging technologies, and new data seemed to confirm many of his early predictions.[13] Persinger called his own version of the Jaynes theory the "vectorial hemisphericity hypothesis," proposing that the human sense of self has two components, one on each side of the brain.

Persinger believed that the Koren helmet approach might be used to create conditions in which contributions to the sense of self from both cerebral hemispheres could be disrupted by interfering with one of the brain's most important electrical activities, called "the binding factor," a wave of electromagnetic activity that runs from the front to the back (from *rostral* to *caudal*) of the human brain every 25 milliseconds, giving it a frequency of 40 Hz. This activity is present during both waking and dreaming periods, but is absent during dreamless sleep, a coma, or periods of traumatic unconsciousness.[14] The binding factor ordinarily inhibits information embedded in external magnetic fields from being sensed, including planetary geomagnetic fields and whatever magnetic signals are emitted by other nearby electrical activity.

Persinger's helmet was designed with the objective of disrupting the binding factor by introducing what he termed "interhemispheric intrusions" in the form of a sequence of magnetic pulses timed to be close to but slightly different in frequency from the binding factor. Formally known as a circumcerebral magnetic stimulation (CMS) device, the so-called helmet (the original design was built using a modified snowmobile helmet) is composed of eight solenoids (electromagnetic coils) set at intervals on a headband fitted around a person's cranium. The solenoids are timed and controlled by a computer program that enables them to rotate precisely configured weak magnetic pulses around the cranium, generating a weak magnetic field that reaches well into the cerebral cortex. This sequence of magnetic pulses partially disrupts the 40 Hz so-called binding factor of the brain that is thought to assist in pulling numerous sensory inputs together into one smooth, seamless perception of the world (i.e., the sensation of self-identity).

Persinger and Koren designed the God helmet in an attempt to create conditions in which contributions to the sense of self from both cerebral hemispheres are disrupted. Put in nontechnical language, this disruption allows normally curtailed or masked information from various operations of the mind-brain system, and in particular the sense of identity from the left cerebral hemisphere, to rise into one's perceptual awareness.

Neither the God helmet, nor technologies derived from it, are examples of what is considered to be transcranial magnetic stimulation (TMS), which apply magnetic fields on the order of one million times stronger than those used in Persinger's lab (Persinger's helmet produces magnetic fields of approximately 1 microTesla). However, effects have been reported to appear that are similar to those described during TMS.

The pattern of fluctuation generated by the magnetic fields of the God helmet is derived from previously recorded physiological sources, primarily from patterns that appear in EEG traces taken from limbic structures. The purpose of exposing magnetic fields patterned after neurophysiological sources (e.g., the burst-firing profile of the amygdala), is to enhance the probability of interaction with the field structure of the brain and thus affect consciousness in some perceivable or therapeutic manner, perhaps by disrupting the normal masking function from which the signal was derived.

In Persinger's laboratory experiments the subject wore the helmet device within an anechoic (soundproof) chamber, constructed to act as a Faraday cage shielding the subject from spurious EMF emissions and radiation other than the Earth's magnetic field. Persinger himself, in summarizing the results from numerous experiments, stated the following:

> At least 80% of participants experienced a presence beside themselves in the room, while others report less evocative experiences of another consciousness or sentient being.[15]

If true, these results would support the Jaynes theory of "the bicameral mind" as well as Persinger's hypothesis that external electromagnetic fields can be made to interact with the mind-brain systems (in some not currently understood manner).

Lacking a consensual theory describing the linkage between consciousness, mind, and brain function, the progress in contemporary brain stimulation devices is entirely pragmatic, driven by trial and error. Such approaches to brain stimulation can be compared to the geographically widespread Neolithic practice of trepanation (fig. 14.12), the oldest surgical procedure for which there is archaeological evidence.[16]

More than 1,500 Neolithic skulls have been found with trepanation holes showing clear ingrowth of bone tissue around the edges, which would indicate that these individuals continued to live well after the procedure.[17] Cave paintings are thought to express the Neolithic belief that carving a hole in the skull could release interior malignant spiritual entities that were thought to be the cause of mental dysfunction. Is the trepanation approach to curing mental ailment terribly different than modern era attempts to alleviate mental symptoms by passing electromagnetic fields through human skulls? Both approaches are based upon nothing but speculative guesswork performed while hoping for a positive outcome.

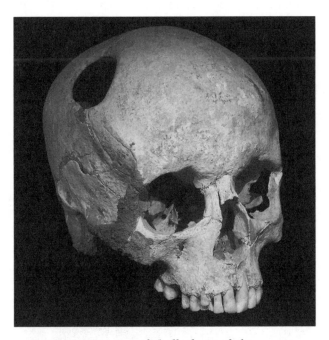

Fig. 14.12. Trepanned skull of a Neolithic woman.

In contrast to these purely trial-and-error approaches, would it not be useful to base future attempts at influencing consciousness upon a wider knowledge base of both electromagnetic communication theory as well as the less explored areas of brain science? The following material presents such areas for consideration.

15

Optical Networks in the Brain and Future Research

In this concluding chapter we move beyond the theories previously discussed to consider how future progress, both in understanding the mechanics of consciousness as well as for the development of truly effective consciousness-interactive hardware systems, might be better advanced through the consideration of a wider, less conventional approach to understanding and mastering a psychophysics of consciousness. The following considerations have been largely neglected by contemporary neurophysiological approaches to the study of consciousness:

1. Harmonic resonance
2. The relevance of scale (the relationship of bandwidth to wavelength size)
3. Signal modulation of electromagnetic waves
4. Photons as information packets
5. Photons in living creatures
6. Optical networks in the brain

HARMONIC RESONANCE

While the lowest frequency of a vibrating string is called its *fundamental frequency,* a vibrating string also generates a number of what are

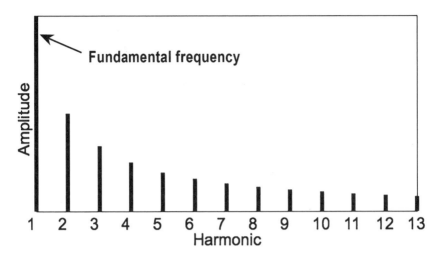

Fig. 15.1. Fundamental and harmonic frequencies

termed *harmonics,* which may be called *acoustic overtones* in musical instruments. A harmonic is defined as an integral (whole number) multiple of the fundamental frequency. In fact, all vibrating energy phenomena produce harmonic overtones of increasingly higher frequency than the fundamental. Generally, however, the fundamental frequency is much stronger in magnitude than the harmonics (fig. 15.1). In musical instruments the generation of these harmonic overtones results in a sound that is perceived as being "richer" or "warmer," having a certain "tone quality" or "color" that is absent if only the fundamental vibrated, devoid of harmonics. In a piano, for example, striking the middle C key produces a first harmonic of 264 cycles per second. The second harmonic is twice this frequency, or 528 cycles per second, which is an octave higher.

In the case of electromagnetic frequencies the same harmonic resonance phenomena occur, and this observation led Jean-Baptiste Joseph Fourier to the previously discussed discovery of the Fourier transform relationship, whereby any signal in space-time can also be viewed as the sum of a series of harmonic frequencies. This fundamental principle has become of primary importance in the design of electromagnetic devices for computing and communications.

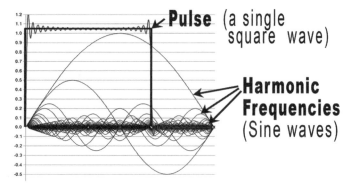

Fig. 15.2. Harmonic frequencies generated by a single pulse

Thus, a "pulse" signal or "square wave" can be viewed as a virtually infinite set of superpositioned harmonic sine waves of decreasing size (fig. 15.2), shrinking down from the wavelength of its fundamental frequency harmonic to ever-smaller harmonic wavelengths, limited only by the Planck length at the bottom of space, 10^{-35} meters. As in the case of musical instruments, the amplitude of these harmonics is small compared to the amplitude of the fundamental. However, engineers have discovered that the greater the number of contributing harmonics, the sharper the resulting composite square wave in space-time.

Similarly, each pulse generated by a transcranial magnetic device contains innumerable harmonics of higher frequencies. It is entirely feasible that there are specific ranges of harmonic frequencies that interact with mind-brain systems through resonance at far higher frequencies than currently supposed (recall EEG research with its focus upon alpha, beta, and delta frequencies, which range from 8 Hz to 40 Hz). Determining which higher frequency transcranial harmonic pulse ranges might interact with the mind-brain would go far toward narrowing the focus upon the "missing link" between consciousness and the brain, the so-called hard problem that has thus far eluded neurophysiologists. One way to locate such higher-frequency ranges would be to selectively filter various frequencies emerging from transcranial devices (using standard electromagnetic filter circuits) in order to determine which frequency ranges maximize the perceived influence on human subjects.

THE RELEVANCE OF SCALE

Understanding the significance of *scale* should be of major consideration when exploring consciousness because it is the close similarity in the size of two objects that becomes the primary factor for predicting resonance. As discussed in previous chapters, the phenomenon called resonance occurs when a physical object is of the same size as the wavelengths of the vibrating energy that intersect that object. This resonance phenomenon offers the possibility for two-way information transfer when information is encoded into the electromagnetic wave. This is why radio antennas are physically scaled to the exact size of the wavelengths that will be received and/or transmitted through use of the antenna, and microwave frequency waveguides are designed so that the hollow inner diameter matches the wavelength of the electromagnetic signal being channeled through the waveguide. Wavelengths are inversely proportional to frequency; in figure 15.3 we see that the higher frequency has a smaller wavelength. We also know from communication theory that more information can be encoded in higher frequencies than in lower frequencies.

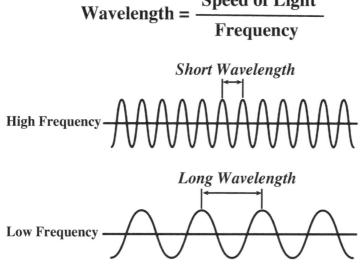

$$\text{Wavelength} = \frac{\text{Speed of Light}}{\text{Frequency}}$$

Fig. 15.3. High frequency and low frequency wavelengths

The following two examples illustrate the relevancy of scale in trying to understand how consciousness and the flow of information may operate in the human body:

1. Electromagnetic voltage fluctuations commonly recorded by EEG scalp electrodes are found to exhibit a frequency of 8 Hz and are called "alpha waves." The steps for calculating the length of an 8 Hz alpha wave is given in table 7, where the alpha signal wavelength is found to be 23,285 miles in length! Accordingly, an alpha wave *could not possibly* resonate electromagnetically with anything within the human body; the scalar sizes are vastly different, precluding resonance.

2. In the same table we see that the peak frequency of 3×10^{13} Hz infrared radiation found in the blood stream is 10 microns (1×10^{-5} m) in wavelength, the precise physical size of the inner diameter of a blood capillary. It is thus feasible that the capillary system may be acting as a waveguide for infrared light signals streaming throughout the human body. This supports the possibility that modulated consciousness is operating at much higher frequencies than those currently being investigated through EEG waveform studies.

TABLE 7. WAVELENGTH CALCULATIONS: BRAIN WAVES VS. BLOOD PLASMA WAVES

Wave type	Frequency (Hz)	Calculation of Wavelength (speed of light/ frequency)	Calculated Wavelength (in meters)	Wavelength (in miles and microns)
EEG Radiation from Alpha Brain Wave	5 Hz	$\dfrac{3 \times 10^8}{5}$	6×10^8	23,285 miles
Infrared Radiation from Blood Plasma	3×10^{13} Hz	$\dfrac{3 \times 10^8}{3 \times 10^{13}}$	1×10^{-5}	10 microns

As discussed in chapter 12, another possible physiological candidate for resonant interaction with a system of electromagnetic consciousness would be microtubules, part of the structural cytoskeleton of all human cells, including neurons. Microtubules are hollow structures with inner diameters of approximately 12 nanometers. Accordingly, microtubules might also act as waveguides, but in this case, for electromagnetic waves of 12 nanometers (or in scientific notation, 1.2×10^{-8}m). This wavelength corresponds to a resonant frequency of 2.5×10^{17} Hz, a frequency that is in the ultraviolet range of the electromagnetic-frequency spectrum and has the potential to encode vast quantities of information as compared even to visible light frequencies that vibrate at lower frequencies.

SIGNAL MODULATION OF ELECTROMAGNETIC WAVES

But discerning these frequency bands of electromagnetic consciousness is only the first and perhaps the easiest step in mastering the physics of consciousness. Once located, the information encoded within the dynamics of the electromagnetic frequencies in that band have to be decoded or demodulated. There are innumerable ways to modulate, or encode, information. Simple AM radio varies the amplitude, or strength, of the signal at the frequency. The variation in time matches precisely the same equivalent variations in the frequency of air motion that our human hearing system interprets as "sound." FM radio, however, varies the frequency itself while maintaining a constant amplitude. The frequency changes up and down within a 2 KHz range to match the equivalent 2 KHz range of audio vibrations that can be heard by most humans. But there are many more ways of sending information via frequencies. Modern digital communication is based on the data "bit," which is simply a binary toggle of "on and off" in the frequency transmission. Other data-modulation schemes can use variable rates of amplitude or frequency over time. The greatest challenge to neurophysiologists, brain scientists, and those involved in consciousness studies is thus to determine how nature, specifically within the human brain, is modulating and demodulating information via electromagnetic fields. How is thought encoded within these nonlinear electromagnetic fields, both in the time domain and in the frequency domain?

PHOTONS AS INFORMATION PACKETS

At this point we must ask the following: By what mechanism might electromagnetic information in these high-frequency bands operate within the physiology of the brain, assuming they have been effectively modulated? Is there any evidence that, in addition to the well-studied molecular chemical communications in human physiological systems, there might very well be some photonic communication network in operation, simultaneously active (but separate from) the chemical-carrier network? Yes, there is: for in recent years a growing body of evidence has shown substantial biophotonic radiation within the human body, and there is a growing conjecture that photons play an important role in the basic functioning of cells![1]

Photons are the fastest and most robust carriers of information over long distances, as can be seen in the ubiquitous global man-made networks supporting the internet, all of which rely on optical communication channels (typically fiber-optic cables routing modulated photons in the infrared range). Photonic communication also offers quantum information processing capabilities with which to support the incredibly high rates of information processing necessary for cognitive operation of the human mind.

PHOTONS IN LIVING CREATURES

Is there evidence of photon emission in the brain? Indeed, experiments over the past several years have proven the existence of biophotons in all living creatures.

All living cells of plants, animals and humans continuously emit ultra-weak biophotons (ultra-weak electromagnetic waves) in the optical range of the spectrum, which is associated with their physiological states and can be measured using special equipment. Neural cells also continuously emit biophotons. The intensity of biophotons is in direct correlation with neural activity, cerebral energy metabolism, EEG activity, cerebral blood flow and oxidative processes.[2]

Biophotons were first discovered in Russia in 1923 by Professor Alexander Gurwitsch, and were widely researched in Europe and the United States in the 1930s. In 1974 German biophysicist Fritz-Albert Popp was able to demonstrate that their origin lies within DNA. In fact, the emission of biophotons appears to be linked to what is called "DNA supercoiling."

In studies as early as those by Gurwitsch in the 1920s researchers have been testing the bio-communication aspects of photonic emission from cells. Gurwitsch put forth the idea that "radiation generates cell division" as early as 1911.[3]

Now, if we assume that these biophotons in plants, animals, and humans are participating in an active communication network linking innumerable physiological subsystems into one whole, then information must somehow be modulated and retrieved via these photonic messengers.

What would be required to support a biophotonic communication network? First of all, photonic communication systems within the brain would require optical waveguides to channel the biophotons while protecting them from decoherence (degradation of their own signal content) due to the myriad larger wavelength EMF activity (referred to as "static" in radio receivers), external "noise" within the brain beyond each waveguide. Typically, waveguides would likely also function to facilitate routing of biophotons to other systems of the mind-brain.[4]

This biophoton emission rate is about 1 photon per neuron per minute.

. . . If one takes such low rate of biophoton emission and considers the fact that there are about 10^{11} neurons in a human brain, there would still be over a billion photon emissions per second.[5]

In discussing the propagation of electromagnetic fields in brain tissue, Giuseppe Vitiello suggests the following:

In biological systems coherent oscillations of dipoles would be confined inside filaments or tubes. . . . The em field [would] thus propagate *only within a network of filaments* inside the correlated water medium, provided the strength of the electric disturbances is sufficiently high. . . . The diameter of the filament in the simplified case of a completely aqueous medium with maximum of polarization may be computed and it turns out to be of the order of 15 nanometers, . . . which is a figure very near to the inner diameter of microtubules. . . . As a matter of fact, the observed dynamical behavior of the cytoskeleton, with its intricate network, with continuous creation and destruction of branches, and with its movements, is a true puzzle to biochemistry.[6]

OPTICAL NETWORKS IN THE BRAIN

A recent study points out the reasonable expectation of an optical communication network within the human mind-brain system.

With the advantages optical communication provides in terms of precision and speed, it is indeed a wonder why biological evolution would not fully exploit this modality.[7]

Communication in the twenty-first-century internet is through a vast network of fiber-optic cables that act as the waveguide for photons connecting our devices to the world. It is interesting to compare the performance of this optical system with the first electrical intercontinental cabling system.

In August 1858 the first message between nations was sent by electrical signals over the new cable, a message from Queen Victoria to President James Buchanan. These first messages were exchanged over the newly laid transatlantic cable, and though the messages were short, they required seventeen hours for transmission via Morse code. Owing to the many unknowns affecting long-range transmission of electrical signals over the underwater cable, it took a full two minutes to transmit even a single character. Over time the technology would improve, but even forty years later the maximum transmission rate over transatlantic cables had only reached 120 words per minute. Yet previously, even a one-way message from Victoria to Buchanan would have had to be sent through a combination of steamship and land telegraph, which would have taken twelve full days. Thus the first transatlantic cable was hailed as "the Eighth Wonder of the World."

By contrast, the average two-way internet rate of information transmission in 2017 was 7,200,000 bits (7.2 megabits) per second. Of course, modern cables are not copper wires but fiber-optic bundles, which stream enormous networks of modulated photons. The estimated total length of underwater intercontinental fiber-optic cable as of 2014 was a total of 550,000 miles.[8]

In the human body, the total length of capillaries branching out from the blood-vessel system is about 60,000 miles, or about one-tenth of the current global internet, offering a suitable waveguide for channeling photonic information within the 10-micron electromagnetic infrared range.

It is interesting to note that the network of photons modulating our internet is powered by carbon dioxide lasers, currently the highest-power continuous-wave lasers available. The CO_2 laser produces a beam of photons that resonate within the infrared wavelength band, between 9.4 microns and 10.6 microns, with the principal wavelength centered on 10 microns, surprisingly (or not surprisingly?) identical to the wavelength of peak radiation that streams throughout the human blood capillary system (human blood radiates electromagnetic energy at a wavelength of 10 microns, the size of the inner diameter of a human capillary). The human body produces over two pounds of carbon dioxide each day, and all of this CO_2 is distributed in the coursing ionic bloodstream flowing throughout the body in the system of capillaries.

DNA SUPERCOILING

Electromagnetic radiation occurs when an electric charge spins ("oscillates") within a specific frequency range. Biophotons are radiated throughout the spectral range of 180–1,000 nanometers, covering the ultraviolet, visible, and near infrared. The corresponding frequency range is from 3×10^{14} to 1.6×10^{15} Hz. The generation of such photons requires two phases: (1) an energy pumping that builds up the charge of the spinning electron to the excited level, and (2) the emission of a photon with the corresponding loss of charge of the spinning electron.[9] Where might we look to discover the source of biophotonic plasma generation? The answer seems to be in DNA supercoiling, a phenomenon that varies with pH as can be seen in the chart of figure 15.4, where DNA rings are seen to move from coiled to uncoiled to coiled again as the pH increases from 11.0 to 13.0 in the chart.

DNA rings have been found to be extremely sensitive to variations in pH, the excess or deficit of electrons in surrounding aqueous fluids. Slight changes in pH result in causing these DNA rings to alternately coil and uncoil. In coiling, the rings store up energy from the surrounding ionic electromagnetic environment; when they relax from a coiled state to a circular state, the additional stored energy is released as biophotons. As mentioned above, it has been determined that biophoton emission rates are about 1 photon per neuron per minute. And given that there are about 10^{11} neurons in the human brain, this would equate to over a billion photon emissions per second, more than sufficient to facilitate transmission of a large number of bits of information, and to offer the possibility of an enormous network of quantum entanglement in the resulting swarm of photonic plasma.[10] It is quite feasible that these biophotons themselves are modulated in some fashion with information transferred from within the DNA configuration.

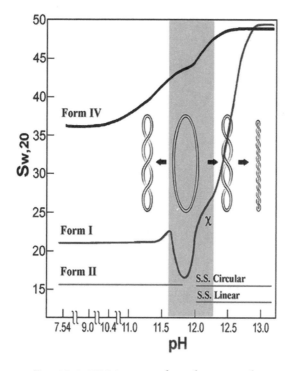

Fig. 15.4. DNA supercoiling changes with pH.
Chart of circular DNA versus pH by Notahelix.

WAVEGUIDES, ELECTROMAGNETIC FIELDS, AND CELL DIVISION

It has been speculated that myelinated axons could serve as waveguides for biophotons traveling within the brain. The widest myelinated axons in the brain have an inside diameter of 10 microns, while the narrowest are 0.2 micron in diameter. Of course, narrower waveguides have the capacity to channel higher frequencies (with the corresponding ability to handle higher rates of information encoding).

Another study has implications for electromagnetic communication among systems within the body. Almost a century ago the idea that electromagnetic fields might govern cell division was put forth in Germany. The communication of information on *cell-loss rate* has long puzzled physiologists. How do systems within the brain govern the rate of cell division without having access to a vast amount of instantaneous information on cell-loss rates in various regions of the body? It has been argued that the growth regulation of organs and tissue is based upon information originating from the death of individual cells, but it is not possible to explain this by the use of "messenger molecules" from individual cells.

A cell is part of a larger structure in which cell loss rate is compensated for rather exactly by the cell division rate, in order to avoid serious disease like abnormal swelling or shrinking of tissues, including cancer. Only electromagnetic field interactions would be suitable for transferring the necessary messages at the required rate.[11]

KIRLIAN PHOTOGRAPHY

One final piece of the puzzle in support of electromagnetic field consciousness is the phenomenon of Kirlian photography, first discovered in 1939 by the Russian electrical engineer Semyon Kirlian. It was found that by placing an object on a photographic plate connected to a high-voltage source, a photographic image of previously unsuspected

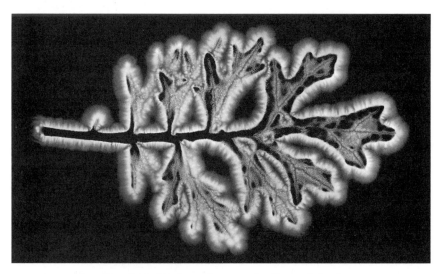

Fig. 15.5. Kirlian photograph of an oak leaf.
Graphic by Mark D. Roberts Photography.

radiation patterns emitted by the object could be produced. This phenomenon has been subsequently called by various names: electrography, electrophotography, corona discharge photography (CDP), bioelectrography, electrophotonic imaging (EPI), and in Russia, Kirlianography.[12] The corona-discharge glow at the surface of an object (fig. 15.5) subjected to a high-voltage electrical field was referred to as a "Kirlian aura" in Russia and Eastern Europe.[13]

FUTURE RESEARCH DIRECTIONS

The topological model set forth in this section provides a feasible solution to Chalmers's "hard problem of consciousness."[14] If consciousness is considered to be manifesting as energy flow in electromagnetic-frequency fields, then one should be able to determine experimentally the location of high information bandwidth channels within human physiology. Such channels must provide the data network infrastructure through which electromagnetic information interchange guides the growth process, effects repair, and catalyzes evolutionary mutation. The widespread assumption of contemporary neuroscience has been that consciousness emerges from neuronal activity in the human brain only as an epiphenomenon.[15] Accordingly, there are regions within which a search would be recommended, outside of the domain of neuronal linkages and synaptic-potential dynamics.

Dimensional analysis indicates that good candidate ranges for testing the electromagnetic field component of consciousness can be found in the near infrared spectrum. This region lies just below the threshold of the visible spectrum that is picked up by the eye's cone structures.[16] Human core body temperatures, ranging from 36.3°C to 37.5°C on a diurnal cycle, indicate that, applying Wien's Law, a search should be conducted within the infrared spectrum in a bandwidth between 9.36425 microns and 9.32808 microns, near the center of the infrared portion of the radiant spectrum.[17]

Converting from wavelength, this range is equivalent to a frequency range of 30.3 gigahertz to 32.0 gigahertz, an enormously wide band compared to, for example, the FM radio frequency band, which ranges from 87.0 to 88.1 MHz.[18] Assuming a bandwidth of 200 KHz (typically used for a single FM station), over 8,000 equivalent FM radio stations could be broadcast within the human infrared radiation band, with no overlapping interference.

One approach in the search for an infrared component of consciousness would be to monitor the dynamics of an infrared spectrum emanating from within the human body in an attempt to detect information-carrying photons escaping the body as modulated infrared radiation. It is possible to detect wavelengths down to 5 microns (the far infrared region) using Fourier transform infrared spectroscopy and to record non-invasively site-specific emissions of infrared radiation issuing from within human organs.[19]

> Interestingly, because biologic materials are transparent to light in
> the near-infrared region of the light spectrum, transmission of pho-
> tons through organs is possible.[20]

The next step would be to demodulate (decode) these photon-packet streams, the difficulty being that even in human communication technology there currently exist dozens of modulation techniques.[21]

An alternate approach would be to search for infrared energy signals flowing as patterns *within* potential physiological waveguide channels located within the human body. The ubiquitous blood capillary system, for example, with typical inner diameters of 10 microns, is a likely candidate to act as an infrared waveguide. Capillaries provide a ready-made network infrastructure within which the flow and resonance of a modulated infrared energy plasma might be discovered. Figure 15.6 suggests the location of feasible electromagnetic bands of consciousness correlated with existing structural systems of the human body.

As indicated in the figure, potential candidates for waveguide structures exist within the human body ranging in diameter (recall that diameter correlates to a dipole wavelength resonant frequency) from ultraviolet radiation in microtubules at a wavelength of approximately

Eight Feasible Bands for Consciousness

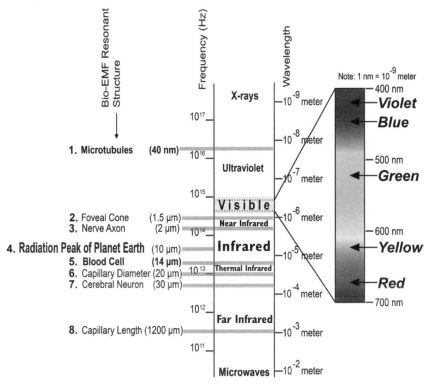

Fig. 15.6. Eight feasible electromagnetic radiation bands of consciousness within existing structural systems of the human body.

10^{-8} m to erythrocyte radiation in capillaries, located in the 10^{-3} m wavelength region.

CONCLUSION

The phenomenon of human consciousness has been explored in this book through the evaluation of numerous nonmainstream approaches to an electromagnetic theory of consciousness. A rather simplified concluding model of human consciousness can be drawn from this material: that consciousness may be viewed as a phenomenon of complex, dynamic feedback between the electrochemical brain itself (the physical neuronal

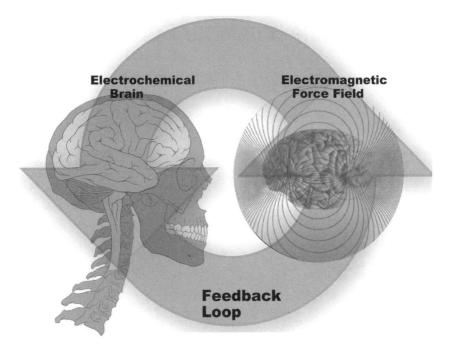

*Fig. 15.7. Feedback loop between the electrochemical brain and
a coterminous electromagnetic force field.*

tissue) and a holographic-like three-dimensional electromagnetic force field that is coterminous with the physical brain (fig. 15.7).

Finally, it is reasonable to speculate about practical implications for this topology on future technology. In considering future technologies, the identification of an energy field manifesting information characteristics in multiple bandwidths of radiant energy associated with biological systems would support the feasibility that, in principle, major components of consciousness might eventually be stored, maintained, and manipulated using nonbiological systems (e.g., fiber optics and silicon, perhaps) instead of wetware (biological tissue). An intriguing implication would be that consciousness might be uploaded from wetware into such a hardware environment. Current mainstream research, however, is almost exclusively directed at neuronal activity and brain wiring, under the tacit assumption that consciousness is somehow an accident of, or— at best—an epiphenomenon of neuronal activity in the brain.

There are numerous avenues of exploration open to future researchers in the study of consciousness. Unfortunately many of these areas of research have been largely ignored by neurophysiologists in their race to map the complex neuronal wiring systems of the brain. It is this author's hope that books such as this might lead to broader avenues of exploration, and eventually result in a deeper understanding of the physics and dynamics of the amazing phenomena that are electromagnetism and consciousness.

Notes

FOREWORD. GROUNDBREAKING THEORIES OF CONSCIOUSNESS

1. Tononi and Koch, "Consciousness: Here, There, and Everywhere?" 1.
2. Koch, "Ubiquitous Minds," 26–29.
3. Koons and Bealer, "Introduction" in *The Waning of Materialism,* Kindle ed., 300–302.

INTRODUCTION. HOW ENTHEOGENS MADE ME CONSCIOUS OF CONSCIOUSNESS

1. Pockett, "Consciousness Is a Thing, Not a Process," 12.
2. Lilly, *Programming and Metaprogramming in the Human Biocomputer.*

CHAPTER 1. TWELVE ELECTROMAGNETIC FIELD THEORIES OF CONSCIOUSNESS

1. Velmans, *Towards a Deeper Understanding of Consciousness,* 200.
2. Velmans, *Towards a Deeper Understanding of Consciousness,* 199.
3. Rose, *Consciousness: Philosophical, Psychological and Neural Theories.*
4. Köhler, *Dynamics in Psychology.*
5. Lashley, "In Search of the Engram."
6. Lashely, "An Examination of the Electric Field Theory."
7. Libet, *The Task of Gestalt Psychology.*
8. Whitehead, *Process and Reality,* 91–92.

9. Burr, "An Electro–Dynamic Theory of Development."

10. Jibu and Yasue, *Quantum Brain Dynamics.*

11. Tiller, *Psychoenergetic Science.*

12. Pockett, "Electromagnetic Field Theory of Consciousness."

13. McFadden, "Conscious Electromagnetic Information (CEMI) Field Theory."

14. Hameroff and Penrose, "Conscious Events as Orchestrated Space-Time Selections."

15. Laszlo, *Science and the Akashic Field.*

16. Sheldrake, *The Presence of the Past.*

17. Pribram, *The Form Within.*

18. Bohm, *Wholeness and the Implicate Order.*

19. Joye, "The Pribram-Bohm Holoflux Theory of Consciousness."

CHAPTER 2. POCKETT'S ELECTROMAGNETIC FIELD THEORY

1. Pockett, *The Nature of Consciousness: A Hypothesis.*

2. Pockett, *The Nature of Consciousness,* 2.

3. Pockett, "Consciousness Is a Thing, Not a Process," 10.

4. Pockett, "Consciousness Is a Thing, Not a Process," 1.

5. Bohm, "The Enfolding-Unfolding Universe," 62.

6. Wheeler, *A Journey into Gravity and Spacetime.*

7. Velmans, "Is Human Information Processing Conscious?" 652.

8. Pockett, "Consciousness Is a Thing, Not a Process," 6.

9. Baars, *In the Theater of Consciousness: The Workspace of the Mind.*

10. Pockett, "Consciousness Is a Thing, Not a Process," 4.

11. Pockett, "Consciousness Is a Thing, Not a Process," 6.

12. Pockett, "Consciousness Is a Thing, Not a Process," 13.

13. Pockett, "Consciousness Is a Thing, Not a Process," 13.

CHAPTER 3. MCFADDEN'S CONSCIOUS ELECTROMAGNETIC INFORMATION FIELD

1. McFadden, *Quantum Evolution,* 26.

2. McFadden, "Synchronous Firing," 23.

3. McFadden, "The CEMI Field Theory: Seven Clues," 164.

4. McFadden, "The CEMI Field Theory: Seven Clues," 154.

5. Engel et al., "Invasive Recordings from the Human Brain," 35.

6. McFadden, "The CEMI Field Theory: Seven Clues," 156–57.

7. McFadden, "The CEMI Field Theory: Seven Clues," 164.

8. McFadden, "The CEMI Field Theory: Seven Clues," 158.

9. McFadden, "The CEMI Field Theory: Seven Clues," 162.

10. McFadden, "Conscious Electromagnetic Information (CEMI) Field Theory," 57.

11. McFadden, "Conscious Electromagnetic Information (CEMI) Field Theory," 56.

12. McFadden, "The CEMI Field Theory: Seven Clues."

13. McFadden, "The CEMI Field Theory: Seven Clues," 386. Italics added.

14. McFadden, "The CEMI Field Theory: Seven Clues," 387.

15. McFadden, "The CEMI Field Theory: Seven Clues," 388.

16. Baars, *Experimental and Theoretical Studies of Consciousness,* 282.

17. Baars, *Experimental and Theoretical Studies of Consciousness,* 389.

18. Baars, *Experimental and Theoretical Studies of Consciousness,* 389.

19. McFadden, "Conscious Electromagnetic Information (CEMI) Field Theory."

20. McFadden, "Conscious Electromagnetic Information (CEMI) Field Theory," 264.

21. Shannon, "A Mathematical Theory of Communication."

22. McFadden, "The CEMI Field Theory: Gestalt Information and the Meaning of Meaning," 179.

23. McFadden, "The CEMI Field Theory: Seven Clues," 394–95.

24. McFadden, "The CEMI Field Theory: Seven Clues," 397.

25. McFadden, "The CEMI Field Theory: Closing the Loop," 164.

26. McFadden, "The CEMI Field Theory: Closing the Loop," 166.

CHAPTER 4. SHELDRAKE'S MORPHIC RESONANCE AND THE MORPHOGENETIC FIELD

1. Sheldrake, *A New Science of Life,* 11.

2. Freeman, "The Sense of Being Glared At," 4.

3. Cavagna et al., "Scale-Free Correlations in Starling Flocks."

4. Cavagna et al., "Scale-Free Correlations in Starling Flocks."

5. Sheldrake, personal communication (email, May 23, 2020).

CHAPTER 5. LASZLO'S THEORY OF THE AKASHA AND THE A-DIMENSION

1. Laszlo, *The Self-Actualizing Cosmos*, 44–45.
2. Laszlo, *Science and the Reenchantment of the Cosmos*, 34–35.
3. Laszlo, *Science and the Akashic Field*, 67.
4. Whicher, "Nirodha, Yoga Praxis, and the Transformation of the Mind," 67.
5. Whicher, "Nirodha, Yoga Praxis, and the Transformation of the Mind," 67.
6. Taimni, *Man, God and the Universe*, 203.
7. Laszlo, *Science and the Reenchantment of the Cosmos*, 34.
8. Laszlo, *The Self-Actualizing Cosmos*, 13–15.
9. Laszlo, *The Self-Actualizing Cosmos*, 95.
10. Sheldrake, *Morphic Resonance: The Nature of Formative Causation*, 158.
11. Laszlo, *The Self-Actualizing Cosmos*, 57.
12. Laszlo, *The Self-Actualizing Cosmos*, 57.
13. Laszlo, *The Self-Actualizing Cosmos*, 56.
14. Laszlo, *Science and the Akashic Field*, 73-75.
15. Smolin, *Time Reborn*, 123.
16. Bohm, *Wholeness and the Implicate Order*.
17. Laszlo, *Science and the Akashic Field*, 76.
18. Bailey, *The Light of the Soul: The Yoga Sutras of Patañjali*, 78.
19. Steiner, *Cosmic Memory: Prehistory of Earth and Man*.
20. Steiner, *Cosmic Memory: Prehistory of Earth and Man*, 39.
21. Todeschi, *Edgar Cayce on the Akashic Records*.
22. Laszlo, *The Self-Actualizing Cosmos*, 95.
23. Joye, "The Pribram-Bohm Holoflux Theory of Consciousness."
24. Laszlo, *Science and the Reenchantment of the Cosmos*, 35.
25. Laszlo, *Science and the Reenchantment of the Cosmos*, 35.

CHAPTER 6. TILLER'S K*SPACE

1. Tiller, *Psychoenergetic Science*.
2. Ostrander and Schroeder, *Psychic Discoveries behind the Iron Curtain*.
3. Tiller, Dibble, and Fandel, *Some Science Adventures with Real Magic*, 35.

4. Tiller, Dibble, and Fandel, *Some Science Adventures with Real Magic,* 35.

5. Tiller, Dibble, and Fandel, *Some Science Adventures with Real Magic,* 36.

6. Tiller, *The Science of Crystallization.*

7. Tiller, *Science and Human Transformation,* 305.

8. Tiller, *Science and Human Transformation,* 303.

9. Bracewell, *The Fourier Transform and Its Applications,* 76.

10. Laszlo, *The Self-Actualizing Cosmos,* 45.

11. Tiller, *Science and Human Transformation,* 55.

12. Tiller, Dibble, and Fandel, *Some Science Adventures with Real Magic,* 9.

13. Tiller, Dibble, and Fandel, *Some Science Adventures with Real Magic,* 9.

14. Tiller, Dibble, and Fandel, *Some Science Adventures with Real Magic,* 9–10.

CHAPTER 7. HAROLD SAXTON BURR'S ELECTRIC FIELDS OF LIFE

1. Burr, *Blueprint for Immortality,* 55.

2. Burr, "An Electro-Dynamic Theory of Development."

3. Bischof, "Introduction to Integrative Biophysics," 55.

4. Olsen, *Electronics: A General Introduction for the Non-Specialist,* 391.

5. Burr, *Blueprint for Immortality,* 43.

6. Burr, *Blueprint for Immortality,* 12–13.

7. Burr, *Blueprint for Immortality,* 48–49.

8. Burr, *Blueprint for Immortality,* 48–49.

9. Burr, *Blueprint for Immortality,* 50.

10. Burr, *Blueprint for Immortality,* 50–51.

11. Burr, *Blueprint for Immortality,* 54.

12. Burr, *Blueprint for Immortality,* 54.

13. Burr, *Blueprint for Immortality,* 59–60.

14. Burr, *Blueprint for Immortality,* 61.

15. Burr, *Blueprint for Immortality,* 63.

16. Burr, *Blueprint for Immortality,* 61.

17. Burr, *Blueprint for Immortality,* 64.

18. Burr, *Blueprint for Immortality,* 64.

19. Burr, *Blueprint for Immortality,* 68–69.

20. Burr, *Blueprint for Immortality,* 64.

21. Burr, *Blueprint for Immortality,* 17.

22. Burr, *The Fields of Our Life.*
23. Burr, "An Electro-Dynamic Theory of Development," 97.
24. Burr, "An Electro-Dynamic Theory of Development," 170–71.
25. Burr, "An Electro-Dynamic Theory of Development," 113.
26. Burr, "An Electro-Dynamic Theory of Development," 108–9.

CHAPTER 8. PENROSE, HAMEROFF, AND THE BRAIN AS BILLIONS OF COMPUTERS

1. Hameroff, *Ultimate Computing,* 38.
2. Hawking et al., G. *The Large Scale Structure of Space-Time.*
3. Kumar, "Cycles of Time: An Extraordinary New View of the Universe by Roger Penrose," 22.
4. The term "Copenhagen interpretation" was not used in the 1930s; it first entered the physicist's vocabulary in 1955, when Heisenberg used it in criticizing certain unorthodox interpretations of quantum mechanics.
5. Penrose and Hameroff, "Consciousness in the Universe," 13.
6. Penrose and Hameroff, "Consciousness in the Universe," 14.
7. Penrose and Hameroff, "Consciousness in the Universe," 14.
8. Penrose and Hameroff, "Consciousness in the Universe," 16.
9. Penrose and Hameroff, "Consciousness in the Universe," 16.
10. Penrose and Hameroff, "Consciousness in the Universe," 15.
11. Hameroff, *Ultimate Computing,* 181–82.
12. Penrose and Hameroff, "Consciousness in the Universe," 30.
13. Hameroff, *Ultimate Computing: Biomolecular Consciousness and Nano-Technology,* 217.

CHAPTER 9. WHITEHEAD'S "ELECTROMAGNETIC OCCASIONS"

1. Whitehead, *The Concept of Nature,* 74.
2. Maxwell first published the equations in his 1865 paper, "A Dynamical Theory of the Electromagnetic Field."
3. Einstein, "Maxwell's Influence on the Evolution of the Idea of Physical Reality," 71.
4. Pribram, *The Form Within,* 92.
5. Hosinski, *Stubborn Fact and Creative Advance,* 46.

6. Whitehead, *Process and Reality*, xiii.

7. Whitehead, *Process and Reality*, 18.

8. Hosinski, *Stubborn Fact and Creative Advance*, 22.

9. Whitehead, *Process and Reality*, 18.

10. Whitehead, *Process and Reality*, 148.

11. Einstein, "On the Electrodynamics of Moving Bodies."

12. The exact speed is 299,792,458 meters/second with a measurement of uncertainty of 4 parts per billion.

13. Susskind, "The World as a Hologram."

14. Whitehead, *Process and Reality*, 91.

15. Whitehead, *Process and Reality*, 89.

16. Whitehead, *Process and Reality*, 91.

17. Whitehead, *Process and Reality*, 91.

18. Whitehead, *Process and Reality*, 91.

19. Whitehead, *Process and Reality*, 93.

20. Whitehead, *Process and Reality*, 96.

21. Whitehead, *Process and Reality*, 98.

22. Whitehead, *Process and Reality*, 92.

23. Whitehead, *Process and Reality*, 92.

CHAPTER 10. PRIBRAM'S HOLONOMIC BRAIN THEORY

1. Pribram, *The Form Within*, 495.

2. Pribram, "Brain and Mathematics," 219.

3. Pribram, *Brain and Perception*, 19.

4. Pribram, *Brain and Perception*, xvii.

5. Broughton and Bryan, *Discrete Fourier Analysis and Wavelets*, 72.

6. Pribram, *Languages of the Brain*, 26.

7. Penfield, *The Mystery of the Mind*.

8. Penfield, *The Mystery of the Mind*, 27.

9. Penfield, *The Mystery of the Mind*, 32.

10. Squire, *The History of Neuroscience*, 314.

11. Talbot, *The Holographic Universe*, 13.

12. Lashley as quoted in Pribram, *The Form Within*, 22.

13. Pribram, *The Form Within*, 24.

14. Pribram, *The Form Within*, 24.

15. Köhler, *The Task of Gestalt Psychology,* 10.

16. Pribram, *The Form Within,* 35.

17. Pribram, *The Form Within,* 35.

18. Pribram, *The Form Within,* 356.

19. Pribram, *The Form Within,* 36.

20. Netter, *Anatomy of the Nervous System.*

21. Köhler and Henle, *The Selected Papers of Wolfgang Köhler.*

22. Pribram, *The Form Within,* 37.

23. Pribram, *The Form Within,* 50.

24. Pribram, *The Form Within,* 54–55, 57.

25. Pribram, *The Form Within,* 458.

26. Pribram, *The Form Within,* 458.

27. Pribram, *Brain and Perception,* xvi.

28. Pribram, *The Form Within,* 16.

29. Pribram, "The Neuropsychology of Sigmund Freud," 445.

30. Johnston, *Holographic Visions.*

31. Gabor, "Theory of Communication."

32. Wasson and Brieger, *Nobel Prize Winners,* 358.

33. Johnston, *Holographic Visions,* 3.

34. Johnston, *Holographic Visions,* 3.

35. Leith and Upatnieks, "Reconstructed Wavefronts and Communication Theory."

36. Johnston, *Holographic Visions,* 4.

37. Johnston, *Holographic Visions,* 7.

38. Johnston, *Holographic Visions,* 7.

39. Leith and Upatnieks, "Photography by Laser."

40. Pribram, *The Form Within,* 42.

41. Lundqvist, *Nobel Lectures, Physics 1971–1980.*

42. Pribram, *Languages of the Brain.*

43. Pribram, *Languages of the Brain,* 140–41.

44. Pribram, *Languages of the Brain,* 19.

45. Pribram, *Languages of the Brain,* 19–23.

46. Borsellino and Poggio, "Holographic Aspects of Temporal Memory."

47. Pribram, *Brain and Perception,* 28–29.

48. Pribram, *The Form Within,* 84.

49. Pribram, *The Form Within,* 69.

50. Pribram, *Brain and Perception,* xvii.

51. Pribram, *Brain and Perception,* 60.

52. Pribram, *Brain and Perception,* 70.

53. Pribram, "What Is Mind That the Brain May Order It?" 323.

54. Pribram, *The Form Within,* 103.

55. Gabor, "Theory of Communication."

56. Pribram, *The Form Within,* 104.

57. Crease, *The Great Equations,* 263.

58. Darling, *The Universal Book of Mathematics,* 151.

59. Alabiso and Weiss, *A Primer on Hilbert Space Theory.*

60. Pribram, "Brain and Mathematics," 221.

61. Gabor, "Theory of Communication," 415.

62. Pribram, *The Form Within,* 364–65.

63. Squire, *The History of Neuroscience,* 322.

64. Squire, *The History of Neuroscience,* 516.

65. Squire, *The History of Neuroscience,* 338.

66. Squire, *The History of Neuroscience,* 142.

67. Pribram, "What the Fuss Is All About," 29.

68. Pribram, "Prolegomenon for a Holonomic Brain Theory."

69. Pribram, *The Form Within,* 495.

70. Pribram, "Brain and Mathematics," 232.

71. Bohm, *Wholeness and the Implicate Order.*

72. Pribram, *The Form Within,* 496.

73. Pribram, *The Form Within,* 87.

74. Pribram, "Brain and Mathematics," 230.

75. Pribram, "Consciousness Reassessed," 8.

76. Pribram, "Consciousness Reassessed," 13.

77. Pribram, "Consciousness Reassessed," 13.

78. Pribram, "What Is Mind That the Brain May Order It?" 322.

79. Dewey, *The Theory of Laminated Spacetime.*

80. Dewey, *The Theory of Laminated Spacetime,* 95.

81. Pribram, *The Form Within,* 106–7.

82. Cazenave, *Science and Consciousness: Two Views of the Universe.*

83. Oates, *Celebrating the Dawn: Maharishi Mahesh Yogi and the TM Technique.*

84. Bohm and Weber, "Nature as Creativity," 35–36.

85. Pribram, Sharafat, and Beekman, "Frequency Encoding in Motor Systems."

86. Squire, *The History of Neuroscience,* 337.

87. Pribram, "What Is Mind That the Brain May Order It?" 320.

88. Pribram, "What Is Mind That the Brain May Order It?" 320.

89. Pribram, "Brain and Mathematics."

90. Pribram, "Brain and Mathematics," 219.

91. Pribram, "Brain and Mathematics,"151.

92. Romanes, *Cunningham's Textbook of Anatomy,* 840.

93. Pribram, *The Form Within,* 109.

94. Baggott, *The Quantum Story,* 64.

95. Baggott, *The Quantum Story,* 71.

96. Baggott, *The Quantum Story,* 74.

97. Born, *The Born-Einstein Letters,* 91.

98. Bohm, *Wholeness and the Implicate Order,* 76.

99. Ringbauer et al., "Measurements on the Reality of the Wavefunction."

100. Ringbauer et al., "Measurements on the Reality of the Wavefunction," 1.

101. Ringbauer et al., "Measurements on the Reality of the Wavefunction," 3.

102. Ringbauer et al., "Measurements on the Reality of the Wavefunction," 5.

103. Karl Pribram authored more than 700 papers and other publications; see Pribram, "Karl Pribram: Bibliography."

104. Pribram, "Mind, Brain, and Consciousness," 129.

105. Pribram, *The Form Within,* 535–36.

106. "Scientists to Speak," *Stanford Daily,* September 26, 1977, 8.

107. Dawson, *Comprehending Cults,* 54.

108. Pribram, *Brain and Perception,* 272–73.

109. Pribram, *Brain and Perception,* 173.

110. Pribram, *Brain and Perception,* 275–330.

111. Pribram, *The Form Within,* 533.

112. Cazenave, *Science and Consciousness.*

113. Cazenave, *Science and Consciousness,* 129–30.

114. As quoted in Talbot, *The Holographic Universe,* 10.

115. As quoted in Squire, *History of Neuroscience,* 342.

116. Pribram, *The Form Within,* 538.

117. Pribram, *Languages of the Brain.*

118. Pribram, *The Form Within,* 531.

119. Bohm, *Quantum Theory,* 1.

CHAPTER 11. BOHM'S CONSCIOUS HOLOFLUX IN THE IMPLICATE ORDER

1. Bohm, "Beyond Limits," 8:00.

2. Bohm, "Beyond Limits," 12:55.

3. Peat, *Infinite Potential*, 193–94.

4. Peat, *Infinite Potential*, 194–95.

5. Bohm and Hiley, *The Undivided Universe*, 1.

6. Bohm and Hiley, *The Undivided Universe*, 31.

7. Peat, *Infinite Potential*, 46.

8. Peat, *Infinite Potential*, 46.

9. Peat, *Infinite Potential*, 47.

10. Peat, *Infinite Potential*, 62.

11. Hiley and Peat, *Quantum Implications*.

12. Peat, *Infinite Potential*, 57–58.

13. Peat, *Infinite Potential*, 58.

14. Peat, *Infinite Potential*, 66.

15. Peat, *Infinite Potential*, 65.

16. Peat, *Infinite Potential*, 64.

17. Bohm and Peat, *Science, Order, and Creativity*, xiii.

18. Peat, *Infinite Potential*, 88.

19. Bohm, *The Special Theory of Relativity*, vi.

20. Hiley and Peat, "The Development of David Bohm's Ideas," 4.

21. Bohm, *Quantum Theory*.

22. Peat, *Infinite Potential*, 120.

23. Peat, *Infinite Potential*, 98–99.

24. Baggott, *The Quantum Story*, 305.

25. Peat, *Infinite Potential*, 120.

26. Peat, *Infinite Potential*, 124.

27. Peat, *Infinite Potential*, 126.

28. Bohm, *Quantum Theory*, 1. Italics added.

29. Bohm, *Quantum Theory*, 29.

30. Peat, *Infinite Potential*, 51.

31. Peat, *Infinite Potential*, 52.

32. Born, *The Born-Einstein Letters*, 91.

33. Peat, *Infinite Potential*, 108.

34. Bohm, "Suggested Interpretation of the Quantum Theory in Terms of 'Hidden Variables.'"

35. Peat, *Infinite Potential,* 148.

36. Peat, *Infinite Potential,* 133.

37. Peat, *Infinite Potential,* 133.

38. Garay, "Quantum Gravity and Minimum Length," 145.

39. Peat, *Infinite Potential,* 48.

40. Peat, *Infinite Potential,* 48–49.

41. Peat, *Infinite Potential,* 168.

42. Bell, *The Speakable and Unspeakable in Quantum Mechanics,* 128.

43. Peat, *Infinite Potential,* 186.

44. Bohm, *Wholeness and the Implicate Order,* 207.

45. Bohm and Krishnamurti, *The Limits of Thought,* vii.

46. Peat, *Infinite Potential,* 213.

47. Bohm and Krishnamurti, *The Ending of Time*; and Bohm and Krishnamurti, *The Limits of Thought.*

48. Peat, *Infinite Potential,* 227–28.

49. Bohm and Krishnamurti, *The Limits of Thought,* vii.

50. Peat, *Infinite Potential,* 229.

51. Peat, *Infinite Potential,* 256.

52. Peat, *Infinite Potential,* 256.

53. Crease, *The Great Equations,* 220.

54. Bohm, *Wholeness and the Implicate Order,* 149.

55. Pylkkänen, *Mind, Matter, and the Implicate Order,* 21.

56. Bohm, "Beyond Limits," 8:00.

57. As discussed shortly, this is the Planck length of 10^{-33} cm.

58. Bohm and Hiley, *The Undivided Universe,* 9.

59. Bohm, *Quantum Theory,* 622.

60. Bohm, *Quantum Theory,* 622.

61. Bohm and Hiley, *The Undivided Universe,* 9–10.

62. Bohm, *Wholeness and the Implicate Order,* 190–91.

63. Bohm, *Quantum Theory,* 18.

64. Bohm and Peat, *Science, Order, and Creativity,* 311–12.

65. Bohm and Peat, *Science, Order, and Creativity,* 86.

66. Gott et al., "A Map of the Universe."

67. Bohm and Hiley, *The Undivided Universe,* 357.

68. Yau and Nadis, *The Shape of Inner Space,* 10.

69. Yau and Nadis, *The Shape of Inner Space,* 10–11.

70. Yau and Nadis, *The Shape of Inner Space,* 12.

71. Yau and Nadis, *The Shape of Inner Space,* 13.

72. Bohm, *Wholeness and the Implicate Order,* 190.

73. Bohm, *Wholeness and the Implicate Order,* 186.

74. Weber, "The Physicist and the Mystic," 187. Italics added.

75. Hiley and Peat, *Quantum Implications.*

76. Hiley and Peat, *Quantum Implications.*

77. Bohm, "Beyond Limits." The source is an interview with Bill Angelos; the quoted dialogue begins 32:23 into the interview. The interview runs 1:08:13 total.

78. Globus, *The Transparent Becoming of World,* 50.

79. Bohm, "A New Theory of the Relationship of Mind and Matter," 51.

80. Bohm, "Meaning and Information," 45.

81. Bohm and Peat, *Science, Order, and Creativity,* 84.

82. Bohm and Peat, *Science, Order, and Creativity,* 84.

83. Bohm, "Meaning and Information," 45.

84. Bohm, "Meaning and Information," 52.

85. Bohm, "Meaning and Information," 52.

86. Bohm, "Beyond Limits," 5:30.

87. Bohm, "Beyond Limits," 1:00.

88. Globus, *The Transparent Becoming of World,* 55.

89. Peat, *Infinite Potential,* 220.

90. Bohm, "Hidden Variables and the Implicate Order," 43.

91. Bohm and Peat, *Science, Order, and Creativity,* 81.

92. Bohm and Peat, *Science, Order, and Creativity,* 81.

93. Bohm and Peat, *Science, Order, and Creativity,* 82. Italics added.

94. Bohm and Peat, *Science, Order, and Creativity,* 82.

95. Bohm and Hiley, *The Undivided Universe,* 38–39.

96. Bohm and Hiley, *The Undivided Universe,* 399.

97. Bohm, "Meaning and Information," 45.

98. Bohm, "Meaning and Information," 46.

99. Bohm, *Wholeness and the Implicate Order,* 196–97.

100. Bohm, *Wholeness and the Implicate Order,* 200.

101. Bohm, in Weber, "The Physicist and the Mystic," 196.

102. Bohm, "The Implicate Order and the Super-Implicate Order," 45–46.

103. Bohm, *The Undivided Universe,* 389–90. Italics added.

104. Bohm, "Beyond Limits," 5:30. Author's transcription.

105. Peat, *Infinite Potential: The Life and Times of David Bohm.*

106. Bohm, "The Enfolding-Unfolding Universe," 62.

107. Bohm and Hiley, *The Undivided Universe*, 381–82.

108. Bohm, "Beyond Limits," 7:20.

109. Carr and Giddings, "Quantum Black Holes," 33.

110. Wong, *The Shambhala Guide to Taoism*, 124–31.

111. Globus, *Quantum Closures and Disclosures*, 175.

CHAPTER 12. JOYE'S SUB-QUANTUM HOLOFLUX THEORY OF CONSCIOUSNESS

1. Chalmers, "Facing Up to the Problem of Consciousness," 5.

2. Hoffman, *The Case against Reality*, 14.

3. Edelman and Tononi, *A Universe of Consciousness*, 215–19.

4. Brodal, *The Central Nervous System: Structure and Function*, 19.

5. Joye, *Sub-Quantum Consciousness*.

6. Chalmers, "Facing Up to the Problem of Consciousness," 217.

7. Gebser, *The Ever-Present Origin*, 312.

8. Bohm, "The Enfolding-Unfolding Universe," 62.

9. Collister, *Journey in Search of Wholeness*, 69.

10. Pribram, *The Form Within*; Bohm, *Wholeness and the Implicate Order*.

11. Pribram, *The Form Within*; Bohm, *Wholeness and the Implicate Order*.

12. Rescher, *G. W. Leibniz's Monadology*.

13. Chalmers, "Facing Up to the Problem of Consciousness."

14. Block, *Consciousness, Function, and Representation*.

15. Bohm, *Wholeness and the Implicate Order*.

16. Teilhard de Chardin, "The Nature of the Point Omega."

17. Laszlo, *Science and the Akashic Field*, 27.

18. Dorf, *Electrical Engineering Handbook*, 1538.

19. Bohm, *Wholeness and the Implicate Order*, 77.

20. Wheeler, *Information, Physics, Quantum*, 207.

21. Susskind, *The Black Hole War*, 119.

22. Wheeler, *Information, Physics, Quantum*, 222.

23. Bekenstein, "Black Holes and Entropy."

24. Romanes, *Cunningham's Textbook of Anatomy*, 137.

25. Joye, "The Pribram–Bohm Holoflux Theory of Consciousness."

26. Bekenstein, "Black Holes and Entropy."

27. Bohm, *Wholeness and the Implicate Order*, 80.

28. Feynman, Leighton, and Sands, *Feynman Lectures on Physics*, 78.

29. Dorf, *Electrical Engineering Handbook.*

30. Dorf, *Electrical Engineering Handbook.*

31. Gowar, *Optical Communication Systems,* 64.

32. Chen, *Introduction to Plasma Physics,* 1.

33. McCraty, *The Energetic Heart.*

34. Turgeon, *Clinical Hematology.*

35. Romanes, *Cunningham's Textbook of Anatomy.*

36. Wick, Pinggera, and Lehmann, *Clinical Aspects,* 6.

37. Fraser and Frey, "Electromagnetic Emission at Micron Wavelengths from Active Nerves."

38. Teilhard de Chardin, "The Activation of Human Energy," 393.

39. Steiner, *An Occult Physiology,* 42.

40. Teilhard de Chardin, "The Activation of Human Energy," 106.

41. Teilhard de Chardin, "The Energy of Evolution," 29.

42. Teilhard de Chardin, "The Activation of Human Energy," 344.

43. Steiner, *An Occult Physiology,* 43.

44. See Pribram, *Languages of the Brain* and "Prolegomenon."

45. Libet, *Mind Time,* 87.

46. Libet, *Mind Time,* 87.

47. Bohm, *Unfolding Meaning,* 128.

CHAPTER 13. QUANTUM BRAIN
DYNAMICS AND NEUROANATOMY

1. Romanes, *Cunningham's Textbook of Anatomy,* 556.

2. Netter, *Anatomy of the Nervous System.*

3. Netter, *Anatomy of the Nervous System.*

4. Herculano-Houzel, "The Human Brain in Numbers," 1.

5. Fields, *The Other Brain.*

6. Vitiello, "Hiroomi Umezawa and Quantum Field Theory."

7. Jibu and Yasue, *Quantum Brain Dynamics and Consciousness,* 164–65.

8. Umezawa and Vitiello, *Quantum Mechanics.*

9. Stuart, Takahashi, and Umezawa, "Mixed System Brain Dynamics: Neural Memory as a Macroscopic Ordered State."

10. Jibu and Yasue, *Quantum Brain Dynamics and Consciousness,* 293.

11. Jibu and Yasue, *Quantum Brain Dynamics and Consciousness,* 293.

12. Dorf, *Electrical Engineering Handbook,* 27.

13. Jibu and Yasue, "Quantum Brain Dynamics and Quantum Field Theory," 288.

14. Pribram, *Brain and Perception,* 277.

15. Chen, *Introduction to Plasma Physics,* 56.

16. Jibu and Yasue, *Quantum Brain Dynamics and Consciousness,* 164–65.

17. Jibu and Yasue, "Quantum Brain Dynamics and Quantum Field Theory," 293.

18. "Brian Josephson," *Encyclopaedia Britannica* online, accessed January 30, 2020.

19. Jibu and Yasue, *Quantum Brain Dynamics and Consciousness,* 146.

20. Jibu and Yasue, *Quantum Brain Dynamics and Consciousness,* 155.

21. Jibu and Yasue, *Quantum Brain Dynamics and Consciousness,* 157.

22. Jibu and Yasue, "Quantum Brain Dynamics and Quantum Field Theory," 293.

23. Dorf, *The Electrical Engineering Handbook,* 27.

24. McCraty, *The Energetic Heart.*

25. Vitiello, *My Double Unveiled,* 57.

CHAPTER 14. PAST AND PRESENT VARIETIES OF ELECTROMAGNETIC BRAIN STIMULATION

1. Parent, "Giovanni Aldini: From Animal Electricity to Human Brain Stimulation."

2. Crabtree, *Animal Magnetism, Early Hypnotism, and Psychical Research, 1766–1925.*

3. As quoted in "Electric Executions," *Lawrence Daily Record,* January 1, 1890, 1.

4. Hotchner, *Papa Hemingway: A Personal Memoir,* 280.

5. Brunoni et al., "Transcranial Direct Current Stimulation for Acute Major Depressive Episodes."

6. "Total DCS Electrode Placement Montage Guide," Total tDCS website.

7. Poreisz et al., "Safety Aspects of Transcranial Direct Current Stimulation Concerning Healthy Subjects and Patients."

8. Kirsch and Nichols, "Cranial Electrotherapy Stimulation for Treatment of Anxiety, Depression, and Insomnia," 169.

9. Morales-Quezada et al., "Behavioral Effects of Transcranial Pulsed Current Stimulation (tPCS): Speed-Accuracy Tradeoff in Attention Switching Task."

10. Rufener et al., "Transcranial Random Noise Stimulation (tRNS) Shapes the Processing of Rapidly Changing Auditory Information."

11. Hammond et al., "Latest View on the Mechanism of Action of Deep Brain Stimulation," 2114.

12. Jaynes, *The Origin of Consciousness in the Breakdown of the Bicameral Mind.*
13. Sher, "Neuroimaging, Auditory Hallucinations, and the Bicameral Mind."
14. Persinger, "Schumann Resonance Frequencies."
15. Persinger and Booth, "Discrete Shifts within the Theta Band between the Frontal and Parietal Regions of the Right Hemisphere and the Experience of a Sensed Presence," 281.
16. Brothwell, *Digging Up Bones,* 126.
17. Wikipedia s.v. "Trepanning," accessed May 28, 2020.

CHAPTER 15. OPTICAL NETWORKS IN THE BRAIN AND FUTURE RESEARCH

1. Tuszynski et al., "Emission of Mitochondrial Biophotons and their Effect on Electrical Activity of Membrane via Microtubules."
2. Tuszynski et al., "Emission of Mitochondrial Biophotons and their Effect on Electrical Activity of Membrane via Microtubules," 1.
3. Litchfield, "The Puzzling Role of Biophotons in the Brain."
4. Tuszynski, "Are There Optical Communication Channels in the Brain?"
5. Creath and Schwartz, "Biophoton Interaction in Biological Systems," 8.
6. Vitiello, *My Double Unveiled,* 57–58.
7. Tuszynski, "Are There Optical Communication Channels in the Brain?"
8. Woollaston, "The World's Nervous System Revealed."
9. VanWijk, "Bio-Photons and Bio-Communication," 187–88.
10. Tuszynski, "Are There Optical Communication Channels in the Brain?" 9.
11. VanWijk, "Bio-Photons and Bio-Communication," 189.
12. Stenger, "Bioenergetic Fields," 626.
13. Antonov and Yuskesselieva, "Selective High Frequency Discharge," 29.
14. Chalmers, "Facing Up to the Problem of Consciousness," 5.
15. Dennett, *Consciousness Explained,* 406.
16. Oyster, *The Human Eye.*
17. Becker, *Cross Currents.*
18. Blakeslee, *The Radio Amateur's Handbook.*
19. Griffiths and de Haseth, *Fourier Transform Infrared Spectrometry.*
20. Cohn, "Near-Infrared Spectroscopy: Potential Clinical Benefits in Surgery," 323.
21. American Radio Relay League, *The ARRL 2016 Handbook for Radio Communications,* 42.

Bibliography

Alabiso, C., and Ittay Weiss. *A Primer on Hilbert Space Theory: Linear Spaces, Topological Spaces, Metric Spaces, Normed Spaces, and Topological Groups.* Switzerland: Springer, 2015.

American Radio Relay League. *The ARRL 2016 Handbook for Radio Communications.* 93rd ed. Newington, Conn.: American Radio Relay League, 2015.

Antonov, A., and L. Yuskesselieva. "Selective High Frequency Discharge (Kirlian Effect)." In *Acta Hydrophysica,* 219–42. Berlin: Institut fur Physikalische Hydrographie, 1985.

Aur, Dorian, and Mandar S. Jog. *Neuroelectrodynamics: Understanding the Brain Language.* Amsterdam: IOS Press, 2010.

Baars, B. J. *Experimental and Theoretical Studies of Consciousness.* Chichester, UK: Wiley, 1993.

———. *In the Theater of Consciousness: The Workspace of the Mind.* Oxford: Oxford University Press, 1997.

Baggott, Jim. *The Quantum Story: A History in 40 Moments.* Oxford: Oxford University Press, 2011.

Bailey, Alice A. *The Light of the Soul: The Yoga Sutras of Patanjali.* New York: Lucis Publishing, 1927.

Becker, Robert O. *Cross Currents: The Perils of Electropollution and the Promise of Electromedicine.* New York: Jeremy Tarcher, 1990.

Becker, Robert O., and Gary Selden. *The Body Electric: Electromagnetism and the Foundation of Life.* New York: Harper, 1985.

Bekenstein, Jacob D. "Black Holes and Entropy." *Physical Review* 7, no. 8 (1973): 2333–46.

Bell, J. S. *The Speakable and Unspeakable in Quantum Mechanics.* Cambridge: Cambridge University Press, 1987.

Benenson, Walter, John W. Harris, Horst Stocker, and Lutz Holger, eds. *Handbook of Physics.* New York: Springer Science, 2006.

Bischof, M. "Introduction to Integrative Biophysics." In *Integrative Biophysics: Biophotonics,* edited by Fritz-Albert Popp and Lev Beloussov. New York: Springer, 2003.

Bisson, Terry. "They're Made Out of Meat." *Omni* 13, no. 7 (1990): 42–45.

Blakeslee, Douglas, ed. *The Radio Amateur's Handbook.* Newington, Conn.: The American Radio Relay League, 1972.

Blinkov, S. M., and I. I. Glezer. *The Human Brain in Figures and Tables: A Quantitative Handbook.* New York: Plenum, 1968.

Block, Ned. *Consciousness, Function, and Representation.* Vol. 1 of *Collected Papers.* Cambridge, Mass.: MIT Press, 2007.

Bohm, David. "Beyond Limits: A Full Conversation with David Bohm." Transcript of 1990 interview by Bill Angelos for Dutch public television. The Bohm-Krishnamurti Project website, March 5, 2011.

———. "The Enfolding-Unfolding Universe: A Conversation with David Bohm." In *The Holographic Paradigm and Other Paradoxes: Exploring the Leading Edge of Science,* edited by Ken Wilber, 44–104. Boulder, Colo.: Shambhala, 1978.

———. "Hidden Variables and the Implicate Order." In Hiley and Peat, *Quantum Implications: Essays in Honour of David Bohm,* 33–45.

———. "The Implicate Order and the Super-Implicate Order." In *Dialogues with Scientists and Sages: The Search for Unity,* edited by Renée Weber, 23–49. New York: Routledge, 1986.

———. "Meaning and Information." In *The Search for Meaning: The New Spirit in Science and Philosophy,* edited by Paavo Pylkkänen, 43–85. Northamptonshire, UK: Aquarian Press, 1989.

———. "A New Theory of the Relationship of Mind and Matter." *Philosophical Psychology* 3, no. 2 (1990): 271–86.

———. *Quantum Theory.* New York: Prentice Hall, 1951.

———. *The Special Theory of Relativity.* Philadelphia: John Benjamins, 1965.

———. "A Suggested Interpretation of the Quantum Theory in Terms of 'Hidden Variables,' Vol. 1." *Physical Review* 85, no. 2 (1952): 166–93.

———. *Unfolding Meaning: A Weekend of Dialogue with David Bohm.* London: Routledge, 1985.

———. *Wholeness and the Implicate Order.* London: Routledge, 1980.

Bohm, David, and Basil J. Hiley. *The Undivided Universe: An Ontological Interpretation of Quantum Theory.* London: Routledge, 1993.

Bohm, David, and J. Krishnamurti. *The Ending of Time: Where Philosophy and Physics Meet.* New York: Harper Collins, 1985.

———. *The Limits of Thought: Discussions between J. Krishnamurti and David Bohm.* London: Routledge, 1999.

Bohm, David, and F. David Peat. *Science, Order, and Creativity.* London: Routledge, 1987.

Bohm, David, and R. Weber. "Nature as Creativity." *ReVision* 5, no. 2 (1982): 35–40.

Booth, J. C., S. A. Koren, and Michael A. Persinger. "Increased Feelings of the Sensed Presence and Increased Geomagnetic Activity at the Time of the Experience during Exposures to Transcerebral Weak Complex Magnetic Fields." *International Journal of Neuroscience* 115, no. 7 (2005): 1039–65.

Booth, J. N., and M. A. Persinger. "Discrete Shifts within the Theta Band between the Frontal and Parietal Regions of the Right Hemisphere and the Experience of a Sensed Presence." *Journal of Neuropsychiatry* 21, no. 3 (2005): 279–83.

Born, Irene, trans. *The Born-Einstein Letters: Friendship, Politics and Physics in Uncertain Times.* New York: Macmillan, 1971.

Borsellino, A., and T. Poggio. "Holographic Aspects of Temporal Memory and Optomotor Responses." *Kybernetik* 10, no. 1 (1972): 58–60.

Bracewell, Ronald. *The Fourier Transform and Its Applications*, 3rd ed. New York: McGraw-Hill, 1999.

Brodal, Per. *The Central Nervous System: Structure and Function.* Oxford: Oxford University Press, 2003.

Brothwell, Don R. *Digging Up Bones: The Excavation, Treatment and Study of Human Skeletal Remains.* London: British Museum of Natural History, 1963.

Broughton, S. A., and K. Bryan. *Discrete Fourier Analysis and Wavelets: Applications to Signal and Image Processing.* New York: Wiley, 2008.

Brunoni, André R., Adriano H. Moffa, Felipe Fregni, Ulrich Palm, Frank Padberg, Daniel M. Blumberger, Zafiris J. Daskalakis, Djamila Bennabi, Emmanuel Haffen, Angelo Alonzo, and Colleen K. Loo. "Transcranial Direct Current Stimulation for Acute Major Depressive Episodes: Meta-Analysis of Individual Patient Data." *British Journal of Psychiatry* 208, no. 6 (2016): 522–31.

Bruskiewich, Patrick. *Max Planck and Black-Body Radiation.* Vancouver: Pythagoras Publishing, 2014.

Burr, Harold Saxton. *Blueprint for Immortality: The Electric Patterns of Life.* Great Britain: C. W. Daniel, 1972.

———. "An Electro-Dynamic Theory of Development Suggested by Studies of Proliferation Rates in the Brain of Amblystoma." *Journal of Comparative Neurology* 56, no. 2 (1932): 347–71.

———. *The Fields of Our Life: Our Links with the Universe.* New York: Ballantine Books, 1973.

Carr, Bernard J., and Steven B. Giddings. "Quantum Black Holes." *Scientific American* 292, no. 5 (2005): 30–35.

Cavagna, Andrea, Alessio Cimarelli, Irene Giardina, Giorgio Parisi, Raffaele Santagati, Fabio Stefanini, and Massimiliano Viale. "Scale-Free Correlations in Starling Flocks." *Proceedings of the National Academy of Sciences* 107, no. 26 (June 2010): 11865–70.

Cazenave, Michel, ed. *Science and Consciousness: Two Views of the Universe.* Edited Proceedings of the France-Culture and Radio-France Colloquium, Cordoba, Spain. Oxford: Pergamon, 1984.

Chalmers, David J. *The Character of Consciousness.* New York: Oxford University Press, 2010.

———. "Facing Up to the Problem of Consciousness." *Journal of Consciousness Studies* 2, no. 3 (1995): 200–19.

Chen, Frances F. *Introduction to Plasma Physics and Controlled Fusion.* Vol 1, *Plasma Physics.* 2nd ed. New York: Springer, 2006.

Cohn, Stephen M. "Near-Infrared Spectroscopy: Potential Clinical Benefits in Surgery." *Journal of the American College of Surgeons* 205, no. 2 (2007): 322–32.

Collister, Rupert Clive. *A Journey in Search of Wholeness and Meaning.* New York: Peter Lang, 2010.

Crabtree, Adam. *Animal Magnetism, Early Hypnotism, and Psychical Research, 1766–1925: An Annotated Bibliography.* New York: Kraus Intl., 1988.

Crease, Robert P. *The Great Equations: Breakthroughs in Science from Pythagoras to Heisenberg.* New York: W. W. Norton, 2008.

Creath, Katherine, and Gary E. Schwartz. "Biophoton Interaction in Biological Systems: Evidence of Photonic Info-Energy Transfer?" In proceedings of SPIE, the International Society for Optical Engineering, vol. 5866, *The Nature of Light: What Is a Photon?* 338–47. Bellingham, Wash.: SPIE, 2005.

Darling, David J. *The Universal Book of Mathematics: From Abracadabra to Zeno's Paradoxes.* Hoboken, N.J.: Wiley, 2004.

Dawson, Lorne L. *Comprehending Cults: The Sociology of New Religious Movements.* New York: Oxford University Press, 2006.

Dennett, Daniel C. *Consciousness Explained.* New York: Back Bay Books, 1991.

Dewey, B. *The Theory of Laminated Spacetime.* Inverness, Calif.: Bartholomew Books, 1985.

Dorf, Richard C., ed. *The Electrical Engineering Handbook.* 2nd ed. Boca Raton, Fla.: CRC Press, 1997.

Edelman, Gerald M., and Giulio Tononi. *A Universe of Consciousness: How Matter Becomes Imagination.* New York: Basic Books, 2000.

Einstein, Albert. *Autobiographical Notes.* Peru, Ill.: Carus, 1979.

———. "Maxwell's Influence on the Evolution of the Idea of Physical Reality." In *James Clerk Maxwell: A Commemoration Volume 1831–1931.* Cambridge: Cambridge University Press, 1931.

———. "On the Electrodynamics of Moving Bodies." *Annalen der Physik* 322, no. 10 (1905): 891–921.

Engel, A. K., C. K. Moll, I. Fried, and G. A. Ojemann. "Invasive Recordings from the Human Brain: Clinical Insights and Beyond." *Nature Reviews Neuroscience* 6, no. 1 (2005): 35–47.

Feuerstein, Georg. *Structures of Consciousness: The Genius of Jean Gebser—An Introduction and Critique.* Lower Lake, Calif.: Integral, 1987.

Feynman, Richard, Robert Leighton, and Matthew Sands. *The Feynman Lectures on Physics.* Vol. 1. Reading, Mass.: Addison-Wesley, 1964.

Fields, R. Douglas. *The Other Brain.* New York: Simon & Schuster, 2009.

Fourier, Jean-Baptiste Joseph. *The Analytic Theory of Heat.* Paris: Firmin Didot Père et Fils, 1822.

Fraser, A., and O. Frey. "Electromagnetic Emission at Micron Wavelengths from Active Nerves." *Biophysical Journal* 8, no. 6 (1968): 731–34.

Freeman, Anthony. "The Sense of Being Glared At: What Is It Like to Be a Heretic?" *Journal of Consciousness Studies* 12, no. 6 (2005): 4–9.

Gabor, Dennis. "Theory of Communication." *Journal of the Institute of Electrical Engineers* 93 (1946): 429–41.

Garay, Luis J. "Quantum Gravity and Minimum Length." *International Journal of Modern Physics* 10, no. 2 (1995): 145–65.

Gebser, Jean. *The Ever-Present Origin: Part One: Foundations of the Aperspectival World.* Translated by J. Keckeis. Stuttgart, Germany: Deutsche Verlags-Anstalt, 1949.

Globus, Gordon G. *Quantum Closures and Disclosures: Thinking-together, Postphenomenology and Quantum Brain Dynamics*. Philadelphia: John Benjamins, 2003.

———. *The Transparent Becoming of World: A Crossing Between Process Philosophy and Quantum Neurophilosophy*. Philadelphia: John Benjamins, 2006.

Gott, J. Richard III, Mario Jurić, David Schlegel, and Fiona Hoyle. "A Map of the Universe." *Astrophysics Journal* 624, no. 2 (2005): 463–514.

Gowar, J. *Optical Communication Systems*. 2nd ed. Hemel Hempstead, UK: Prentice Hall, 1993.

Griffiths, P. R., and J. A. de Haseth. *Fourier Transform Infrared Spectrometry*. 2nd ed. Hoboken, N.J.: Wiley Interscience, 2007.

Hameroff, Stuart R. "Is Your Brain Really a Computer, or Is It a Quantum Orchestra?" *Huffington Post*, July 9, 2016.

———. *Ultimate Computing: Biomolecular Consciousness and NanoTechnology*. Amsterdam: Elsevier Science Publishers, 1987.

Hameroff, Stuart R., Travis J. A. Craddock, and Jack A. Tuszynski. "Quantum Effects in the Understanding of Consciousness." *Journal of Integrative Neuroscience* 13, no. 2 (2014): 229–52.

Hameroff, Stuart, and Roger Penrose. "Conscious Events as Orchestrated Space-Time Selections." *Journal of Consciousness Studies* 3, no. 1 (1996): 35–53.

Hammond, C., R. Ammari, B. Bioulac, and L. Garcia. "Latest View on the Mechanism of Action of Deep Brain Stimulation." *Movement Disorders* 23, no. 15 (2008): 2111–21.

Harnad, Stevan. "Why and How We Are Not Zombies." *Journal of Consciousness Studies* 1, no. 1 (1994): 18–23.

Havelka, D., M. Cifra, O. Kucera, J. Pokorny, and J. Vrba. "High-Frequency Electric Field and Radiation Characteristics of Cellular Microtubule Network." *Journal of Theoretical Biology* 286, no. 7 (2011): 31–40.

Hawking, Stephen W., G. F. R. Ellis, P. V. Landshoff, D. R. Elson, D. W. Sciama, S. Weinberg. *The Large Scale Structure of Space-Time*. Cambridge: Cambridge University Press, 1975.

Herculano-Houzel, Suzana. "The Human Brain in Numbers: A Linearly Scaled-Up Primate Brain." *Frontiers in Human Neuroscience* 3, no. 31 (2009): 1–11.

Hertz, Heinrich. *Electric Waves: Being Researches on the Propagation of Electric Action with Finite Velocity Through Space*. London: MacMillan, 1893.

Hiley, B. J., and F. David Peat, eds. "The Development of David Bohm's Ideas from the Plasma to the Implicate Order." In Hiley and Peat, *Quantum Implications: Essays in Honour of David Bohm,* 1–32.

———, eds. *Quantum Implications: Essays in Honour of David Bohm.* London: Routledge, 1987.

Hoffman, Donald. *The Case against Reality: Why Evolution Hid the Truth from Our Eyes.* New York: W. W. Norton, 2019.

Hosinski, Thomas E. *Stubborn Fact and Creative Advance: An Introduction to the Metaphysics of Alfred North Whitehead.* Maryland: Rowman & Littlefield, 1993.

Hotchner, A. E. *Papa Hemingway: A Personal Memoir.* New York: Bantam Books, 1967.

Jaynes, Julian. *The Origin of Consciousness in the Breakdown of the Bicameral Mind.* New York: Houghton Mifflin Harcourt, 1976.

Jibu, Mari, and Kunio Yasue. *Quantum Brain Dynamics and Consciousness: An Introduction.* Philadelphia: John Benjamins, 1995.

———. "Quantum Brain Dynamics and Quantum Field Theory." In *Brain and Being: At the Boundary between Science, Philosophy, Language and Arts,* edited by Gordon Globus, Karl Pribram, and Giuseppe Vitiello, 267–90. Philadelphia: John Benjamins, 2003.

Johnston, Sean F. *Holographic Visions: A History of New Science.* New York: Oxford University Press, 2006.

Joye, Shelli R. *Sub-Quantum Consciousness: A Geometry of Consciousness Based upon the Work of Karl Pribram, David Bohm, and Teilhard de Chardin.* Viola, Calif.: The Viola Institute, 2019.

———. 2016. "The Pribram–Bohm Holoflux Theory of Consciousness: An Integral Interpretation of the Theories of Karl Pribram, David Bohm, and Pierre Teilhard de Chardin." Ph.D. diss., California Institute of Integral Studies, 2016. UMI No. 1803306323.

Kafatos, Menas, Rudolph E. Tanzi, and Deepak Chopra. "How Consciousness Becomes the Physical Universe." *Journal of Cosmology* 14 (2011): 1318–28.

Kirsch, D. L., and F. Nichols. "Cranial Electrotherapy Stimulation for Treatment of Anxiety, Depression, and Insomnia." *Psychiatric Clinics of North America* 36, no. 1 (March 2013): 169–76.

Koch, Christof. "Ubiquitous Minds." *Scientific American Mind* 25, no. 1, (January 2014), 26–29.

Köhler, Wolfgang. *Dynamics in Psychology: Vital Applications of Gestalt Psychology.* New York: W. W. Norton, 1940.

———. *The Selected Papers of Wolfgang Köhler*. Edited by Mary Henle. New York: W. W. Norton, 1971.

———. *The Task of Gestalt Psychology*. Princeton: Princeton University Press, 1969.

Koons, R. C., and G. Bealer, eds. *The Waning of Materialism*. Oxford: Oxford University Press, 2010.

Kuehn, Kerry. *A Student's Guide through the Great Physics Texts*. Vol. 1, *The Heavens and The Earth*. New York: Springer, 2014.

Kumar, Manjit. "Cycles of Time: An Extraordinary New View of the Universe by Roger Penrose—Review." *Guardian*. (October 16, 2010). Accessed May 27, 2011.

Lashley, Karl. "An Examination of the Electric Field Theory of Cerebral Integration." *Psychological Review* 58, no. 2 (1951): 123–36.

———. "In Search of the Engram." *Symposium of the Society for Experimental Biology* 4 (1950): 454–82.

Laszlo, Ervin. *The Immortal Mind: Science and the Continuity of Consciousness beyond the Brain*. Rochester, Vt.: Inner Traditions, 2014.

———. *Science and the Akashic Field: An Integral Theory of Everything*. Rochester, Vt.: Inner Traditions, 2007.

———. *Science and the Reenchantment of the Cosmos: The Rise of the Integral Vision of Reality*. Rochester, Vt.: Inner Traditions, 2006.

———. *The Self-Actualizing Cosmos: The Akasha Revolution in Science and Human Consciousness*. Rochester, Vt.: Inner Traditions, 2014.

Leckie, Robert. *Delivered from Evil: The Saga of World War II*. New York: Harper & Row, 1987.

Leith, Emmet N., and J. Upatnieks. "Photography by Laser." *Scientific American* 212, no. 6 (1965): 24–35.

———. "Reconstructed Wavefronts and Communication Theory." *Journal of the Optical Society of America* 52, no. 10 (1962): 1123–30.

Libet, Benjamin. *Mind Time: The Temporal Factor in Consciousness*. Cambridge, Mass.: Harvard University Press, 2004.

Libet, B., C. A. Gleason, E. W. Wright, and D. K. Pearl. "Time of Conscious Intention to Act in Relation to Onset of Cerebral Activity (Readiness Potential): The Unconscious Initiation of a Freely Voluntary Act." *Brain* 106, no. 3 (1983): 623–42.

Lilly, John. *The Deep Self: Consciousness Exploration in the Isolation Tank*. New York: Simon & Schuster, 1977.

———. *The Mind of the Dolphin: A Nonhuman Intelligence.* New York: Doubleday, 1967.

———. *Programming and Metaprogramming in the Human Biocomputer: Theory and Experiments.* Victoria, Australia: Communication Research Institute, 1968.

Litchfield, Gideon. "The Puzzling Role of Biophotons in the Brain." *MIT Technology Review*, December 17, 2010.

Lundqvist, Stig, ed. *Nobel Lectures, Physics 1971–1980.* Singapore: World Scientific, 1992.

MacKenna, Stephen. *Plotinus: The Enneads.* New York: Larson Publications, 1992.

McCraty, Rollin. *The Energetic Heart: Bioelectromagnetic Interactions within and between People.* Boulder Creek, CA: Institute of HeartMath, 2003.

McCraty, Rollin, M. Atkinson, D. Tomasino, and R. T. Bradley. "The Coherent Heart: Heart-Brain Interactions, Psychophysiological Coherence, and the Emergence of System-Wide Order." *Integral Review* 5, no. 9 (2009): 10–115.

McCraty, Rollin, Annette Deyhle, and Doc Childre. "The Global Coherence Initiative: Creating a Coherent Planetary Standing Wave." *Global Advances in Health and Medicine* 1, no. 1 (2012): 64–77.

McFadden, Johnjoe. "The CEMI Field Theory: Closing the Loop." *Journal of Consciousness Studies* 20, nos. 1–2 (2013): 153–68.

———. "The CEMI Field Theory: Gestalt Information and the Meaning of Meaning." *Journal of Consciousness Studies* 20, nos. 3–4 (2013): 152–82.

———. "The CEMI Field Theory: Seven Clues to the Nature of Consciousness." In *The Emerging Physics of Consciousness,* edited by Jack A. Tuszynski, 385–404. Berlin: Springer-Verlag, 2006.

———. "Conscious Electromagnetic Field Theory." *NeuroQuantology* 5, no. 3 (2007): 262–70.

———. "The Conscious Electromagnetic Information (CEMI) Field Theory: The Hard Problem Made Easy." *Journal of Consciousness Studies* 9, no. 8 (2002): 45–60.

———. *Quantum Evolution: The New Science of Life.* New York: W. W. Norton, 2000.

———. "Synchronous Firing and Its Influence on the Brain's Electromagnetic Field: Evidence for an Electromagnetic Field Theory of Consciousness." *Journal of Consciousness Studies* 9, no. 4 (2002): 23–50.

McGinn, Colin. "Consciousness and Space." In *Explaining Consciousness: The Hard Problem,* edited by Jonathan Shear, 97–108. Boston: MIT Press, 1997.

Morales-Quezada, Leon, Jorge Leite, Sandra Carvalho, Laura Castillo-Saavedra, Camila Cosmo, and Felipe Fregni. "Behavioral Effects of Transcranial Pulsed Current Stimulation (tPCS): Speed-Accuracy Tradeoff in Attention Switching Task." *Neuroscience Research* 109 (August 2016): 48–53.

Netter, F. H. *A Compilation of Paintings of the Normal and Pathologic Anatomy of the Nervous System.* Summit, N.J.: CIBA, 1972.

Nilson, Arthur R., and J. L. Hornung. *Practical Radio Communication: Principles, Systems, Equipment, Operation, Including Very High and Ultra High Frequencies and Frequency Modulation.* 2nd ed. New York: McGraw-Hill, 1943.

Oates, B. *Celebrating the Dawn: Maharishi Mahesh Yogi and the TM Technique.* New York: Putnam Books, 1971.

Olsen, George Henry. *Electronics: A General Introduction for the Non-Specialist.* New York: Plenum, 1968.

Ostrander, Sheila, and Lynn Schroeder. *Psychic Discoveries behind the Iron Curtain.* Englewood Cliffs, N.J.: Prentice Hall, 1971.

Ouspensky, P. D. *In Search of the Miraculous: Fragments of an Unknown Teaching.* London: Harcourt, 1949.

Oyster, Clyde W. *The Human Eye: Structure and Function.* Sunderland, Mass.: Sinauer Associates, 1999.

Parent, G. "Giovanni Aldini: From Animal Electricity to Human Brain Stimulation." *Canadian Journal of Neurological Sciences* 31, no. 4 (2004): 576–84.

Peat, F. David. *Infinite Potential: The Life and Times of David Bohm.* Reading, Mass.: Addison-Wesley, 1997.

Penfield, Wilder. *The Mystery of the Mind: A Critical Study of Consciousness and the Human Brain.* Princeton, N.J.: Princeton University Press, 1975.

Penrose, Sir Roger. *Cycles of Time: An Extraordinary New View of the Universe.* New York: Alfred A. Knopf, 2010.

Penrose, Sir Roger. *The Emperor's New Mind: Concerning Computers, Minds and the Laws of Physics.* New York: Oxford University Press, 1989.

Penrose, R., and Stuart Hameroff. "Consciousness in the Universe: Neuroscience, Quantum Space-time Geometry and Orch OR Theory." Selected from *Journal of Cosmology,* vol. 14. Cambridge: Cosmology Science, 2011.

Penrose, R., Stuart Hameroff, and S. Kak, eds. *Consciousness and the Universe: Quantum Physics, Evolution, Brain & Mind.* Selected from *Journal of Cosmology,* vols. 3 and 14. Cambridge: Cosmology Science, 2011.

Persinger, Michael A. "Schumann Resonance Frequencies Found within Quantitative Electroencephalographic Activity: Implications for Earth-Brain Interactions." *International Letters of Chemistry, Physics and Astronomy* 30 (2014): 24–32.

Persinger, Michael A., and John Nichols Booth. "Discrete Shifts within the Theta Band between the Frontal and Parietal Regions of the Right Hemisphere and the Experiences of a Sensed Presence." *Journal of Neuropsychiatry and Clinical Neurosciences* 21, no. 3 (2009): 279–83.

Pizzi, Rita, Giuliano Strini, Silvia Fiorentini, Valeria Pappalardo, and Massimo Pregnolato. "Evidences of New Biophysical Properties of Microtubules." In *Artificial Neural Networks,* edited by Seoyun J. Kwon, 1–17. New York: Nova Science Publishers, 2010.

Planck, Max. "On the Law of Distribution of Energy in the Normal Spectrum." *Annalen der Physik* 309, no. 3 (1901): 553–63.

Pockett, Susan. "Consciousness Is a Thing, Not a Process." *Applied Sciences* 7, no. 12 (2017): 1248.

———. "Difficulties with the Electromagnetic Field Theory of Consciousness: An Update." *NeuroQuantology* 5, no. 3 (2007): 271–75.

———. *The Nature of Consciousness: A Hypothesis.* Lincoln, Neb.: Writers Club, 2000.

———. "Problems with Theories that Equate Consciousness with Information or Information Processing." *Frontiers in Systems Neuroscience* 8, no. 255 (2014): 225–29.

Poreisz, C., K. Boros, A. Antal, and W. Paulus. "Safety Aspects of Transcranial Direct Current Stimulation Concerning Healthy Subjects and Patients." *Brain Research Bulletin* 72, nos. 4–6 (2007): 208–14.

Pribram, Karl H. "Brain and Mathematics." In *Brain and Being: At the Boundary Between Science, Philosophy, Language and Arts,* edited by Gordon Globus, Karl Pribram, and Giuseppe Vitiello, 215–40. Philadelphia: John Benjamins, 2004.

———. *Brain and Perception: Holonomy and Structure in Figural Processing.* Hillsdale, N.J.: Lawrence Erlbaum, 1991.

———. "Consciousness Reassessed." *Mind and Matter* 2, no. 1 (2004): 7–35.

———. *The Form Within: My Point of View.* Westport, Conn.: Prospecta Press, 2013.

———. "Karl Pribram: Bibliography." Karl Pribram.com. Accessed December 20, 2018.

———. *Languages of the Brain: Experimental Paradoxes and Principles in Neuropsychology.* Englewood Cliffs, N.J.: Prentice Hall, 1971.

———. "Mind, Brain, and Consciousness: The Organization of Competence and Conduct." In *Science and Consciousness: Two Views of the Universe,* edited by Julian Davidson and Richard Davidson, 115–32. New York: Springer, 1984.

———. "The Neuropsychology of Sigmund Freud." In *Experimental Foundations of Clinical Psychology,* edited by Arthur J. Bachrach, 442–68. New York: Basic Books, 1962.

———, ed. *Origins: Brain and Organization.* Hillsdale, N.J.: Lawrence Erlbaum, 1994.

———. "Prolegomenon for a Holonomic Brain Theory." In *Synergetics of Cognition,* edited by H. Haken, 150–84. Berlin: Springer-Verlag, 1990.

———. "What Is Mind That the Brain May Order It?" In *Proceedings of Symposia in Applied Mathematics: Proceedings of the Norbert Wiener Centenary Congress,* vol. 52, edited by V. Mandrekar and P. R. Masani, 301–29. Providence, R.I.: American Mathematical Society, 1994.

———. "What the Fuss Is All About." In *The Holographic Paradigm and Other Paradoxes,* edited by Ken Wilber, 27–34. Boulder: Shambhala, 1982.

Pribram, Karl H., A. Sharafat, and G. Beekman. "Frequency Encoding in Motor Systems." In *Human Motor Actions: Bernstein Reassessed,* edited by H. T. A. Whiting, 121–56. Amsterdam: Elsevier Science Publishers, 1984.

Pylkkänen, Paavo. *Mind, Matter, and the Implicate Order.* New York: Springer, 2007.

Rendek, Kimberly N., Raimund Fromme, Ingo Grotjohann, and Petra Fromme. "Self-Assembled Three-Dimensional DNA Nanostructure." *Acta Crystallographica Section F: Structural Biology and Crystallization Communications* 69, no. 2 (2013): 141–46.

Rescher, Nicholas, ed. *G. W. Leibniz's Monadology: An Edition for Students.* Pittsburgh: University of Pittsburgh Press, 1991.

Ringbauer, M., B. Duffus, C. Branciard, E. G. Cavalcanti, A. G. White, and A. Fedrizzi. "Measurements on the Reality of the Wavefunction." *Nature Physics* 11, no. 2 (2015): 249–54.

Romanes, G. J., ed. *Cunningham's Textbook of Anatomy.* 10th ed. New York: Oxford University Press, 1964.

Rose, D. *Consciousness: Philosophical, Psychological and Neural Theories.* New York: Oxford University Press, 2006.

Rufener, K. S., P. Ruhnau, H. Heinze, and T. Zaehle. "Transcranial Random Noise Stimulation (tRNS) Shapes the Processing of Rapidly Changing Auditory Information." *Frontiers of Cell Neuroscience* 11 (2017): 162.

"Scientists to Speak." *Stanford Daily* 172, no. 2 (1977): 8.

Shannon, C. E. "A Mathematical Theory of Communication." *Bell System Technical Journal* 27, no. 3 (1948): 379–423.

Sheldrake, Rupert. *Morphic Resonance: The Nature of Formative Causation.* Rochester, Vt: Park Street Press, 1989.

———. *A New Science of Life: The Hypothesis of Morphic Resonance.* Rochester, Vt: Park Street Press, 1981.

———. *The Presence of the Past: Morphic Resonance and the Memory of Nature.* New York: Times Books, 1988.

Sher, Leo. "Neuroimaging, Auditory Hallucinations, and the Bicameral Mind." *Journal of Psychiatry & Neuroscience* 25, no. 3 (2000): 239–40.

Smolin, Lee. *Time Reborn.* London: Penguin Books, 2013.

Squire, Larry R., ed. *The History of Neuroscience in Autobiography.* Vol. 2. London: Academic Press, 1998.

Stapp, Henry P. *Mind, Matter, and Quantum Mechanics.* 3rd ed. New York: Springer-Verlag, 2009.

Steiner, Rudolf. *Cosmic Memory: Prehistory of Earth and Man,* translated by K. E. Zimmer. San Francisco: Harper & Row, 1959.

———. *An Occult Physiology: Eight Lectures by Rudolf Steiner, given in Prague, 20th to 28th March, 1911.* 2nd ed. London: Rudolf Steiner Publishing, 1911.

Stenger, Victor J. "Bioenergetic Fields." *Scientific Review of Alternative Medicine* 3, no. 1 (1999): 625–43.

Stuart, C. I. J., Y. Takahashi, and H. Umezawa. "Mixed System Brain Dynamics: Neural Memory as a Macroscopic Ordered State." *Foundations of Physics* 9, nos. 3–4 (1979): 301–7.

Susskind, Leonard. *The Black Hole War: My Battle with Stephen Hawking to Make the World Safe for Quantum Mechanics.* New York: Little, Brown and Company, 2008.

———. "The World as a Hologram." *Journal of Mathematical Physics* 36, no. 11 (2008): 6377–96.

Taimni, I. K. *Man, God and the Universe*. Madras, India: Theosophical Society, 1969.

Talbot, Michael. *The Holographic Universe*. New York: Harper Collins, 1992.

Teilhard de Chardin, Pierre. "The Activation of Human Energy." In *Activation of Energy*, translated by René Hague, 385–93. London: William Collins Sons, 1976.

———. *The Appearance of Man*. Translated by J. M. Cohen. New York: Harper & Row, 1956.

———. "The Energy of Evolution." In *Activation of Energy*, translated by René Hague, 359–72. London: William Collins Sons, 1976.

———. "The Nature of the Point Omega." In *The Appearance of Man*, translated by J. M. Cohen, 271–73. New York: Harper & Row, 1956.

Tiller, William A. *Psychoenergetic Science*. Walnut Creek, Calif.: Pavior Press, 2007.

———. *Science and Human Transformation: Subtle Energies, Intentionality and Consciousness*. Walnut Creek, Calif.: Pavior Press, 1997.

———. *The Science of Crystallization: Macroscopic Phenomena and Defect Generation*. Cambridge: Cambridge University Press, 1991.

Tiller, William A., Walter E. Dibble, and J. Gregory Fandel. *Some Science Adventures with Real Magic*. Walnut Creek, Calif.: Pavior Press, 2005.

Todeschi, Kevin J. *Edgar Cayce on the Akashic Records*. Norfolk, Va.: A.R.E. Press, 1998.

Tononi, Giulio, and Christof Koch. "Consciousness: Here, There and Everywhere?" *Philosophical Transactions of the Royal Society Biological Sciences* 370, no. 1668 (2015): 1–16.

Tudzynski, P., T. Correia, and U. Keller. "Biotechnology and Genetics of Ergot Alkaloids." *Applied Microbiology and Biotechnology* 57, nos. 5–6 (2001): 593–605.

Turgeon, Mary Louise. *Clinical Hematology: Theory and Procedures*. Baltimore: Lippincott Williams & Wilkins, 2004.

Tuszynski, Jack A. "Are There Optical Communication Channels in the Brain?" New York: Springer-Verlag, 2017.

———, ed. *The Emerging Physics of Consciousness*. New York: Springer-Verlag, 2006.

Tuszynski, J., N. Rahnama, I. Bokkon, N. Cifra, P. Sardar, and V. Salari. "Emission of Mitochondrial Biophotons and Their Effect on Electrical Activity of Membrane via Microtubules." *Journal of Integrative Neuroscience* 10, no. 1 (2011): 65–88.

Umezawa, Hiroomi, and Giuseppe Vitiello. *Quantum Mechanics: Monographs and Textbooks in Physical Science: Lecture Notes (Book 1)*. Pittsburgh: Bibliopolis, 1986.

VanWijk, R. "Bio-Photons and Bio-Communication." *Journal of Scientific Exploration* 15, no. 2 (2001): 183–97.

Velmans, Max. "Is Human Information Processing Conscious?" *Behavioral Brain Science* 14, no. 4 (1991): 651–69.

———. *Towards a Deeper Understanding of Consciousness*. New York: Routledge, 2017.

Vines, B. W., D. G. Nair, and G. Schlaug. "Contralateral and Ipsilateral Motor Effects after Transcranial Direct Current Stimulation." *Neuroreport* 17, no. 6 (2006): 671–74.

Vitiello, Giuseppe. "Hiroomi Umezawa and Quantum Field Theory." *NeuroQuantology* 5, no. 3 (2011):402–12.

———. *My Double Unveiled: The Dissipative Quantum Model of Brain*. Philadelphia: John Benjamins, 2001.

Wasson, Tyler, and Gert Brieger. *Nobel Prize Winners: A Biographical Dictionary*. New York: H. W. Wilson, 1987.

Weber, Renée. "The Physicist and the Mystic: Is a Dialogue Between Them Possible?" In Wilber, *The Holographic Paradigm and Other Paradoxes*, 187–214.

Wheeler, John Archibald. *Geons, Black Holes, and Quantum Foam: A Life in Physics*. New York: W. W. Norton, 1998.

———. *Information, Physics, Quantum: The Search for Links*. Austin: University of Texas Press, 1990.

———. *A Journey into Gravity and Spacetime*. New York: Scientific American, 1990.

Whicher, Ian. "Nirodha, Yoga Praxis, and the Transformation of the Mind." *Journal of Indian Philosophy* 25, no. 1 (1997): 1–67.

Whitehead, Alfred North. *The Concept of Nature*. Cambridge, UK: Cambridge University Press, 1964.

———. *Process and Reality: An Essay in Cosmology. Gifford Lectures, 1927–28*. New York: Simon & Schuster, 1978.

———. *Science and the Modern World*. New York: MacMillan Company, 1925.

Wick, Manfred, Wulf Pinggera, and Paul Lehmann. *Clinical Aspects and Laboratory Iron Metabolism*. Vienna, Austria: Springer-Verlag, 2003.

Wilber, Ken. *A Brief History of Everything*. Boston: Shambhala, 1996.

———, ed. *The Holographic Paradigm and Other Paradoxes: Exploring the Leading Edge of Science.* Boulder: Shambhala, 1982.

———. *Integral Spirituality: A Startling New Role for Religion in the Modern and Postmodern World.* Boston: Integral Books, 1997.

———, ed. *Quantum Questions: Mystical Writings of the World's Great Physicists.* Boston: Shambhala, 1985.

Wiltschko, Wolfgang, and Roswitha Wiltschko. "Magnetic Orientation and Magnetoreception in Birds and Other Animals." *Journal of Comparative Physiology A: Neuroethology, Sensory, Neural, and Behavioral Physiology* 191, no. 8 (2008): 675–93.

Wiseman, Howard M., Fuwa Maria, Shuntaro Takeda, Marcin Zwierz, and Akira Furusawa. "Experimental Proof of Nonlocal Wavefunction Collapse for a Single Particle Using Homodyne Measurements." *Nature Communications* 6 (March 24, 2015): 192–203.

Wong, Eva. *The Shambhala Guide to Taoism.* Boston: Shambhala, 1997.

Woolf, N. J. "Microtubules in the Cerebral Cortex: Role in Memory and Consciousness." In Tuszynski, *The Emerging Physics of Consciousness,* 49–94.

Woollaston, Victoria. "The World's Nervous System Revealed." *Daily Mail,* January 31, 2014.

Yau, Shing-Tung, and Steve Nadis. *The Shape of Inner Space: String Theory and the Geometry of the Universe's Hidden Dimensions.* New York: Basic Books, 2010.

Zizzi, Paola. "Consciousness and Logic in a Quantum Computing Universe." In Tuszynski, *The Emerging Physics of Consciousness,* 457–81.

Index

BOOKS OF RELATED INTEREST

Developing Supersensible Perception
Knowledge of the Higher Worlds through Entheogens, Prayer, and
Nondual Awareness
by Shelli Renée Joye, Ph.D.
Foreword by Robert McDermott

Morphic Resonance
The Nature of Formative Causation
by Rupert Sheldrake

Science and the Akashic Field
An Integral Theory of Everything
by Ervin Laszlo

The Immortal Mind
Science and the Continuity of Consciousness beyond the Brain
by Ervin Laszlo
with Anthony Peake

The Intelligence of the Cosmos
Why Are We Here? New Answers from the Frontiers of Science
by Ervin Laszlo
Afterword by James O'Dea
Foreword by Jane Goodall

Searching for the Philosophers' Stone
Encounters with Mystics, Scientists, and Healers
by Ralph Metzner, Ph.D.

Mindapps
Multistate Theory and Tools for Mind Design
by Thomas B. Roberts, Ph.D.

Dark Light Consciousness
Melanin, Serpent Power, and the Luminous Matrix of Reality
by Edward Bruce Bynum, Ph.D., ABPP

INNER TRADITIONS • BEAR & COMPANY
P.O. Box 388
Rochester, VT 05767
1-800-246-8648
www.InnerTraditions.com

Or contact your local bookseller